CHINES

Hong Kong University Press thanks Xu Bing for writing the Press's name in his Square Word Calligraphy for the covers of its books. For further information, see p. iv.

Echoes: Classics of
Hong Kong Culture and History

The life of Hong Kong has been described and explored in many books, literary, historical and scholarly. Sadly many of those books are no longer in print. The purpose of *Echoes* is to reprint those special books about Hong Kong and its region, to bring their insights and the reading pleasure that they offer to new readers, and to bring back memories for those who knew these books before.

CHINESE CHRISTIANS
Elites, Middlemen, and the Church in Hong Kong

CARL T. SMITH

New introduction by Christopher Munn

香港大學出版社
HONG KONG UNIVERSITY PRESS

Hong Kong University Press
14/F Hing Wai Centre
7 Tin Wan Praya Rd
Aberdeen
Hong Kong

© Hong Kong University Press 2005

First published in 1985 by Oxford University Press

This edition published by Hong Kong University Press in 2005

ISBN 962 209 688 3

British Library Cataloguing-in-Publication Data
A catalogue entry for this book is available from the British Library.

www.hkupress.org
secure on-line ordering

Printed and bound by Pre-Press Limited in Hong Kong, China.

Hong Kong University Press is honoured that Xu Bing, whose art explores the complex themes of language across cultures, has written the Press's name in his Square Word Calligraphy. This signals our commitment to cross-cultural thinking and the distinctive nature of our English-language books published in China.

"At first glance, Square Word Calligraphy appears to be nothing more unusual than Chinese characters, but in fact it is a new way of rendering English words in the format of a square so they resemble Chinese characters. Chinese viewers expect to be able to read Square Word Calligraphy but cannot. Western viewers, however are surprised to find they can read it. Delight erupts when meaning is unexpectedly revealed."

— Britta Erickson, *The Art of Xu Bing*

Contents

Plates

Introduction to the Paperback Edition

Christopher Munn

Every so often a work of history appears that radically changes our understanding of people, place and period. *Chinese Christians*, first published in 1985, is such a work. This book asked questions about Hong Kong that had never been asked before. It showed that the leaders of Chinese society had a far greater role in shaping early Hong Kong history than earlier historians had believed. It also demonstrated, for the first time, that Chinese society in early colonial Hong Kong had coherence and continuity.

Dispensing with the traditional governor-by-governor approach to Hong Kong history, *Chinese Christians* explores the lives of some 200 men and women who came into contact with Christian missionaries in early Hong Kong and who used their connections to achieve wealth and status. Its themes are the building of communities in colonial Hong Kong and the "middlemen" who linked the Chinese and colonial communities. These were the people who laid the foundations of Hong Kong society. Many of them became influential beyond Hong Kong through their connections with the colonial community and its official religion. Yet, with the exception of Sir Robert Ho Tung, Yung Wing, Sun Yat-sen and perhaps one or two others, few of the characters in this book are remembered much today. Even the important among them find little place in the standard histories of colonial Hong Kong. Many of the men and women here are representative rather than significant — people who are known simply because they happened to be recorded as members of congregations or schools. Some, like the indignant Chu Tak-leung or the déclassé Taiping royals, are utterly unimportant. They are no less interesting for that.

In rescuing these lives from obscurity, Carl Smith has shown that the history of early colonial Hong Kong is more than just a narrative of governors, opium wars, merchant houses and grand reclamation projects: it is also the experience of ordinary people — and of a few extraordinary men and women who saw the opportunities thrown up by British rule and tried to make something of them. In *Chinese Christians* these people speak clearly across the years: some of their voices are loud and impressive; others are moving; a few are angry and accusing. By bringing them together in this book, Carl Smith made a singular contribution to Hong Kong history. Together with his other writings on people and society in Hong Kong, *Chinese Christians* has, perhaps more than any other body of work, turned the field of Hong Kong history on its head.[1]

Chinese Christians was first published by the Oxford University Press in 1985 to mark the twenty-fifth anniversary of the founding of the Hong Kong Branch of the Royal Asiatic Society: Carl Smith was a driving force in the Society then, as he is today. The chapters that make up *Chinese Christians* were, however, published even earlier as separate articles in a number of Hong Kong journals and bulletins, one as early as 1969. Most of these journals are difficult, if not impossible, to track down. *Chinese Christians* itself has also become something of a rare book. It is now difficult to obtain from libraries. It is not to be found in bookshops, new or second-hand, and whenever it appears for sale on the Internet (which is not often) large sums are demanded. No book of this kind should be so inaccessible for so long. Twenty years on, this reprint seeks to remedy the problem.

This edition of *Chinese Christians* reproduces the original in its entirety, without revision and with the pagination and original foreword by James Hayes preserved.[2] All that has been added is this new introduction, which has been written with Carl Smith's consent and warm co-operation. The main intention of this new introduction is to bring out some of the themes and significance of *Chinese Christians* and to examine the author's working methods.

* * *

For a book that has been assembled, without much modification, from essays and articles written over the course of over a dozen years, *Chinese Christians* achieves a remarkable coherence and consistency. Each chapter forms a discrete unit and can be read on its own, as Smith originally intended. Taken together, however, and read in sequence, the chapters add up to a book that is far more satisfying than the sum

---

1. Nineteen of Smith's other essays on Chinese élites, neighbourhoods, women and labour, missionaries and communities are collected in *A Sense of History: Studies in the Social and Urban History of Hong Kong* (Hong Kong: Hong Kong Educational Publishing Co., 1995). Many more are scattered among a variety of books and journals.
2. The Wade-Giles romanization of Chinese characters is also preserved, and is used, for the sake of consistency, in this new preface.

of its parts. Smith has structured *Chinese Christians* so that the discussion moves progressively from the particular to the general. After a brief introduction sketching the early Protestant communities in China and Hong Kong, the book begins with studies of particular institutions, families and connections: all of these studies are enriched with thick description and a great deal of quotation. The book then turns to the formation of élites in the first half-century or so of colonial Hong Kong. Finally, the view broadens, with three concluding chapters on the complex, often contradictory, relationships between people, Church and government.

Despite holding together well as a book, *Chinese Christians* is not always an easy work to navigate. It does not have the single narrative sweep of many comparable urban or social histories (though there is chronological development within articles and, to some extent, among them). The richness of detail and the anecdotes that make the book such a pleasure to read often lead us away from the main point of each chapter: sometimes, indeed, the "point" is in the detail — in conveying an impression of the complexity and the muddle of so much of Hong Kong's history. This is not a fault, but a product of Smith's unusual methodology and of his reluctance to generalize. It might, however, be helpful to readers to provide a brief outline of the book and its main themes.

Chinese Christians is divided into two parts. In Part I, Smith examines the products of missionary education in a series of sketches that centre mainly on the schools and institutions in which they were taught. Chapter 1 draws on an extraordinary collection of letters and school essays to examine, mainly through the eyes of the students themselves, the effects of missionary education on a group of Chinese boys at the Morrison Education Society School in Macau and Hong Kong. This study is remarkable not just for its subjects — most of these boys grow up to be substantial figures in the modernization of China — but also for its touching vignettes of life at school, and for the cultural conflicts that it uncovers. In Chapter 2, Smith takes three of the graduates of this school, the Tong brothers, and traces their lives from humble childhood in Kwangtung Province of the 1830s and 1840s to wealth and fame in Hong Kong, Canton, Shanghai and Tientsin later in the century. This chapter illustrates one of the central arguments in *Chinese Christians*: the importance of an English-language education in launching careers in government, trade and industry. Chapter 3 enlarges on this theme, with an account of the lives of some of the translators, compradors and advisers — the archetypal middlemen — who transmitted knowledge and mediated in transactions between Chinese and Europeans. The central part of this chapter contains Smith's well-known essay on Wei Akwong, another Morrison School student, who rose from hungry beggarboy in Macau to become one of Hong Kong's richest and most respected citizens.

In Chapter 4, Smith pauses to remind us that not all contact with missionaries led to Christian enlightenment, personal wealth and social advancement. Here he explores the part played by Christian missionaries in and around Hong Kong in the Taiping Rebellion of the mid-nineteenth century. The Taiping Rebellion devastated much of southern China over a period of 20 years and resulted in the deaths of more than 20 million people. Christianity provided some of the inspiration for the bizarre and corrupted mixture of beliefs that made up the Taiping ideology. Hong Kong was the centre of some of this inspiration and became a refuge for some of the rebels and their families. Smith's interest is not so much in ideas but in the details of the contacts between missionaries in Hong Kong and the Taiping rebels and their families. His study also traces the work of missionaries in preparing the most prominent of these rebels, Hung Jen-kan, for his vain attempt to introduce a truer version of Christianity into the Taiping capital at Nanking. The chapter concludes with a touching account of the fate of some of the remnants of the Taiping movement: the minor members and friends of the Taiping royal families who sought refuge in Hong Kong and help from missionaries to regain the life they had before the Taiping kingdom.

The final chapter in Part I (Chapter 5) examines the Hong Kong connections of a more successful revolutionary figure, Sun Yat-sen. Sun's baptism in Hong Kong by an American missionary in 1883 was an important step towards his relationships with overseas Chinese communities, which later helped him raise funds for his various revolutionary enterprises. Smith also takes up here a theme explored in his study of the businessman Tsang Lai-sun in Chapter 4, and of the Tong brothers in Chapter 2: the formation of a network of interconnected Chinese families stretching beyond Hong Kong along the China Coast.

Part II of *Chinese Christians* takes us deeper into the Chinese community of nineteenth-century Hong Kong, with two chapters that are among Carl Smith's most original — and certainly his most influential — contributions to Hong Kong history. In place of the traditional generalizations about a murky, leaderless rabble of transients and criminals, Chapter 6 offers a detailed and documented anatomy of an organized Chinese community, with a clear leadership and sense of identity. For much of this chapter, Chinese Christians give place to generally non-Christian contractors, merchants and government employees, who organized and gave shape to Chinese society prior to the formation of the Tung Wah Hospital — the headquarters of Chinese power — in the early 1870s. Here we meet some of early Hong Kong's most colourful citizens: Loo Aqui, the sleazy head of the colony's gambling and retail drug empires, and the main reason why early British rulers were so concerned about the kind of people settling in the colony; the wealthy Tam Achoy and Kwok Acheong, who became leaders of the early Chinese community; and the newspaper editor, Chan Oi-ting, who was to become China's first Consul-General in Havana.

The final part of Chapter 6 notes the importance of Christian missions in producing leaders who could work out more effective and lasting relationships with the colonial government. This point is further brought out in Chapter 7, which explores the institutions and experiences that served as launching pads or stepping stones to success in nineteenth-century Hong Kong: the Church, western-style education, government employment, marriage or liaison with Europeans, previous experience in other colonies, professional status, community service, and — common to nearly all of these categories — proficiency in the English language. While Chapter 6 deals with a kaleidoscope of characters and situations prior to the establishment of the Tung Wah Hospital, Chapter 7 presents a more certain route to dynastic power and influence in Hong Kong — the acquisition of English — a tool which had its origins in the old Canton system and which has continued to wield importance long after the period covered by this book.

The final three chapters contain Carl Smith's reflections on the topics covered in *Chinese Christians*. These reflections take us into more abstract spheres. But they are still grounded in solid fact and gain strength from carefully chosen vignettes that sharply illustrate the conflicts and contradictions of nineteenth-century Hong Kong. The reader who wishes to know Smith's personal view of Hong Kong history should look here rather than in the largely narrative introduction. The earlier chapters deal with largely progressive events and processes: the formation of communities, for example, the growth of understanding between people of different backgrounds, and the building of careers and family fortunes. These final chapters take us into darker regions, and the observations in them are not comfortable ones.

In Chapter 8, Smith dwells on the racial and cultural barriers between European missionaries and Chinese Christians, and on the anomalies in the position of missionaries in nineteenth-century China: their reliance on imperial power and on funding from opium merchants; the contradictions between Christian values and the behaviour of Europeans in China; the layers of distrust between missionaries and their students. Like the other concluding chapters, this one is packed with telling anecdotes and quotations, including a scathing attack on Christian hypocrisy from Chu Tak-leung, a language teacher who was dismissed by his missionary employers after they found opium-smoking equipment in his room. Chapter 9 reflects on the role of the Church in what Smith refers to as "the Hong Kong situation": the city's complex meaning for its Chinese inhabitants as a place of refuge, freedom and opportunity, yet also as a place in which they were marginalized from both the colonial community and their own origins. The final chapter (Chapter 10) explores another awkward issue in the early Church in Hong Kong — the conflicts, and the areas of concurrence, between traditional Chinese values and Christian teaching. Out of conflict comes much confusion and frustration, but also some progress: a large part of this chapter discusses, with great sensitivity, the role of the Church in the quiet liberation of Chinese women in Hong Kong.

* * *

It should be clear even from the bald summary above that *Chinese Christians* is not a simple book. Nor is it one that can be easily categorized. It contributes substantially to practically all aspects of Hong Kong history — social, economic, political, cultural — yet it cannot be described as a conventional "general history". The title highlights Chinese Christians and Hong Kong. But some of the most important material in the book deals with people who barely came into contact with Christianity, and its geographical scope stretches the whole length of the China Coast, down to the Chinese communities in Southeast Asia, and across to California. This is a work primarily of social and cultural history, not of religious or church history: even the "Christians" are (according to ancient Hong Kong usage) exclusively Protestants, and not members of the larger community of Roman Catholics. The most seminal chapter — on the emergence of a Chinese élite in early Hong Kong — deals with men who hardly came into contact with Christianity at all. The focus of *Chinese Christians* is on social élites, yet many of its most memorable characters are those who fell by the wayside.

Most striking of all, particularly to students of Hong Kong history brought up on the works of Endacott, Eitel and Sayer, *Chinese Christians* pays almost no direct attention to the colonial side of Hong Kong society. Compare this book, for example, with G.B. Endacott's *Biographical Sketch-book of Early Hong Kong*, first published in 1962, just a year or two after Carl Smith arrived in Hong Kong (and read John Carroll's new introduction to this work for an explanation of Endacott's entirely eurocentric approach).[3] *Chinese Christians* moved the discussion of Hong Kong history away from its whiggish colonial framework, and away from the small number of Europeans who ran the official side of the colony, towards an understanding of the people who lived *with* (rather than *under*) colonial rule. The colonial presence is there, but it is a shadowy presence: governors, officials and European merchants are distant shadows, while men and women prominent in the Chinese community, but unheard of in most other histories, move to centre stage. The picture that emerges is not that of a passive, faceless Chinese community thriving under British tutelage, but one of men and women using the machinery of colonialism to launch professions, gather riches, secure political influence and build dynasties. *Chinese Christians* shows continuity, development, organization and self-awareness within the Chinese community, and particularly in its élites. In doing this, it quietly demolishes one of the central tenets of the traditional colonial histories: that the Chinese in Hong Kong were a passive, fragmented, loosely organized community of sojourners, who did not begin to look on Hong Kong as home until well into the twentieth century.

One of the other tenets of traditional historical writing about Hong Kong has been the idea that important sources for Hong Kong history have disappeared, whether through periodic clearing-out exercises, through destruction during the Japanese occupation, or through consumption by white ants, or some other scourge. There is much truth in this idea. But often it was an excuse for assuming that the few sources that survived had been exhausted, and that there was not much that one could say about some aspects of Hong Kong history — particularly the Chinese experience — even if one wanted to. *Chinese Christians* decisively overturned this notion by showing how imagination, persistence, and careful cross-referencing could throw up all kinds of materials for producing a detailed and coherent picture of

---

3. G.B. Endacott, *A Biographical Sketch-book of Early Hong Kong* (with an introduction by John Carroll) (Hong Kong: Hong Kong University Press, 2005).

Chinese life in the colony. It introduced new sources, used new methodology, and achieved a degree of accuracy that, among other things, makes it possible to reprint this work without the need of corrections, despite all of the new research that has been carried out since its original publication.

Prior to Carl Smith's research (and with the exception of the notable work done on the rural areas by James Hayes and others), the source base for Hong Kong history had been notoriously narrow. Those few, such as Endacott, who bothered to research primary materials tended to stick to the core colonial archives, and to borrow many of their observations and conclusions from governors and senior officials. Those with insight and originality, like H.J. Lethbridge, bothered little with primary research. Smith's investigations into the sources are exhaustive. They cover the colonial canon as a matter of course, though they take little from it. They extend to newspapers, missionary archives, Chinese-language materials, private letters and other sources. In a pioneering way, they also find rich material in land records, wills and other sources that had hardly been glanced at. Smith's historical research is unprecedented in Hong Kong for its depth and detail, and it set new standards for Hong Kong history.

Smith's methodology is first to ask large questions and then to answer them by distilling masses of carefully organized research material into answers. There is a hint of how this process works on page 167 of *Chinese Christians*, where, having outlined the anatomy of the English-speaking Chinese élite in nineteenth-century Hong Kong, Smith says (with customary understatement) that his purpose in writing the chapter is "to refine some of the raw material, to systematize some of the data, before any positive sociological statements ... could be made". This process of refinement can be roughly summarized as follows:

- Information is gleaned from the primary sources and added (originally by hand and later by typewriter) to 8" by 5" library index cards, which are organized in filing cabinets according to individual names. Smith has, during nearly 50 years of research, accumulated some 140,000 of these index cards. Further records are organized according to neighbourhoods, streets and landholdings.
- Big questions — Did becoming Christians make converts less Chinese and more westernized? Did their social and economic position change? — are asked, and answers are sought from the huge mass of material accumulated on the index cards.

- The information on the index cards is pieced together according to topic, family, neighbourhood or institution and then transferred into a more narrative or explanatory format.
- The text is refined and moulded into material suitable for publication.
- Broad reflections and conclusions are added.

The style of *Chinese Christians* reflects this methodology. The work contains arguments and observations that are often strikingly original and sometimes controversial. But it is not a tightly organized thesis with the usual exposition, development and recapitulation: one important reason for this is that the research comes before, rather than after, the development of hypotheses, so that almost no fragment of information, however commonplace, is left ungleaned. The first impression may be that *Chinese Christians* is simple narrative or description, and, because it is largely biographical or prosopographical, much of it is indeed storytelling, though of a concentrated kind. Every so often, however, Smith steps back to observe the significance of what he has just described: the brief but focused conclusions to each chapter reveal that all of the detailed material in it serves to answer a clear set of questions, or to demonstrate broad observations. Smith himself compares this to "looking at a tree or a shrub in a great forest, perhaps getting lost for a while, and then beginning to see what this tree or that shrub had in relation to its neighbours, and suddenly seeing the whole ecological picture".[4]

There are three further ingredients in Smith's methodology. His remarkably precise memory of his own research tells him where to look among these thousands of index cards and gives him a control over his sources that is not readily available to the many researchers who use his cards for casual reference. His historical imagination, which ranges across the decades and into the very streets and homes of people in nineteenth-century Hong Kong, enables him to think through the choices, experiences and preoccupations of his subjects. His judgement and common sense, combined with the soundness of the research, never fail to maintain the confidence of the reader.

* * *

4. Quoted in May Holdsworth, *Foreign Devils: Expatriates in Hong Kong* (Hong Kong: Oxford University Press, 2002), 147.

Chinese Christians, along with works by Henry Lethbridge, James Hayes, Elizabeth Sinn, David Faure, Chan Wai-kwan and Tsai Jung-fang, is one of the key texts in what might be called the Hong Kong school of Hong Kong history. Although its practitioners have never consciously claimed to be promoting a school, they can be easily differentiated from the Colonial school and the Nationalist school by their focus on Hong Kong and its people, rather than on the problems of colonial government or on Hong Kong as a topic in diplomatic relations. The Hong Kong schools tends to place Hong Kong's inhabitants, with all their complex experience and relationships, in the foreground, and to push the governors and officials who dominate the colonial and nationalist accounts into the background. In its methodological approach, the Hong Kong school makes wide use of previously untapped sources, particularly Chinese-language sources, and deploys the traditional colonial sources in a new and more critical way. Its centre of gravity, to use Smith's words, is in the life of ordinary people "and how they adapted or did not adapt to a colonial situation and the reasons for it".[5]

More broadly, and looking beyond Hong Kong, Smith's work on élite formation and social organization in Chinese and colonial cities can be likened to the work of William Rowe and Ho Ping-ti on China, and of Christopher Bayly and David Arnold on India. These historians have, like Smith, pioneered research into structures of power and continuity that complement or compete with those laid down by governments. Smith himself makes reference to earlier writings by Max Weber and R.H. Tawney in explaining the function of Christianity (or more specifically Protestantism) in the creation of wealthy élites.[6] Outside of a few footnotes on works by other Hong Kong historians, this is the extent of his reference to other scholars. When asked about how his work fits into a larger historiography, he says that he is just filling in the gaps left by the more official colonial historians. If asked about his influence on other scholars, he tends to talk about graduate students who have recently sparked an interest.

This is characteristic Smith understatement, and a reminder that his consuming passion is pure historical search rather than theorizing or self-reflection. Needless to say, his influence has been far greater than he would have us believe. It extends to practically all of the

---

5. Ibid.
6. Smith, *Chinese Christians*, 193. The works referred to are Max Weber, *The Protestant Ethic and the Spirit of Capitalism* and R.H. Tawney, *Religion and the Rise of Capitalism*.

historians who have worked on Hong Kong over the last three or four decades: there are few among them who have not drawn material and ideas from his published works, and many who would have written a very different version of events had these works not existed. This influence comes not just from the contents of these works, but in what Smith has revealed about the source base for Hong Kong history and in the exceptionally high standards he has set for accuracy. Equally important, Smith's massive card index, a copy of which is now kept at the Hong Kong Public Records Office, has been delved into by researchers into all aspects of Hong Kong's past and treated almost as a canon of primary sources on early Hong Kong society. This is no small achievement for a historian who began his research as a sideline to his vocation in the Church.

Carl Thurman Smith was born on 10 March 1918 at Dayton, Ohio: Dayton was at that time a moderately large industrial city, and the home of Orville and Wilbur Wright, the pioneers of aviation. Smith took a Bachelor of Arts degree at DePauw University, Greencastle, Indiana in 1940 and graduated from the Union Theological Seminary, New York as a Master of Divinity in 1943. In the same year he was ordained as minister in the Evangelical and Reformed Church (now the United Church of Christ). After two years as Pastor of Dewey Avenue Reformed Church, Rochester, New York, he became Founding Pastor of St Stephen's United Church of Christ at Philadelphia. Then, in 1960, he decided he wanted go into missionary work and joined the United Board for World Ministries, which sent him, after a few months of Cantonese training at Yale University, to the Hong Kong Council of the Church of Christ in China. In Hong Kong he lectured in theology first at the Church's Theological Institute in Tuen Mun, and then between 1962 and 1983 at Chung Chi Seminary and its successor, the Chinese University of Hong Kong.

While still a schoolboy, and later during his time as pastor in Philadelphia, he developed an interest in family history and genealogy — both his own and that of other people in the places in which he lived. In Hong Kong, when asked to teach a course on the history of the Protestant Church in China, he discovered that most of the books on this subject "dealt with what the missionaries did and not who the Chinese converts were". Smith was not willing to teach the subject just from the missionary point of view.

> I thought to myself — the students are young Chinese who would be working with Chinese people, and they ought to know more

about the origins of the Church as it affected Chinese lives. I thought I would try and get as much material as I could about early Chinese converts in the missions, particularly in this area of China, using the same methodology that I had employed for my genealogical research in the USA and looking at all the archives I could find.[7]

This, then, was the stimulus for the research that went into *Chinese Christians*, and the explanation of its unusual methodology: fundamental questions about the impact of Christianity on individual lives; and genealogical research transformed into historical research into communities and social networks.

In 1983 Smith formally retired from teaching, although he continued to give courses at various universities in Hong Kong. He then devoted most of his time and energy to his research into Hong Kong and China Coast history. In 2002, at the age of 84, when he might be expected to start to take life easy, he took on a full-time position with the Instituto Cultural of Macau, under whose auspices he is continuing work begun some years ago on the history of society and social élites in Macau. He now spends most of his time in Macau, returning to Hong Kong from time to time for meetings, seminars and other events. There has been no relaxation in his work routine, which begins early in the morning and stretches into the evening, although it now usually includes a generous afternoon nap.

We might expect a man who spends most of his waking hours sifting through land records and old newspapers to be a somewhat solitary, obsessive figure, with perhaps little time or inclination for socializing. Carl Smith is quite the opposite of this. He has often said that the greatest reward from his work is the large number of friends that it has introduced him to. These are friends, new and old, from all parts of the world and from all walks of life, who visit or correspond with him about all aspects of Hong Kong history. His home is rarely free of visitors, who come not just for the index cards but to find what cannot be set down in writing or tracked in footnotes: the advice, insights and guidance of a scholar with nearly half a century of research behind him. Many have gone to him to clarify facts or fill gaps, but have come away with new ideas and questions about the patterns and shapes of Hong Kong history.

---

7. Quoted in Holdsworth, *Foreign Devils*, 144.

Yet it would be misleading to present Carl Smith as some grand patriarchal figure, or as a solemn oracle with an answer for everything and an aversion to small talk. He has many questions of his own to ask, and (after research) his great passion is conversation. His interest is in people, and he listens as much as he speaks. Like all good conversation, talk with him tends to stray well beyond its starting point, and, given his curiosity about the foibles of historical figures (living and dead), often becomes irreverent. The welcome he gives to those who consult him, and the complete absence of any sense of proprietorship over his research have set the tone for the collegial way in which Hong Kong history is practised. The humour and the warmth have created many lasting friendships. The interest he takes in other people's research makes him the greatest single source on what other Hong Kong scholars are working on at any given time.

Chinese Christians was first published when Hong Kong's transition from British colony to Special Administrative Region of China had just begun. A year before, in 1984, Great Britain and China had made their Joint Declaration on the future of Hong Kong. Although the declaration gave many reassurances, there were concerns about whether people in Hong Kong would continue to enjoy their traditional way of life after 1997. In the spirit of the times, and in keeping with the subject matter of the book, the introduction and epilogue to *Chinese Christians* raises questions about the prospects for freedom of research and religion in the territory, and the future path of institutions such as the Royal Asiatic Society (which co-published the book) and the Christian Church. Twenty years on, many of these questions are now being answered. People still worship freely. The Hong Kong Branch of the Royal Asiatic Society held on to its royal connections in 1997 and now has more members than it had in 1985. Stimulated by world interest in Hong Kong in the run-up to 1997, academic research is flourishing, especially in the field of Hong Kong studies. In many ways, *Chinese Christians* asks, and goes a long way towards answering, more fundamental historical questions about the nature and origins of Hong Kong society. This book is important to anyone with an interest in Hong Kong's development as a city, and particularly to those who may believe that a "Hong Kong identity" was a creation of the late twentieth century.

Foreword

IT is a great honour for me to be able to provide a foreword to this study of élites, middlemen, and the Chinese Protestant Church in Hong Kong by my friend, the Revd Carl T. Smith. In it, I shall touch on the importance of his work for present-day Hong Kong and on the record of the Hong Kong Branch of the Royal Asiatic Society, since this book, a joint venture with Oxford University Press, marks the twenty-fifth anniversary of the re-establishment of the Society in Hong Kong.*

Carl Smith, a Vice-President of our Society, is the most assiduous and knowledgeable researcher into Hong Kong society among local Western scholars. He has made a long and careful search among all kinds of source material for the history of this port-city over many years and has written a great many articles on various aspects of its history and development. His work has tended to concentrate on Chinese social organization in the city, especially its leading institutions, and, as befits a clergyman and teacher of theology, on the establishment and development of the Chinese Christian community in Hong Kong. He has concentrated on urban work, in contrast to most other researchers, who have tended to apply themselves mainly to the much older, rural communities of the New Territories. It is fitting that, at this time in Hong Kong's history, that hitherto-neglected subject, the urban history of Hong Kong, is coming into its own. Fortunately, more scholars are now aware of its intrinsic interest, and the public is more ready for the results of their work. This book, focusing as it does on the people and their institutions against the background of their times, will be a stimulus to other researchers, and a useful research aid to further effort.

Its intrinsic value apart, Carl Smith's work takes on a new importance at this time of preparation for a largely autonomous Hong Kong after 1997, when the territory will become a Special Administrative Region within the People's Republic of China. Hong Kong people, whether they want to or not, have to overcome their long-standing lack of interest in government and politics in order to participate in the current constitutional changes, with their intended politicization of local—including district—

affairs, which are designed to provide a politically as well as economically viable Hong Kong by 1997. Carl Smith's careful description of our earlier social development and the insights he provides are required reading for those who seek to understand our present-day society. They show, too, that the part which Hong Kong people now have to play in preparing for their future is not as foreign to them as some may think.

The message of this book must, I think, be that, although the urban population has been mobile and largely male until relatively recently, local society, even under colonial rule, took firm steps almost from the beginning towards creating a community, viewed in its many parts and as a whole. In this respect, the Chinese genius for community organization, so marked by researchers working in the rural parts of the Hong Kong region, has been more developed in the urban areas than one would think. This is not in itself surprising, since studies of overseas Chinese communities in Singapore, the Philippines and Indonesia, especially Jakarta, have shown what impressive organizations have been created, and managerial capacity amply demonstrated, by peasant immigrants and petty shopkeepers there, in precisely the same way as experienced in nineteenth- and early twentieth-century Hong Kong.

I turn now to an account of the Society, reproduced from a leaflet prepared by Dr J.R. Jones, CBE, MC, our first President until his retirement in 1970.

> The Hong Kong Branch of the Royal Asiatic Society was originally founded in 1847, but it ceased to exist at the end of 1859. Exactly a century later, on December 28, 1959, it was resuscitated with the approval of the parent society in London—The Royal Asiatic Society of Great Britain and Ireland.
>
> The (Royal) Asiatic Society was founded in London in March 1823 'for the investigation of subjects connected with and for the encouragement of science, literature and the arts, in relation to Asia'. It received its Charter of Incorporation as a royal society from His Majesty King George IV on August 11, 1824. The Royal Asiatic Society is the oldest and most important Society of its kind in Europe, and its standing as the doyen of Societies promoting the study of Asia has been maintained by the devotion of generations of eminent scholars, explorers and others who have contributed through

its Journal, in public addresses and in many other ways, a rich harvest of knowledge, both academic and practical, in the service of Western understanding of the East.

A large part of the Society's work has always been done through its branches and affiliated Societies in the East. Branches were formed at Bombay and at Madras about 1838, and in Ceylon in 1845. The Hong Kong Branch followed in 1847, the North China Branch at Shanghai in 1857, the Japanese in 1875, the Malayan in 1878, and the Korean in 1900, etc. etc.

The Hong Kong Branch grew out of a Medico-Chirurgical Society founded in 1845. This Society, however, in accord with the contemporary spirit of inquiry and the enthusiasm for better knowledge of Asia in general and China in particular, had contemplated setting up a Philosophical Society; but the movement ended in the establishment of the Asiatic Society with laws drafted by Andrew Shortrede, Editor of the *China Mail*, and based upon those of the Royal Asiatic Society. Sir John F. Davis, the Governor, by reason of his known literary and scientific acquirements rather than his official rank, was asked to be President. He suggested that the Society should seek to be admitted as a Branch of the Royal Asiatic Society with which, as a founder member, he was in close touch and with whose active President, the Earl of Auckland, he had discussions on these lines before he left England.

So in January 1847 the Hong Kong Branch of the Royal Asiatic Society was founded, and all the members of the Medico-Chirurgical Society who wished to join were admitted without ballot or entrance fee on condition of their Society's apparatus and books being handed over to the new body.

Besides the Governor and Shortrede, the first office-bearers included Major-General D'Aguilar, Peter Young the Colonial Surgeon, Mercer the Colonial Treasurer; John Bowring the younger (of Jardines); and also Thomas Wade, the celebrated interpreter and Envoy to China, who later became famous as inventor of the Wade System of romanization of Chinese still in general use today. As Sir Thomas Wade he was to become President of the Society in London in 1887.

In his Inaugural Address as President of the Hong Kong Branch, Sir John Davis stressed the importance of directing the Society's attention to practical projects and to natural history, geology and botany, as well as to literary pursuits, and suggested that he could get the sanction of the Colonial Office to the grant of a moderate piece of ground for a Botanical Garden. Sir John left the Colony in 1848; but, as the result of a stirring appeal by the Rev. C. Gutzlaff, the missionary, at a meeting of the Society in August 1848, the project was approved, although it was not carried into effect until the governorship of Sir John Bowring (the younger John Bowring's father), and then the Garden was placed under Government control and not under that of the Society.

During the twelve years of its life, the Society was dogged to some extent by the personal animosities prevalent in Hong Kong in the early days; but it flourished under the inspiration of Sir John Davis, and also for a time under Sir John Bowring, who enjoyed a European reputation as a scholar—as President he preferred to be called *Dr.* Bowring—and who animated the Society with his personal influence and by his contributions to its discussions. The Society had no permanent home of its own, but in 1849 it was granted by Sir S.G. Bonham a room in the Supreme Court building. It published six volumes of Transactions, the first in 1847 and the last in 1859. The Hong Kong Branch now possesses a microfilm of these six volumes.

With the departure of Sir John Bowring in May 1859 and the death in the September following of the Branch's devoted Secretary—Dr. W.A. Harland, M.D.—the Society collapsed. The efforts of Dr. James Legge, as well as those of Sir Hercules Robinson, the new Governor, as President, of the Bishop of Victoria and of the Acting Chief Justice as Vice-Presidents and of Harry (later Sir Harry) S. Parkes were of no avail.

The collapse of the Society came at an unfortunate time and deprived it of the prestige and momentum which it would undoubtedly have gained from the work of some of its famous members. Legge was on the eve of publishing his famous translation of the Chinese Classics, which eventually appeared only through the generosity of Joseph Jardine (and

his successor Sir Robert Jardine) and of John Dent, the
heads of the two largest merchant houses in the Colony. A
little later, in 1865, T.W. Kingsmill had to resort to the aid of
the Shanghai Branch for the publication of his studies on the
geology of Hong Kong.

The North China Branch started in Shanghai in 1857 under
the name of the Shanghai Literary and Scientific Society. Its
first President was the Rev. E.C. Bridgman, D.D., the first
American missionary in China and the founder and manager
of the *Chinese Repository*. Its first Journal appeared in 1858
in the name of the Literary and Scientific Society, but in that
year the Society became affiliated to the Royal Asiatic Society as its North China Branch. Except for a brief period
between 1861, when Dr Bridgman died, and 1864 when the
Society was reanimated through the unremitting efforts of Sir
Harry Parkes as President, it maintained for nearly 85
years—until the outbreak of the second world war [in Asia]
in December 1941—almost an unbroken vigour and a high
reputation as one of the principal centres for the study and
discussion of Oriental culture in Central China. It kept up a
high standard of scholarship and of cultural appeal in its
Journal, which appeared unfailingly every year. After the
war it continued its work until, in 1949, it was forced through
political troubles to cease its activities. The last issues of the
Journal were published with the cooperation of the Interna-
tional Institute of China.

From its earliest days the Society in Shanghai was fortu-
nate in the support of a generous public and of the British
Government, which in 1868 provided it with a site at a
nominal rent for its own building, completed in 1871. Later
the property was conveyed to the Society in perpetuity or for
so long as it was used for the Society's purpose. Thus, in 1931
the Society was able, with the aid of public subscriptions and
generous municipal grants, to build in Museum Road close to
the British Consulate a commodious building of its own; it
contained a lecture hall named after the donor who was the
late Dr. Wu Lien-teh, a floor to accommodate its Oriental
Library of 12,000 volumes and adjacent reading rooms, as
well as space for an excellent natural history museum and for
the exhibition of Chinese paintings and other works of art,

with Arthur de Carl Sowerby as Curator in whose memory a member of the Society gave a donation of HK$10,000 to the Hong Kong Branch.

In 1941 the Society in Shanghai had nearly 800 members, including most of the leading Oriental scholars, explorers and travellers. Amongst the outstanding personalities who had been associated with the North China Branch a few may be mentioned—Dr. Joseph Edkins, Thomas W. Kingsmill, Dr. Emil Bretschneider, Henri Cordier (at one time the Society's Librarian), P.G. van Mollendorf, Sir Robert Hart, Sir Harry Parkes, Sir Byron Brenan, W.H. Medhurst, Sir Edmund Hornby (the first British Judge in China), Sir Rutherford Alcock, H.A. Giles, E.H. Parker, H.B. Morse, A.P. Parker, Alexander Hosie, Samuel Couling, Sir Sidney Barton and Dr. J.C. Ferguson, an American, former President of Nanking University and a man of profound learning and wisdom who, in the course of half a century, served the Society as President, Secretary and Editor of the Journal.

The Hong Kong Branch was resuscitated as the outcome of a meeting attended by some thirty interested persons, held at the British Council Centre on December 28, 1959. The meeting adopted a constitution approved by the parent Society in London, and formed an interim Council to hold office until a General Meeting should be held. The following were elected to the Council:—President: Dr. J.R. Jones; Vice-Presidents: The Hon. Sir Tsun-nin Chau and Dr. [later Sir] Lindsay Ride; Hon. Secretary: Mr. J.D. Duncanson; Hon. Treasurer: Mr. T.J. Lindsay; Hon. Editor of the Journal: Mr. J.L. Cranmer-Byng; other Councillors: Dr. Marjorie Topley and Messrs. James Liu, Holmes Welch, and G.B. Endacott. His Excellency the Governor, Sir Robert Black, graciously consented to become the Patron of the revived Hong Kong Branch of the Royal Asiatic Society. He was a life member of the Society and in recognition of his active and valuable service to the Society he was elected an Honorary Member.

The Inaugural Meeting was held on April 7, 1960, in the Loke Yew Hall of Hong Kong University. It was to have been presided over by His Excellency the Governor, had illness not prevented it. The Inaugural Address was delivered by Professor F.S. Drake, Professor of Chinese at Hong Kong

University, on 'The Study of Asia: a Heritage and a Task'.

On January 23, 1961, Sir Robert Black presided over a meeting of the Branch in his capacity as Patron, and thus restored a tradition after a lapse of a hundred years.

In reviewing the work of the Society since its inauguration, one may say that, in a quiet way, it has been fulfilling the expectations of its founders. We do contribute to the knowledge of China and East Asia, with special reference to Hong Kong, through our lecture programmes, our local and overseas tours to places of historical interest, and our *Journal*. Our library, too, has been built up over the years and now comprises over 3,000 volumes of books about China, many of them of abiding interest and value. Whatever we may have achieved is, of course, due to the contributions of many interested authors, here and abroad, to the work of the Council, and to the support given by members of the Society.

Against this modest achievement, one must admit that there are factors which operate to our disadvantage. In the first place, Hong Kong has always been a very busy place. Unless retired, and sometimes not even then, most of us have full-time, demanding jobs which leave little time or energy for other pursuits. Whilst we have never found it difficult to recruit Council members, there has always been a limit to the amount each of us can do for the Society. Councillors are either librarians, editors, secretaries, or the like, but no one yet has been able to combine several posts or take up additional duties. This has hit us particularly hard with regard to promotion of and publicity for the Society and its work. We find it very difficult to deal with this kind of situation, which results in a fundamental dilemma: until we carry out more promotion and publicity, our membership will remain low and our publications will not sell as well as they ought or reach their full potential public. We have addressed these problems again recently and are trying to improve the position.

Now is also the time for the Society to look ahead, especially in anticipation of the severing of the link with Britain and the establishment of a highly autonomous Special Administrative Region of the People's Republic of China. There are those who conclude that the Royal Asiatic Society has no place in the new situation. Its name alone, they say, however honourable in itself, is sufficient indication that we cannot expect to continue after 1997, when Hong Kong will no longer be a colonial appendage of Great Britain and the whole emphasis and outlook of the territory will have changed and when, in the words of Chairman Deng Xiaoping, 'Hong Kong people will govern Hong Kong'.

I do not deny that change is necessary and this may even involve a change in title, but what is in a name? Surely it is the content of what one does which is important, and the question is whether there will still be a need in Hong Kong for work in the English language on China past and present in all its diversity and complexity. We can surely expect that there will be a continuing interest in the subject among Hong Kong residents. If a name is the only barrier to progress, we could become the Asiatic Society of Hong Kong, and I am sure the mother society would not sever our association for such a trifle.

Perhaps more to the point, we should now be considering whether to move towards a bilingual presentation in our lectures and publications for it is arguable that, through creating a wider potential interest and membership, the resources of the Society would broaden and extend so as to enable us to move away from the narrow base of the first twenty-five years.

In short, we should be assessing our situation and the options open to us and be taking steps to move in the right direction like other bodies faced with similar problems. In this way, we will be able to look forward more confidently to celebrating our fiftieth anniversary in 2010, which will also be the 163rd anniversary of the founding of the first branch of our Society in Hong Kong.

JAMES HAYES
President

---

*Strictly speaking, although the earlier branch seems to have been popularly referred to as the Hong Kong Branch, and our first President, Dr J.R. Jones, has used this term in the account quoted below, its official title was the *China Branch* of the Royal Asiatic Society.

Preface

SHORTLY after my arrival in Hong Kong in 1961 to teach in a theological school, I was asked to conduct a course on the history of the Christian Church in Hong Kong. As this was an area I had not studied previously, I sought out material on the subject. I was immediately struck by the paucity of detailed information about the Chinese converts. From what social and economic group had they come? How did becoming a Christian affect their relationship with non-Christians? Did they become less Chinese and more Westernized? Did their social and economic position change? To what extent were they alienated from their cultural tradition?

Although these matters were referred to in the literature, much more attention was devoted to the missionaries and their activities. This emphasis on the missionary troubled me. I was to teach Chinese students; should not the emphasis be on the Chinese side of the story? I acknowledged that I was not Chinese, nor was I acquainted with the Chinese literature on the subject, but I still felt an obligation, in preparing the course, to emphasize the Chinese aspects of the development of the Church more than the missionary aspects, though, admittedly, until a fully independent Chinese Church had been established, the two strands could not be separated.

As a local historian and genealogist by avocation, I decided to apply the methodology I had acquired in these fields to find what material I could about the origins and careers of Chinese Christians in Hong Kong. This approach resulted in the gathering of many isolated items which formed a base on which to build up biographies and recreate the community setting of the lives of Chinese Christians. Only after I had ferreted out the details and placed them in order could I formulate general principles.

This volume represents the result of my studies. The chapters were originally published as separate articles in *Ching Feng*, a quarterly of the Ecumenical Study Centre at Tao Fong Shan, the *Chung Chi Bulletin*, the *Chung Chi Journal*, the *Journal of the Hong Kong Branch of the Royal Asiatic Society*, and a symposium publication of that society entitled *Hong Kong: the Interaction of Tradition and Life*. They are reproduced here with the kind permission of the relevant journals.

CARL T. SMITH
April 1985

Introduction

THIS introductory chapter provides a framework for the more detailed studies in succeeding chapters. It sketches the introduction of Christianity into China and the organization of Chinese Protestant congregations in Hong Kong in the nineteenth century; it makes selected reference to some of the Chinese workers in these congregations, describes the missionary's attitude towards those who were not Christians and his educational philosophy, and explains the role of missionary schools in the creation of a new type of China-coast middleman.

Christianity, like Buddhism, was brought to China from the West. Buddhism was introduced into China from India. Christianity came by trade routes from Central Asia. The first certain evidence of Christianity in China is in the Tang dynasty. A stele at Hsianfu erected in AD 781 records the arrival of a Nestorian Christian, 'A-lo-pen', in AD 635. The Nestorian form of Christianity, even though it took on certain Chinese characteristics in its new environment, slowly withered into insignificance. Roman Catholic missionaries from Europe arrived in China at the end of the thirteenth century. With the collapse of the Mongol domination of China, Christianity again died out. In the sixteenth century, the Portuguese pioneered another wave of Catholic missionaries. Since then, a Christian presence has been continuously maintained in China through periods of favour and disfavour.

Protestant clergy accompanied the Dutch in their occupation of Formosa in the seventeenth century and made an attempt to convert the natives of the island. After this effort, which had no lasting results, no Protestant missionary came to China until 1807, when the Revd Robert Morrison arrived at Canton. He was not welcomed by the East India Company, which controlled British trade with China. Indeed, the attitude of the Company towards missionaries forced Morrison to arrive on an American ship and to take up residence as a guest of an American firm whose partners were eager to see Protestant mission work begin in China. Two years after his arrival, Morrison was offered the post of translator for the East India Company. His acceptance regularized his residence at Canton and Macau. Though his missionary interest was not welcomed by the Company, his language skills were. The missionary and his students, who were educated in the English language, were used as necessary language links between foreigners and Chinese.

The first conversion of Chinese by Protestant missionaries occurred in overseas Chinese communities, principally at Malacca, Penang, Singapore, Batavia, and Bangkok. (A list of converts up to 1843 is given in the Appendix.)

By the Treaty of Nanking, signed in 1842, five ports in China were opened for foreign residence. Though the missionary would have wished for completely free access to China, he welcomed the opportunity the treaty provided; and with the cession of Hong Kong to the British, there was an area on the edge of China where he could be free from the expected hostility and harassment of Chinese officials. It was soon recognized, however, that Hong Kong was not China and that relations between foreigners and Chinese in a colony were different from those in Chinese cities. The missionaries had ambivalent feelings about these differences.

The first Chinese to come to the new settlement of Victoria on Hong Kong Island did not represent a cross-section of Chinese society. They came for economic advantage or to escape from Chinese jurisdiction. Later, Hong Kong became a refuge for those fleeing disturbances in China.

For missionaries Hong Kong was a place to bide until the terms of the treaty between England and China had been fixed, signed, and ratified, and had become operative. Most of the missionaries who had been working in the Chinese communities in South-east Asia and those living in Macau came to Hong Kong before moving on to the treaty ports. Some, however, remained to establish the Chinese Protestant Church in Hong Kong.

Within days of the unfurling of the British flag on Possession Point on Hong Kong Island in 1841, a party of missionaries came from Macau to look over the island to see whether it would be a suitable field for their work. A year later, in February 1842, the first missionary took up permanent residence: the Revd Issachar J. Roberts, a Baptist, moved over from Macau. A month later, he was joined by the Revd J. Lewis Shuck and his wife, Henrietta. She was the first foreign lady to reside in Hong Kong. In the same year, their colleague, the Revd William Dean, and his wife arrived from Bangkok. The relationship between Roberts and Shuck was strained and Roberts moved to the village of Stanley. For a short time he conducted a school there.

A Baptist congregation was organized in Hong Kong in May 1842 , and in July a chapel was opened on Queen's Road west of its junction with Wellington Street. In April 1843, the Baptist Church had nine European and three Chinese members. A month later, Dean organized a separate Chiu Chow-speaking congregation of three members.

The Baptist mission opened a boarding-school in the spring of 1844 with fifteen pupils. Dr Thomas T. Devan arrived in October 1844 and, shortly afterwards, opened a dispensary in Kowloon City. Both the school and the dispensary were short-lived, for Devan and Shuck, along with nine Chinese assistants, the entire Cantonese-speaking congregation, moved to Canton in April 1845. Roberts also moved to Canton, taking a few converts with him.

Dean remained in Hong Kong. His work among Chiu Chow speakers was extended to Stanley, to the village of To Kwa Wan on the Kowloon peninsula, and to the island of Cheung Chau. The American Baptist Mission in Hong Kong was closed in 1860 and its work transferred to the newly opened port of Swatow. However, a small Chiu Chow-speaking congregation continued in Hong Kong. Fifteen years later, in 1875, the widow of the Revd John Johnson organized a school for girls and was active in the affairs of the congregation. The members of the congregation were gradually shifting from the Chiu Chow dialect to the Cantonese.They received occasional visits from the missionaries of the Southern Baptist Convention at Canton. A report dated 1889 states that there were sixty members on the books but only twenty were counted as faithful.

A wealthy American lady visited Hong Kong in 1896 and donated money for a building for the congregation which, through the years, had been meeting in rented premises. In 1901, the Hong Kong Chinese Baptist Church was organized as a self-supporting congregation with thirty-eight members in a newly opened building on Peel Street. This congregation is the present Caine Road Baptist Church.

The Revd James Legge of the London Missionary Society moved the station at Malacca to Hong Kong in May 1843. He brought with him a small group of nine converts, several of whom were young people. They formed the nucleus of a reorganized

Anglo-Chinese College which had originally been founded at Malacca in 1819 by the Revds William Milne and Robert Morrison. Legge closed both it and his Theological College in 1856, at the time considering them to have been failures.

In Hong Kong Legge organized a Union Church for foreigners and also gathered a Chinese congregation. A Chinese pastor, the Revd Ho Fuk-tong, was ordained in 1846. Elders and deacons were elected in 1847. At the time, the church had twenty members. In 1875, a constitution was adopted for 'The Independent Chinese Church of Hong Kong'. The congregation increasingly assumed its financial obligations. In 1863, two auxiliary chapels were opened—one to the west in Tai Ping Shan, the other to the east in Wan Chai. To build these the Chinese contributed $1,300. A few years later they raised $1,000 to build a chapel at Fat Shan (Fo San) in Kwangtung Province. By 1884, they were able to provide full support for their newly elected pastor, the Revd Wong Yuk-cho.

Through the years, the congregation had met on Sunday afternoons in the Union Church. In 1888, they occupied a part of their own new building on Hollywood Road near Aberdeen Street. As a fully independent congregation, they adopted the name 'To Tsai Church'. In 1926, this congregation moved to Bonham Road under a new name, Hop Yat Church.

In the 1880s, the area in which the Tai Ping Shan chapel had been built was resumed by the Government as a plague-prevention measure. The work there was transferred to Yee Wo Street at Causeway Bay. In 1919, this congregation was moved to Eastern Hospital Road, So Kon Po, as Shing Kwong Church of the Church of Christ in China.

Work was started by the London Missionary Society and To Tsai Church in Sham Shui Po in Kowloon in 1892. Out of this work the present Shum Oi Church, of the Church of Christ in China, was organized. In the same year that work was started at Sham Shui Po, a chapel was opened in a store at Yau Ma Tei. The members of Union Church and To Tsai Church organized the New Territories Evangelization Society in 1898 to send evangelists to this newly acquired area.

Although a colonial chaplain, the Revd Vincent Stanton, arrived in Hong Kong in 1843, work among the Chinese by the Anglican Church was slow in getting under way. Stanton was interested in such work but his main responsibility was the spiritual welfare of the British community. In 1847, however, he gathered some Chinese boys into a class. In 1850, the first Bishop of Victoria, the Right Revd George Smith, brought with him to Hong Kong funds and plans to reorganize Stanton's school on a larger scale as St. Paul's College. Three of its students were baptized in June 1851. They were followed by other students from the College, the Diocesan Native Female Training School (1860) and schools conducted by Miss Magrath and Miss Baxter. The student converts worshipped with the Cathedral congregation.

The first Anglican missionary sent to Hong Kong to establish a Chinese congregation was the Revd Thomas Stringer, who arrived in 1862. Two years later, a site on Gap Street—now a part of Hollywood Road—was secured for a church. St. Stephen's was opened there in 1866. It was hoped that the new congregation would have the support of the Christian old boys from St. Paul's, but they showed little interest.

Stringer left after three years and his successor, the Revd Charles Warren, was also in Hong Kong for only three years. Their short tenures impeded the proper growth of the congregation in spite of the continuity provided by their Chinese assistant, the Revd Lo Sam-yuen. The congregation only began to show substantial growth under the pastorate of the Revd Kwong Yat-sau (Matthew Fong), who served from 1883 to 1902. In 1888, St. Stephen's was moved to Pok Fu Lam Road and today is on Bonham Road.

The Church Missionary Society worked intermittently on the Kowloon peninsula at Yau Ma Tei. Evangelical work was begun in 1890 but was soon discontinued. It was resumed from 1894 to 1898 and out of this work All Saints' Church was established at Ho Man Tin in 1903. In 1898, the Anglicans organized mission work at Ping Shan in the New Territories, not far from Yuen Long.

The Revd Charles Gutzlaff, while serving as the Chinese Secretary to the Hong Kong Government, organized the Chinese Union in 1844. This was an important means of broadcasting Christian ideas in China and planted seeds which contributed to the Christian element in the ideology of the Taiping movement. To assist him in his work, Gutzlaff recruited young men from the Basel, Rhenish and Berlin Missionary Societies. After a brief stay in Hong Kong, they were sent into the interior of Kwangtung Province. When the second Sino-British war broke out, these missionaries sought refuge in Hong Kong. While there, they gathered a group of followers for worship. When peace came, the missionaries returned to their stations on the mainland but the Revd Rudolph Lechler of the Basel Missionary Society remained in Hong Kong. Under his direction, a church was built for a Hakka-speaking congregation in 1863 on High Street in Sai Ying Pun.

A church was built for Hakka settlers at Shau Kei Wan in 1861. Another group of Hakkas formed a congregation at Sham Shui Po in Kowloon in 1886 and yet another at Lung Yeuk Tau near Fanling in the New Territories in 1898. All of these congregations are now part of the Tsung Tsin Church in Hong Kong, the successor of the Basel Missionary Society.

The Rhenish Missionary Society established a church in 1898 for members who had moved to Hong Kong from their country churches in Kwangtung Province. They occupied a site on Bonham Road that now lies just east of the University of Hong Kong.

The mission board of the Congregational Church, in response to appeals from Chinese converts at their California mission, sent the Revd Charles Hager to Hong Kong in 1883. He organized a congregation in a building rented on Bridges Street for use as a school and residence. One of the congregation's first members was Sun Yat-sen, then a student at Queen's College. About the turn of the century, a church was built on Ladder Street for this group, called the China Congregational Church—in Chinese, Kung Lei Tong.

The Wesleyan Methodists established a congregation in Hong Kong in 1884. Like the Rhenish Church, it was formed of members who had moved to Hong Kong from Kwangtung. After worshipping at a number of sites, the congregation built a church on Hennessy Road in Wan Chai in 1936.

Congregations are made up of people. The early Churches in Hong Kong were organized by missionaries, but to have a congregation they needed followers and assistants. The influence of the Church on people's lives is the theme of this book. A brief account follows of some of the Chinese who worked with the missionaries to build the Hong Kong Church. In other chapters fuller details are given of the careers of some of those mentioned.

When the Revd I.J. Roberts, the first Protestant missionary to live in Hong Kong, came over from Macau, he was accompanied by an old, frail, and sickly follower named Chan. Before attaching himself to Roberts, Chan had been a member of a beggar group in Macau. He was baptized in the waters at Stanley village in June

1842, four months after his arrival, the first Chinese to be baptized on Hong Kong Island. Roberts moved to Canton in May 1844 and took Chan with him, but he died the following year. At that time Roberts paid him the following tribute, 'He has done me much assistance and has often made my heart glad that I came to China.'

Roberts' colleague, the Revd J.L. Shuck, took under his patronage a young man named Julian Ahone or, to give him his Chinese name, Wei Ng. Julian had brought with him from the United States in 1843 a letter of introduction to the Baptist missionaries in Hong Kong from a congregation in Baltimore, Maryland, where he had been baptized and received as a member. After a time, Shuck's assistant began to act strangely. He went about the neighbourhood claiming to be a king seeking his queen. He was arrested for theft and given a public flogging; Shuck tried to rehabilitate him but was not successful.

When the Revd William Dean joined Roberts and Shuck in Hong Kong, he was accompanied by several converts he had made in Bangkok. One of these was killed in April 1843 when he intervened as a peacemaker in a street quarrel.

The Revd Elijah Bridgman of the American Board mission came over from Macau in 1843. He opened a small building in the Lower Bazaar as a chapel, school, and dispensary, though most of his time was devoted to the editing and publishing of the *Chinese Repository*. He had two assistants, Wei Akwong, the first student taken under the patronage of the Morrison Education Society, and Liang Tsin-tih, son of the first ordained Chinese evangelist, Liang A-fa.

Of the few remaining converts of the London Missionary Society station at Malacca, James Legge brought with him to Hong Kong in 1843 Ho Fuk-tong, Ho A-sam, and Kueh A-gong (otherwise known as Wat Ngong). Ho Fuk-tong was the first Chinese pastor ordained in Hong Kong and rendered years of valuable service to the congregation organized by the London mission. Ho A-sam had a block-cutting and print shop next to the Lower Bazaar Chapel of the mission and did evangelistic work in his spare time. Kueh A-gong was assistant and evangelist at the Medical Missionary Hospital on Morrison Hill.

The first Bishop of Victoria, the Anglican Bishop who founded St. Paul's College in 1851, brought with him from England a young Chinese, Chan Tai-kwong, whom he planned to prepare for holy orders. But, after a few years, the glint of gold became too alluring and Tai-kwong left the Bishop's care for a business career in the Chinese Bazaar, but he soon became bankrupt after over-extending himself as the opium monopolist.

The Bishop had the assistance of Lo Sam-yuen at St. Paul's College from 1850 to 1855. In the latter year, Lo Sam-yuen emigrated to Australia, where he served as a catechist in the gold fields under the Bishop of Melbourne. He returned to Hong Kong in 1862. The following year he was ordained a deacon. He assisted the Church Missionary Society agents in organizing and caring for St. Stephen's congregation until his retirement.

Lo Sam-yuen was succeeded at St. Stephen's by another returned Australian sojourner, Kwong Yat-sau, also known as Matthew Fong. Upon returning to Hong Kong in 1874, Kwong attached himself to the Anglicans but soon moved to assist in the work of the London Missionary Society congregation. From there, he returned to the Anglicans in 1883 when he was ordained a deacon. In the following year he became priest. He served at St. Stephen's until 1902, when he retired to Kowloon City.

The Revd Karl Friedrich August Gützlaff—Anglicized to Charles Gutzlaff—organized the Chinese Union in June 1844. It had twenty-one members, all Chinese except for Gutzlaff and Roberts. Its purpose was to train men to distribute scriptures and tracts in all parts of China and to spread the Christian faith. The Chinese Union grew rapidly and within four years reported six hundred converts. When Gutzlaff visited Europe in 1849 to raise funds, he left the Revd T. Hamberg in charge of the Union. Hamberg and other missionaries questioned the sincerity of the majority of the members of the Union. An investigation was held and many were dismissed. Hamberg reported that of two hundred members, fifty were opium-smokers and seventy to eighty had given false names and places of their work.

When Gutzlaff returned to Hong Kong in 1850, he tried to re-vitalize the Chinese Union, but he died the following year. Though his widow and the Revd R. Neumann, whom Gutzlaff had recruited from the Berlin Missionary Society, tried to keep the work going, when Neumann left in 1855 the Chinese Union ceased to exist.

From its members the Rhenish and Basel Missionary Societies inherited a few faithful workers. The Union did penetrate into China with the Christian message and literature. These had an influence on some of the leaders of the Taiping movement.

Roman Catholic and Protestant missionaries brought with them the idea of Christendom and its correlative attitude towards those beyond Christendom. The concept of Christendom had a triple heritage: religiously it drew upon the Hebrew-Christian faith, culturally it looked to Greece, and politically its model was the Roman Empire. Each strand contributed to the definition of the person beyond Christendom. From the religious standpoint he was the gentile infidel to be converted, culturally he was the barbarian to be civilized, and politically he was the enemy to be subdued. The imperialism of the nineteenth century added to these three objectives the economic incentive of commercial exploitation under the name of 'free trade'.

The missionary seldom freed himself from this understanding of those beyond Christendom. His primary objective was the evangelization of the heathen. He came to extend what he regarded as the civilizing benefits of Christendom. The Christian message of peace made him uneasy about excessive use of military force in the process of domination, but he rationalized its use as the wrath of God working for the salvation of souls.

The missionary brought these views to his work among the Chinese. Their religious practices were idolatrous, their customs were inferior, their morality was degrading, their intellect was stunted, and their educational system was outmoded. The missionary task was to convert, to civilize, to improve, and to educate. The relationship implicit in this task was that of superior-inferior. The missionary had something to give, his listeners and followers were expected to receive. The missionary was to set the example, the convert was to imitate. The missionary, who realized the dangers in this relationship, struggled to assist the Chinese Christians to arrive at maturity, equality, and independence.

It was a painful struggle. Once one had agreed with the criticism of old ideas and practices, become a follower, had been under instruction, and had accepted the tasks assigned, it was not easy to become creative, to assume leadership, to teach, and to direct. A reversal of roles and a transfer of power became necessary. Though such changes were difficult, they were inevitable.

The Chinese Church today is living in a different era. The concept of Christendom has lost its force; colonial imperialism is all but gone; there is a greater appreciation of values in cultural traditions other than one's own. There are no missionaries, as such, in China; in Hong Kong, they are a dying breed.

The problem of relating to another culture had to be faced in the early schools conducted by missionaries, particularly in those which provided an English-language education. The missionaries opened such schools because there was an urgent need for Chinese who could translate and write Christian literature. In addition, they hoped that some of their students, when converted, would continue their studies to prepare themselves as catechists, evangelists, and pastors.

In the early period of Protestant missions there were few, if any, theological, homiletic, or pastoral books in Chinese. This meant that students needed to be able to read English if they were to meet the standards the missionaries regarded as necessary for workers in the Church. The missionaries had a low opinion of traditional Chinese educational methods and questioned the value of a comprehensive knowledge of the Chinese classics and the ability to write essays in the traditional style.

The missionaries wished their students to have a knowledge of world and biblical history, mathematics, natural and moral philosophy, and a scientific understanding of the world. It was hoped that they could be trained to approach these subjects with a questioning mind. In short, they wished to produce students who would have enough ability in the Chinese language to translate from it and write literature in it. Yet, at the same time, they were to be versed in the English language and have a knowledge of subjects considered necessary in a Western-style education.

The results of their educational efforts were not what they planned. They created a man who stood between two cultures, a man who was not altogether at home in either. He was not wholly in the Chinese model, nor was he altogether Western. This dual aspect of his thought and outlook enabled him to fill a needed place in the meeting of the Chinese nation with foreigners promoting trade and commerce. The foreign merchant needed a Chinese to supervise the Chinese side of his business. Chinese merchants trading with foreigners needed a Chinese who understood the foreigner and who could speak his language. The Governments of both China and Hong Kong needed translators and interpreters. In Hong Kong, the colonial Government needed a group of Chinese who could advise them about policies affecting the Chinese under their jurisdiction. Beginning with Commissioner Lin's seizure of the opium of foreign merchants at Canton and continuing through the succeeding years of the Ch'ing dynasty, Chinese officials needed the advice and assistance of Chinese who were well acquainted with foreign practices and ways of thought. The English-educated Chinese found themselves in demand on the China coast.

This group of Chinese interpreters, compradores, advisers to officials and Government, and men in various professions created a distinct culture in the China coast cities. Their way of life was a mixture of their Chinese inheritance overlaid with an understanding of Western ways and thoughts.

The emergence and functions of this new type of middleman in China in the later part of the Ch'ing dynasty have been the subject of numerous studies. Most of these have considered the activities of these middlemen within China and their role in its industrial and commercial modernization and in the reform/revolutionary movement. This volume deals with these developments from the standpoint of Hong Kong.

Some of the earliest English-language schools on the China coast were at Hong Kong. The students trained in these schools were among the first to beome middlemen within newly evolving relationships between foreigners and Chinese on the China coast. Many of these students remained in Hong Kong as interpreters, translators, compradores, and advisers to government officials. Others went to China to serve the same functions. Some went overseas. There they became links between their host country and the overseas Chinese communities. Of the several scores of students who went through the schools before 1860 not all rose to positions of leadership. For some, there are few records of their subsequent careers and they have slipped back into the mists of history.

In Hong Kong, the students of the English-language mission schools became a significant element in the emergence of a Chinese élite. Just as the students and other élites in Hong Kong adapted themselves to the ways of colonial administrators, so the Church adapted itself to the special conditions of a colony. At the same time, it made certain adjustments to Chinese cultural values and social patterns. These adjustments were a part of the struggle of the Church towards maturity and independence.

PART I
MISSION SCHOOLS AND THEIR PRODUCTS: A NEW TYPE OF CHINA COAST MIDDLEMAN

1 The Morrison Education Society and the Moulding of its Students

THE Morrison Education Society was formed by foreign merchants at Canton in 1835 in memory of the Revd Robert Morrison, the first Protestant missionary to China. The Revd Samuel R. Brown was the first principal of the Society's school, which was opened in 1839 at Macau and moved to Hong Kong in 1842. After Brown left in 1846 to return to the United States for reasons of health, the school continued under Mr William A. Macy for three years and then closed.

The Revd Samuel Brown was an educationalist. Before being chosen by the Morrison Education Society to come to China, he had taught at the New York Institution for the Deaf and Dumb. He was attracted to his new position by the challenge of teaching students of another culture and language. As he studied his task he formulated certain ideas and procedures by which he hoped to achieve his missionary objectives.

Within the context of his own historical period and theological understanding, Brown attempted to introduce the type of education which would best fulfil his missionary expectations. This involved an evaluation of the traditional Chinese system of education, the relation of this system to Chinese society, culture and religion, and the effect of his educational programme on his students in their identification of themselves as Chinese. Traditional Chinese education was in conflict with the Western idea of education as a training of the mind for creative thought operating within a world view of progress. The missionary educator and his Chinese students were caught in this conflict.

The missionary regarded the conservative nature of Chinese culture as a sign of backwardness. Western education, he hoped, would free the mind of China, it would open it to the 'benefits' of Western civilization, it would enlighten the prevailing darkness.

Brown's Philosophy of Education

Samuel R. Brown defined his task as the education of the 'Christian man', but a Chinese Christian man. He did not want to remove his students from the stream of Chinese life: 'All those whom we educate will return to their own people, and be associated with them in after life, and while they will be improved (we hope) in many respects, they will still be Chinese.'[1] Brown wished his students to remain Chinese as a necessary requirement for their role as transmitters of Western knowledge in Chinese forms. For them to be able to perform this function they needed a thorough knowledge of the literature of China. Without this knowledge, they would not have the tools to convey the 'benefits' of Western learning, nor would they command respect among their own people, where literary ability was the road to eminence and distinction. Brown's interest in the traditional literature of China lay not in its inherent value as the foundation for a way of life valid in its own right, but as a necessary 'tool' for the introduction of another approach to life.

In his review of the traditional texts used in Chinese schools, Brown found little of educational value other than their use as a vehicle for the memorization of characters and an understanding of the structure of the language.[2] He viewed the traditional method of studying the Chinese classics as a journey across an arid desert of ancient lore though he acknowledged that there were a few green patches of enlightened thought. Having made the trip, the student might then go back and try to understand the meaning of what he had memorized and develop a style imitative of the books he had studied. The purpose of Chinese education, according to Brown, was to acquire a knowledge of the language. The method prevented creative intellectual development.

The mind of the nation has been systematically taught not to think, and the reasoning faculty, like their written language, has long ago been arrested in its improvement so that what another has said of Egypt, is as true of this country,—and China 'is a petrification'.[3]

Brown brought a dynamic Western understanding of society and thought to his evaluation of Chinese education. Its end result, in his opinion, was to foster an enervating conservatism and to impede the development of the search for truth. It sustained a static social order in which 'manners, customs, even opinions, have been about equally unvarying from age to age'. It produced 'industrious and quiet servants of the state'. Repressing the spirit of spontaneous enquiry, it created 'peaceable machines'. He was not able to appreciate a system that preserved a culture which stressed the primacy of harmonious relationships between individuals, the social orders, and society and the cosmos. He came from a tradition where education was directed towards fostering activity in terms of abstract 'truths', rather than sustaining the delicate balance of an ordered cosmos. It was the self-sufficiency of China, its unwillingness to change, its rejection of new ideas from the West that irritated the foreigner. Brown sensed that to 'open up' China, its traditional mode of education must be supplanted by one which would foster independent, critical thought. The subsequent course of events, particularly as influenced by his students, proved the correctness of Brown's analysis.

Brown was interested in the structure of language. Before coming to China, as a teacher in the New York Institution for the Deaf and Dumb, he had been involved in basic problems of language communication. He knew that there was a reciprocal relation between language and basic thought patterns. The Chinese language was structured to express the thought of the people. As long as education was confined to the traditional material the language fulfilled its function, but Brown was interested in introducing new ideas into China. He wished the thought of the Chinese 'to diverge a little from the beaten track, to take in a wider range of objects, to become familiar with new truths'. This would require a new vocabulary. Only someone thoroughly imbued with the delicate nuances of a language can coin new words for it. One of the purposes of the Morrison Education Society should be to train a body of men 'who have been educated through the medium of a foreign tongue, and thereby gained a knowledge of the new facts that call for new words to represent them, and at the same time have received a good Chinese education'.[4]

Brown was sensitive to the importance of language as a key to mutual understanding between cultures. He understood the necessity for the Western teacher of the Chinese to have a competent mastery of the Chinese language. Good education arises from the teacher understanding the minds of those he instructs. 'Language is the portrait of the mind in action, and he who would be familiarly acquainted with it must become qualified to judge of its picture with the skill of an artist.' If language is the key to understanding the mind within a homogeneous culture and language group, then it is indispensible for a proper understanding between differing groups.

It is because this attainment is so rare that there is so much misconception and ignorance respecting the peculiar feelings, prejudices, habits, and history of the Chinese. We meet them day after day, but our interviews respect the most palpable and common-place things, while in other points, our minds and theirs are widely removed from mutual contact. There is little or no play of sympathies between us.[5]

Brown believed that the quality of the education undertaken by Westerners for the Chinese would count more than the quantity they educated. His objectives were a nation-wide change in the centuries-old pattern of Chinese education, and an arousing and awakening of China from its 'long hibernation'. The means would be effected through a handful of scholars trained in the best of Chinese lore and the best of Occidental learning. 'We can do much to inspire some individuals with new activity, and make them powerfully react upon the slumbering multitude.'[6] Brown lived to watch his students play a direct role in the opening of China to Western education, medicine, business methods, and technology. Their changed minds were enlisted in the 'self-strengthening' of China. The scholar-official class trained in the traditional Chinese manner turned to them for the new—the ways of the West.

The Effect of Brown's Educational Methods on his Chinese Students

In what specific ways were the students of Brown prepared for the role they played in adult life? What particular influences shaped and moulded them so that their outlook and ways of thinking were different from those of other Chinese? Were they able to remain within the stream of Chinese life even though Brown's objective was to inspire them with 'new activity'?

These questions are not easy to answer. A part of their answer lies in the inner area of the mind and spirit and the changes that may or may not have taken place there. But there are various suggestions of what happened to the Chinese boy who was educated in two different streams of educational material and method. Brown's description of entering students provides a background against which to judge the changes produced in the students by their residence and education at the school:

When a pupil is received into our school, he is young, ignorant of almost everything but the little affairs of his home, prejudiced against all that is not of Chinese origin, the dupe of superstition, trembling at the shaking of a leaf as if earth and air were peopled with malignant spirits, trained to worship all manner of senseless things, and in short having little but his mental constitution to assimilate him to the child of Christendom, or to form the nucleus of the development we would give him. ... When looking for the first time on a class of new pupils ... there is usually almost a universal expression of passive inanity pervading them. The black but staring glassy eye, and open mouth, bespeak little more than stupid wondering gaze out of emptiness.[7]

The description, of course, is coloured by a lack of real understanding of the underlying values of traditional Chinese social patterns; it emphasizes the effect of popular superstition upon the child. Brown also had a very poor opinion of the moral state of the Chinese boys. He thought every single one of them came into the school with an 'utter disregard of truth, obscenity, and cowardliness'.

Brown considered that the entering student had no factual information of his world. He was filled with 'a vast accumulation of false and superstitious notions', and was the victim of bad habits. As their teacher, Brown felt that his task was to rid their minds of superstitions and to replace these with truth, to develop a scientific attitude and arouse a curiosity towards the facts of the world, and to replace evil habits with good. It would be difficult to change the minds and values of the students. Brown asked whether:

It is [sic] possible to quicken the minds into a healthy activity—to awaken in them a relish for inquiry and discovery—to change their present vacancy into busy thought? Is it possible to transform these beings, who have grown up hitherto in the impressible [sic] and formative period of their lives, under a false and defective training, into enlightened Christian men?[8]

Difficult as the task might be, he was eager to try and change them: 'For this purpose they are sent here, and the trial must be made. Here are the subjects; now for the mode of treatment.'[9] The place to begin was in the affections of the boys. Their confidence must be won. Their prejudices against the 'foreign devils' must be overcome. Brown was sure that kind treatment would soon meet with a ready response.

Even the physical setting for the education of the boys would have its effect on their pattern of life. The comparative spaciousness of the quarters provided for the boys must have been in contrast with the crowded conditions of their homes. It served to accustom them to a different pattern of life from the one into which they had been born. When the school moved to Hong Kong, each boy had his own separate room. Brown felt that this arrangement would encourage better morals, simplify housekeeping problems, provide privacy for spiritual meditation, and cultivate self-respect in the student.

For the Chinese lad brought up in the congested quarters of a poor Chinese home, the opportunity to be master of his own domain with its attendant responsibilities was a drastic change. Under crowded conditions the Chinese had not developed the same type of housekeeping order made possible by the more spacious accommodation to which their Western teacher was accustomed. Brown found that occasional visits to the rooms of the boys were sufficient to correct 'any slovenliness or negligence' that did not conform to his New England standards.

An opportunity for privacy would also be in striking contrast to the Chinese home-life of the boys. While contemplation was a traditional Chinese value, it was usually thought of as a retreat to the quiet of nature or intense concentration which would remove external distractions in the midst of social activity. The opportunity for quiet withdrawal to a private chamber was the privilege of the wealthy.

The boys had constant opportunity to observe the manners and conventional polite social forms of Western society. Mr and Mrs Brown considered the boys to be a part of their family. They were welcomed into the family circle, which reflected the best of small-town New England society. The school was the object of frequent visits by people from government, military, and commercial circles in Hong Kong. Teas were held for visiting dignitaries. The students had ample opportunity to observe the ritual social forms of Western society, which were in many respects in marked contrast to Chinese etiquette, and sometimes in outright violation of it. In their association with foreigners the boys were expected to adopt Western social customs. They were to be as polite and well-mannered as the students of any New England academy or British public school. The training was effective in moulding a different social being. In 1845, one of the boys was sent to Shanghai to serve as interpreter in the British Consulate. One of his fellow passengers reported on the boy's ability to fit in easily among Westerners: 'The boy will make friends wherever he goes. He won the esteem of all on board.'[10] This lad may well have been Tong A-chick, as he was one of the two boys sent to Shanghai in 1845. In 1852, while in California, he represented the Chinese community of California, presenting a memorial on their behalf to Governor Bigler at Sacramento. Here he was wined and dined at the Governor's mansion.[11] The knowledge of European manners he had acquired at the school in Hong Kong prepared him to fit into the Western social and political world.

The close-knit family community fostered at the school tended to break some of the natural attachments of the student to his own home. The students would also be influenced by the attitudes their parents had towards their school life and the type of education they were receiving. What was the reaction of the students' parents to the English education their sons received? At first they were suspicious. The only parents willing to place their boys under the charge of Westerners were the very poor, or those in some way connected with the missionaries or the foreign patrons of the school, or parents who had been observant enough to realize that a knowledge of English paid well in the business circles of Canton, Macau, and Hong Kong.

Yung Wing, a student of the Morrison Education Society School, in recollection, had difficulty in understanding how his parents could have so broken with customary Chinese practice as to send him in 1835, at the age of 7, to the school conducted by Mrs Gutzlaff in Macau.[12]

I can only account for the departure thus taken on the theory that as foreign intercourse with China was just beginning to grow, my parents, anticipating that it might soon assume the proportions of a tidal wave, thought it worthwhile to take time by the forelock and put one of their sons to learning English that he might become one of the advanced interpreters and have a more advantageous position from which to make his way into the business and diplomatic world.[13]

If Yung Wing's parents were attracted by the possibility of English-language education as a means for economic and social advancement, his own personal experience reinforced this expectation.

Yung Wing did not stay long at Mrs Gutzlaff's school, for she soon discontinued the experiment of a mixed school and the boys were sent away. He returned home and, after his father's death in 1840, the family had a difficult time making ends meet. One of the ways of achieving this was to send Yung Wing at harvest time to glean in the rice fields. He was usually accompanied by his sister. One day she told the head reaper that her brother could speak, read, and write English. This aroused the man's curiosity to hear a strange tongue, as he had never heard the 'Red Hair Men's talk' before. Yung Wing was bashful, but he was urged on by his sister, who tried to bribe him with the suggestion that the reaper might give him a large bundle of rice if he would perform. The boy yielded and repeated the alphabet. A crowd of workers gathered round and 'stood in vacant silence, with mouths wide open, grinning with evident delight'.[14] The reaper was true to his word and rewarded the 12-year-old boy with several sheaves of rice. Thus, early in life, Yung Wing learned that a knowledge of English could be profitable.

The boys of the Morrison Education Society School were well motivated to participate in the learning opportunity offered by the school. Factors which might have made them resistant to the new ways and thoughts to which they were exposed were gradually removed. One of the pupils who had been in the school for more than six years wrote an essay in 1846 on the topic, 'Why do you wish to get an education?'. The essay illustrates the original motivation of the boys and the manner in which this changed under the type of education they received.

The object led me to come [sic] was to learn English, so that I might make money by dealing with the English, and I had no hope of becoming a scholar. But this was a low object when we look at the desire of those people who support us. The people in Christian countries look at this vast empire full of all sorts of wickedness, a land where the name of Christ is not known, with compassion and pray for it. ... The only hope they cherish is that China may be enlightened and turn to a Christian country, and that its people may share the blessing which they themselves enjoy.

Now this is the hope that all Christians have, and shall we who are the objects of their hope, waste the money which they subscribe in desiring merely that we may get a fortune by means of the education which we receive in this school, and make their ardent desire of no effect? We ought to know better than that, after being under the instruction of a Christian teacher for years. It is our duty to learn to be good, and then with all our power to do or help others to do good.[15]

The boys were aware of the changes that had taken place in their lives. In an essay written by a student in the second class in 1846 we read: 'If you convey a heathen boy to a place filled by Christian and delightful boys, he will soon be like one of them; and if you transmit a Christian boy to a heathen village, it is certainly true he will soon work the same deeds as they.'[16]

The school gave the students a new perspective. It provided them with the dynamism of Western thought which drives the mind in the quest for knowledge and 'truth' for its own sake. In his report to the Trustees of the school for 1844, Brown states that the boys' education had awakened their minds to question the given, to habits of observation and reflection, and to a drive to know the truth of a matter.[17] They were beginning to adopt a Western approach to knowledge, which leads to the scientific method. Thus, their structures of thought were changing.

In morality they were coming under the tensions created by the concept of a supernatural Deity who sets forth absolute ethical standards. As Brown states it: 'They were once without God.... They now know that there is but one living and true God'. With knowledge of a super-mundane God came also an awareness of the Will of this God as a standard for conduct. 'Conscience has become enlightened.... Its existence was at first scarcely perceptible, of course it could serve but little to regulate their actions. It seldom caused them shame or remorse.' Now they had come under the rule of a demanding and judging God. This awakened in them 'the sentiment of duty, and reverence for God and his laws'. Whether this was an improvement each must decide for himself; at least in the opinion of Brown it made them less Chinese. He had instilled into them Western attitudes towards truth and falsity as based on the abstract concept of an absolute 'Truth' rather than the Chinese understanding that abstract truth is subordinate to the necessity of maintaining harmonious relations between people. This strain of 'absolutism' in the education of the boys was the product of Brown's own training in a nineteenth-century theology weighted on the side of a Puritan legalism. It sharpened the dichotomy between the Western conception of truth and the subordination of the place of truth in Chinese ethics to the maintenance of harmonious personal relationships. Though Puritan legalism no longer has a strong influence in theology, the tension between a Western and Chinese understanding of the ethics of 'truth' is not yet altogether resolved within the context of the Chinese Church.

Brown had overheard students who had noticed an instance 'of falsehood or low cunning' among Chinese, say 'with a look of disgust, "that is Chinese"'. The boys had learned the 'value' of truth, and Brown expected that when they left the school, they would be 'men of truth'. It would be of great value to the foreign community to have Chinese who were different because they had been trained in Western values.

To have a class of Chinese young men, on whom we may depend for truth, even though partially educated, living among us in our public and private offices, will assuredly be worth to the foreign community all that their education costs. Nor will it be to our comfort and advantage alone, for such a class will influence others that have not enjoyed equal advantages with themselves.[18]

Brown saw the influence of the boys as not only of value for the foreign community but also for China.

The good implanted in the minds of a few will not die with them, but by its self-propagating virtue, will be diffused more and more widely as time advances. In addition to this, if those who are first sent forth into the world from the school, shall, any of them, go not as they came, idolaters and full of all manner of superstition, but changed by the transforming influence of our holy religion, happier still will it be for us, for them and for their country.[19]

Brown's pious sentiments were prophetic of the important role the students would play, not particularly in the total evangelization of China as he probably hoped, but in the introduction of Western thought to China.

What effect did education in the English language and the use of Western educational methods have upon the minds of Chinese students? How did these affect their view of their cultural heritage? A series of letters and essays from the students of the school throws some light on these questions. Most of these were written between the years 1840 and 1846 by students of the first class.[20] The subject-matter covers a variety of topics, but the letters provide us with material which offers glimpses into the effect on the students of their education and environment. Inasmuch as this first class of the Morrison Education Society School included

Yung Wing, the initiator of the Chinese Educational Mission, Wong Shing, one of the pioneers in Chinese newspaper journalism, Wong Fun, the first Chinese graduate of a Western medical school, and Tong A-chick, later associated with the China Merchants' Steam Navigation Company and other business and industrial enterprises in China, what hints we can get from these letters on the mental development of these students in the formative years of their youth will help us to understand the important role they played in the introduction of Western ideas and techniques into China in the second half of the nineteenth century.

In June 1840, the boys wrote letters to Mr Brown's former pupils in the New York Institution for the Deaf and Dumb. This was their first attempt to write a letter in English. They had been studying English for six months. The letters, of course, are very simple and reflect a beginner's struggle with the English language, but they show that several of the students had made rapid progress in English. Two of the letters were printed in the *New York Observer* and they both express the boys' happiness and gratitude at being in the school under the charge of Mr Brown. One of the writers, Auseule,[21] must have been particularly impressed with the close family atmosphere for he mentioned the Browns' 4-year-old daughter (perhaps he missed his own little sisters) and with youthful directness said, 'I love Mrs. Brown'. They describe the typical school day, emphasizing that they wash on arising and play in the garden, where they pick flowers and 'catch butterflies and bugs to give to Mr. Brown', who puts them in boxes. The influence of religious instruction is particularly evident. Each boy wrote a sentence or two regarding God as the creator of all things. 'God makes grow flowers can smell. Dead flowers cannot smell.' Awai emphasized that though God made the world 'one day did not make because it is Sabbath day'. On this day they read the Bible and 'we with Mrs. Brown and Mr. Browne and Mr. Abeel and Mr. Milne in parlor pray to God'.

The boys were absorbing, or at least reflecting, the 'missionary line'. For an 11-year-old boy, Awai sounds very pious when he writes: 'I want to learn the Bible because God spake all these words. I had not Bible in my father's house. My countrymen have no Bible. I want to teach them learn the Bible.'[22] Already, the mark of division was becoming evident. The boy in the mission school had the Bible, neither his family nor his countrymen had it. Therefore, he had a mission: to give them something they did not have; in this case, the Bible. Thus, early in their education the idea was implanted that China was deficient in something of value that the West could provide, and it was the duty of the 'enlightened' Chinese to transmit it.

Though there may have been a degree of prompting and help in the composition of these letters, they do reflect the impressions a new life and association had upon an 11- or 12-year-old Chinese boy: family life, the chore of keeping clean, play periods, and the impact of religious instruction and observance.

The next group of letters show an even deeper rift between the boys and their Chinese background. These letters are dated 14 January 1842 and are, of course, more mature, though they may not represent the true independent thinking of the boys. The letters reflect the same criticism of Chinese education that their teacher set forth in his annual report to the Trustees of the school for the year 1842. Yung Wing wrote somewhat prophetically in the light of his later role in the promotion of the Chinese Educational Mission:

The Chinese have schools, but they learn but few things, and their learning is different from that of other nations. They only repeat their lessons, without thinking or understanding them. When they have learned five or six years, their teacher explains to them a little out of the book. I think there is not one school in China as good as the schools in the United States or in England. There are a great many Chinese boys and girls not educated as in your country, because the Chinese are stingy fellows. That is the reason they can't have good education.[23]

The process of providing a different criterion for moral conduct was under way. Brown commented that 'in manners and habits they are much changed, and their convictions of what is right and wrong are clear and manifest'. This is illustrated by Tong A-chick's reference to the delinquencies of a schoolmate: 'When the school was formed it had five boys.... Afterwards eldest of them, whose name was Aling, went home, because he did a very bad thing and committed a great sin against God, as in the law of Moses and the prophets.' Lee Kan, writing on Chinese schools, also reflected a growing awareness of 'sin'. He said that in Chinese schools the students sometimes 'worship their idol Confucius.... They think it will make them more understanding. Although they worship and serve it, it cannot help them at all, and besides it is a sin against the true God'.[24]

The nineteenth-century Protestant theological emphasis on man as sinner and the need for repentance produced a training that emphasized an inflexible Holy Will in terms of law and an awareness of guilt at its violation. Guilt for the Chinese was not a result of disobedience to laws given by a transcendental God, but a result of the violation of human relationships, particularly regarding the obedience due to superiors in family, school, or government.

In May 1842, Chow Wan wrote to the mother of Mr Brown in the United States. The letter was quite critical of his Chinese countrymen. He had been influenced by the missionary reaction to the difficulties encountered in tract distribution:

The English and American have made a great many Chinese books about Jesus Christ, and give them to the Chinese. Sometimes when walking round about the streets, some men ask them, and they give them to them. By and by the Chinese men look at them, and find out about Jesus Christ, and God in the book, and mock, and laugh. Sometimes the Chinese tear them into shreds, and burn them up. Some of them go to a distance with the books, and meet with Chinese soldiers, and they are beaten.[25]

Chow Wan probably shared the general Chinese view of the corruption of many of the mandarins. He described the pomp and ceremony involved in the public appearance of a high Chinese official and the deference required on the part of the populace: 'The Tso-Tong sits in a sedan chair, and all the men go before him through the streets, and everybody stands up. If they don't do so, they beat them with whips.' He gave examples of the unequal judgments made by officials. If an opium smuggler was caught, large sums of money were extracted from him if he was rich. He was then set free. If he was poor, he was put in prison for life or beheaded. There is little doubt that the ordinary Chinese person resented the abuse of power and the corruption that characterized the Chinese Government at this time, but it is doubtful if they would have so sweepingly condemned the Chinese people as does Chow Wan after his two-year exposure to Western views in the Morrison Education Society School: 'The Chinese are proud, and easily provoked, and envy each other, and everyone is bad. They care for nothing but money.' This criticism of the Chinese was also expressed by Yung Wing, who also wrote in a letter to Mrs Brown: 'In our country the people are so proud that they swell up as balloons.'[26]

The theme of administrative corruption is taken up again in an essay written in 1846 on 'Chinese Government'.[27] The essay analysed the Chinese political structure, the hierarchy of government bureaucracy, and the corrupt practices of the official class from top to bottom.

Indeed the hearts of the Chinese are comparatively dark and foolish; and most Chinese officers are vicious, cruel and selfish; the only object they pursue is wealth. It is a very fine thing to have wealth, but we ought to get it by fair dealings; but on the contrary they are out of the true way and use unjust means to get it.

The student was sensitive to Western opinion of China's Government and expressed the hope for a better day.

It is lamented that such things occur throughout the whole country. I regret very much that the Chinese officers are so ignorant of virtue and all other excellent attributes of government. I hope that they will soon become better, and that justice, liberty, and happiness may be promoted and diffused over the country; and every individual in the empire will exhibit his civilization so that our nation may deserve commendation of all others.[28]

Another set of essays was written at the request of the Corresponding Secretary of the Society for the first public examination of the school by its patrons and Trustees. The essays were all concerned with the difference between Chinese and English education. The estimates of the students reflect statements made by Mr Brown in his annual reports to the Trustees of the school.

English education covered a broader range of subjects than Chinese education. 'The English learn of many useful things, such as astronomy, geometry, algebra, true religion, and many other things that I cannot mention to you now.'[29] In contrast, Chinese instruction taught 'only about Confucius, how he acted in his lifetime, and [how] his followers praised him'. Chinese education was directed towards acquiring the skills necessary to read and write in the classical style. This was entirely different from colloquial modes of expression. In their Chinese studies the boys encountered an antiquated and unfamiliar style: 'In the poetical classic I find many words which I never heard people speak in my life, and I believe they are seldom used through the Empire, except when they want to make a dictionary.' Not only did the classics concentrate on an uncommon style removed from daily life, but they fostered an attitude which disdained manual labour: 'The Chinese say a learned man should never do anything that is laborious, as a common man does.'

The crux of the difference between Chinese and English was

that of social conservatism and stability in contrast to a continuing quest for truth which fostered change and progress.

But the great difference between the English and Chinese is this: the Chinese look back into ancient times, but the English are always looking to the present and the future, to discover the truth, therefore the Chinese are always about the same, while the English become better and better.[30]

In one of these 1842 essays the idea that the Westerner came with values that China lacked is expressed in a somewhat more sophisticated style than in the letter written by Awai in 1840, but the typical Western sense of benevolent 'mission' is the same:

The Chinese have no Bible and they do not know Jesus Christ who created the universe. They are full of superstitions and ignorance; besides their government rules with injustice. How glad we ought to be when a light came from the other side of the world, not called here by our own countrymen, but sent by foreigners to enlighten our minds, and clear off the superstitions from us.[31]

A more practical appreciation of the significance of Western knowledge for the future of China is expressed in an essay written in 1846:

Knowledge is important to every individual, and it is especially so to us. We are born in a country where science is not much known, and art is in a rude state, and the modern improvements of the West are unknown. In our time China is open to free trade with foreigners, and the eye of China is open, and perceives that there are some things good in the Fan-qui which she did not know, and she watches them carefully, waiting to see in them that which has made them so superior to herself. If we had not the opportunity of being educated, we might hope in vain to improve our nation.[32]

These remarks by one of the students are of special interest because they set the context within which the students were to play their future role in furnishing China with knowledge and techniques of the West in its policy of 'self-strengthening' initiated after 1861 as a response to the superior power of the West.

A group of essays were written by the first class in 1843 on the history of Hong Kong. These show that the boys were learning their history from the Western point of view. They had been indoctrinated with the Western rationalization of the British seizure of Chinese territory and its pressured cession: 'This island is safe place to the English, a place governed by their own laws. They can carry on trade with China, in which it seems an outlet of their manufactures. I hope this island will become more dignified by spreading over the country light and knowledge.'[33] Another student was more specific as to how 'light and knowledge' would spread: 'I hope that through the influence of pious missionaries, the Christian religion will be spread over the island produce the fruits of holiness.'

At the time of the arrival of Caleb Cushing, the United States Commissioner to China, one of the students, Lee Kan, expressed the hope that the visit would result in the opening of China to further trade relations with Western powers:

I have heard of Mr. Cushing who came to this country from America to make a treaty with the emperor for your country, and I hope the emperor will be very glad to have foreigners come here to trade with his own subjects. If so, I think this country will have an extensive commerce, and that it will be a great advantage to China, America, England, and other countries.... This country has been shut up a great many years.[34]

The students were repeating nineteenth-century Western political and religious interpretations of the role of China and the West.

Western-style education implanted an appreciation of the practical values of science. Wong Shing, who later managed the printing establishment of the London Missionary Society in Hong Kong and who in 1872 was invited to set up a printing plant with movable type at the Tsungli Yamen (Chinese Foreign Office in Peking), writing as a student in 1842, noted the value of geometry and algebra. They formed the basis of navigation, the art of drawing and building, and the essence of geography.

These sciences teach us the general truths of natural things and how to reason, so that we by these may discover a great many other truths ... God gives us ... a mind to cultivate.... All knowledge helps us to think of God's mighty power, goodness, and to serve him better. Therefore every man ought to study and learn.... I hope when we boys grow up to be men, we shall teach boys, in the same manner as Mr. Brown treats us.[35]

In 1864, Wong Shing was called to Shanghai to take charge of the foreign language school that was opened there by the Chinese Government. He also used his ability in science and mechanics to produce, in collaboration with Wang T'ao, a Chinese work entitled *Drawings on Gunnery*. The dependence of the scholar-official class on a handful of Western-educated Chinese for a knowledge of Western technology is illustrated by the following account by

Wang T'ao of the manner in which the book on gunnery was produced:

One day Hwuang Seng chanced to tell me that the supervisor Ting Jih-
ch'ang who was then at Soochow, under instruction from Li Hung-chang
had often written inviting him for a visit. The Supervisor was then in
charge of the arsenal, and guns produced there were very good.... I told
Hwuang Seng that the military situation was now tense and that what was
needed to suppress the rebels was good weapons. Why did you not offer
what you knew to him? This might be a help to him.... Hwuang Seng
took out a few English books and the five translated pieces on smelting,
moulding, installation for furnaces, boring of barrels and gun-powder.
Then he took out various tables of survey and a supplement on the
management of guns. I rephrased them, added something here, and
deleted something there, all based on my own limited knowledge and
what I had learnt recently. All the arguments came from my humble
mind, but the theory of the resistance of air and wind was borrowed
from the English books.[36]

Wong Shing not only profited from the scientific aspect of
his education but was also affected by the religious influence the
students experienced in the school. In several successive annual
reports Brown refers to the gratifying religious and moral development of Wong Shing. This serious side of his nature is evi-
denced by a composition he wrote in 1844. It was an assignment
occasioned by the death of the wife of the Revd Dyer Ball, an
American missionary. A few sentences extracted from the essay
will give the tenor of this 18-year-old youth's view of death:

Death is the door between this world and the other world. When the idea
of death comes to our minds, how solemnly it affects us.... How dreadful
when death occurs to a man who loves not God, for he knows that there is
no forgiveness in the grave, and his conscience tells him that he has been
sinning all the time, and he feels that he must suffer the punishment of
that great God.... Shall we sin against that almighty God without ceas-
ing? O stop, stop, let us think before we go any farther. Can we have a
seat in heaven by this sinful life.[37]

These words would have been quite appropriate in an old-
fashioned New England pulpit.

It is interesting, however, to contrast this view of death with an
essay written by one of the students in 1845 on 'Notions of the
Chinese in regard to a future state'.[38] The essay is an interesting
exposition of popular religion in China. To the Western observer it

has the appearance of an accurate description. It described the Chinese conception of '*t'ien*', the future world above the earth, and '*yin chien*', the place of shades. The various Chinese holidays were described with their religious implications. He mentioned the practice of 'buying the souls out of Hell' and of the use of sorceresses to call back the souls of the dead. The essayist pointed to the Buddhist influence on Chinese popular religion in the form of the transmigration of souls and the ascetic, contemplative practices of priests and nuns.

Though they spend their life in doing so, alas they are hopeless and woe to them surely. Because the benignant Creator has given us the precious Bible, which is likened to a guide-board, which shows to the traveler the way which is safe and that which is dangerous.

After his training by Western Christians, he saw no value in the magic-oriented popular religion of China for he had been taught that there is but one way to heaven.

The use of the Scriptures as a guide to salvation was the theme of an essay by another student:[39] 'If a person is ignorant of the Scriptures, he cannot find the true light which will guide him to the way of salvation. He will always be in the state of gloom, and not know what will become of his soul.' Since the Scriptures 'teach the way of salvation, and true religion will support us under the trials of this world, and prepare us for that which is to come', the translation of the Scriptures into Chinese and the promotion of their circulation by missionaries was essential.

I hope that the Scriptures will be openly circulated among the Chinese, for hundreds of millions are going mad after their dumb idols. From these considerations we must rank the effect of Holy Scriptures among the vital interests of mankind.

The hours in the school schedule devoted to the study of the Bible and its explanation, as well as morning and evening prayer and Sunday worship, had impressed upon the boys the primacy of the Bible in the Protestant tradition.

An essay by a student in 1846 illustrates the impression that the study of the catechism made on his mind. The topic is the first question of the Westminster Catechism: 'What is the chief end of man?' The essay is another example of Puritan theology:

As we are eager to supply our mind with temporal knowledge, we should be more eager to store up that of spiritual concerns, involving our duties to God, and his appointments for us.... Men are created to accomplish the object predestinated by him who worketh all things after the counsel of his own will ... Life is short ... Let us learn to prize the hours—learn to esteem life as it deserves. It is not bestowed in vain, but to serve the purposes of God. He has determined to glorify himself, and has so planned the universe, that everything should work for his own glory. He has created man to be his special instrument to execute this work.[40]

In place of the balanced cosmic order of traditional Chinese thought in which the duty of each was to preserve a given harmony as expressed in nature, social relationships, and political life, the student had received a theology of predestination in which a Deity greater than the cosmic order controls the affairs of His creation so that it contributes to His glory. The primary duty of man is conformity to God's divine will.

Along with a predestinarian theology the students received Protestant ethical values. Protestant work ethics are reflected in a student's essay on labour. The values of labour are in contrast to the traditional disdain for manual labour of the Chinese literati.

According to my own opinion, and with reference to what God has designed, I think it is necessary that we should work with our own hands, and secure happiness by our own labour: for we love and enjoy those things produced by our hands, a great deal more than that which is granted for nothing.

Labour is a prerequisite for true happiness and has religious significance:

In order to secure our happiness, it is necessary that men should labour. It is the inevitable lot of men, but it is a blessing, which lays the foundation of future happiness as well as present. Now let us labour; labour not for riches: labour for good: labour for our fellowmen: labour for the glory of our Creator: and remember that our labour will not be in vain. The Lord will reward us in this world, and that which is to come.[41]

With this kind of philosophy no wonder several of the graduates made large fortunes and died wealthy. For mature life is built on the foundations laid in youth. This is the title of another of the essays: 'The life of man a building, and youth the foundation':

No man has a well cultivated mind, and habits which qualify him to discharge the serious duties of life, unless he has laid a good foundation for all these things when he was a youth. On this foundation whether good or bad, we must build the superstructure in middle life and age.[42]

We have examined at some length the foundations laid for the students of the Morrison Education Society School. These were quite different from those provided for the average Chinese boy in the traditional Chinese school. The preparation for adult life laid by Samuel R. Brown in the school was the result of his effort to provide an education in the Western tradition and at the same time to train the student so that he could identify himself with the Chinese community and the welfare of his country. Brown hoped that his students would be able to transmit the benefits of their Western education into Chinese forms and so make them available to China for its 'enlightenment' and advancement.

Conclusion

The problems faced by Samuel R. Brown as principal of the Morrison Education Society School are still encountered when Christian faith meets other cultural traditions. How can the essential nature of the faith be expressed in another tradition? Brown wanted his students to remain Chinese, yet at the same time he wished to free them from the conservatism of their culture and broaden their thought. In trying to do so, he faced the basic problem of language and communication. How can the thought forms of one culture express the truths of Christian faith? For Brown, the solution to the dilemma lay in education in both streams. English-language education would train the mind in reasoning and creativity, education in the Chinese language and classics would equip the student to cast Western ideas into Chinese forms. Brown's basic approach was an educational imperialism. This merely reflected the basic Western imperialistic approach of the nineteenth century.

How can a correlation be made between the essential intent of Christian faith and the basic intentions expressed in distinctive Chinese cultural structures and thought forms? Today, the problem is complicated because traditional Chinese values have already been broken up by the impact of the West in the course of modern history. Already alien secular patterns are being incorporated into Chinese life. We are tempted to pose the problem in the static terms of the past. But the issue is to be found in the dynamic interaction and change taking place in Communism striving to find its identity within a Chinese context, or in the fluid interactions between modern secular structures and an outmoded colonialism in the historically marginal Chinese community of Hong Kong, or the frequently reactionary attempts of those Chinese cut off from the mainland to re-create a Chinese 'way of life' that has long since been undercut by historical change. In each of these three situations the problem for Christian faith lies not so much in the Chinese patterns of the past as in a reckoning with the fast-paced changes the movement of history is producing upon traditional Chinese values and modes of thought.

2 The Formative Years of the Tong Brothers, Pioneers in the Modernization of China's Commerce and Industry

THE three Tong brothers, who were students at the Morrison Education Society School in Hong Kong in the 1840s, may be considered to be representative of a new class of commercial bourgeoisie that emerged in the China coast cities at the end of the Ch'ing dynasty. This new class within the Chinese social system was composed of entrepreneurs, business men, financiers, and industrialists. They were key figures in the industrial and commercial modernization of China following the impact of the West upon traditional China.

The three brothers were Tong Mow-chee (T'ang Mao-chih) (唐茂枝) (alias T'ang T'ing-chih) (唐廷植), known in his youth as A-chick (亞植), born in 1828 and who died in 1897; Tong King-sing (T'ang Ching-hsing) (唐景星) (alias T'ang T'ing-shu) (唐廷樞), known in his youth as Akü, born in 1832 and who died in 1892; and Tong Ting-keng (T'ang T'ing-keng) (唐廷庚) (perhaps also known as Tong Ying-sing), known in his youth as Afu or A-foo (亞扶), born in 1845. Tong King-sing was the most prominent of the brothers, but although several biographical notices and monographs have been written on aspects of his life, none of them trace his formative years in much detail.[1] More information is available on the youthful years of Tong Mow-chee than on the other brothers.

An account of the 61st birthday celebration of Tong Mow-chee in 1888 states that 'the Tong family has played an important part in the history of the trade relations between foreigners and Chinese in Shanghai, and they may be said to be the leaders of the party of progress in the initiation and development of commerce after the style of foreign countries'.

A study of the formative years of the three Tong brothers illustrates the background from which the new bourgeois class arose in China. One of their classmates at the Morrison Education Society School wrote an essay entitled, 'The life of man a building, and youth the foundation'.[2] The youthful essayist asks how a man can

have 'a well cultivated mind and habits which qualify him to discharge the serious duties of life, unless he has had laid a good
foundation for all these things when he was a youth. On this
foundation whether good or bad, we must build the superstructure
in middle life and age'.[3]

The location of their home district, their education by the Morrison Education Society, their youthful services as interpreters,
and their first ventures into the business world all laid the foundations for the Tong brothers' contribution to their country's progress.

Their Home Village

The home of the Tong brothers was the village of Tong-ka in the
Heung Shan District of Kwangtung Province.[4] The district is situ-
ated between Macau and Canton, the two centres for early European commerce in China. The villagers had grown accustomed to
the presence of the 'red-haired barbarians' with their strange ways,
as the Cumsingmoon anchorage for the opium ships was in the bay
just off shore from the village. The lesson that an ability to deal
with the European might be financially profitable was not lost on
them.

When the Morrison Education Society recruited its first students, the majority by far, if not all, were from the Heung Shan
District. At that time, only a Chinese family that was too poor to
provide its sons with a traditional Chinese education or one that
intended its sons to enter the service of foreigners would consider
sending its sons to a school operated by foreigners, where English
would be one of the languages of instruction. It is likely that some
members of Tong King-sing's family had had previous contacts
with Europeans and realized the financial value of a good command of English.[5]

The Presbyterian missionary, the Revd Dr A.P. Happer, who
opened an Anglo-Chinese school at Macau after the Morrison
Education Society had moved its school to Hong Kong, considered
that the home village of King-sing was particularly favourable for
Christian influence. The Morrison Education Society School had
eight boys enrolled from the village or vicinity, three of them being
the Tong brothers, and the Presbyterians also had eight. Happer
thought of Tong-ka village as a possible location for his English-
language school. When this did not seem practicable, he suggested

to his mission board that the Chinese schools there should be given a grant, on the understanding that they would include the study of the Bible in their curriculum, the intention being that with this preparation the village might make a good mission station at some time in the future.[6]

Student Years at the Morrison Education Society School

The father of the three Tong brothers enrolled them as students of the Morrison Education Society School. He was required to sign an agreement giving the school jurisdiction over his sons for a period of eight years or until their education had been completed. In turn, the Society agreed to provide board, clothing, and schooling. The brothers' father admitted to the school's principal in 1845 that it required some courage to hand his boys over. Principal Brown quotes him as saying:

We could not understand why a foreigner should wish to feed and instruct our children for nothing. Perhaps it was to entice them away from their parents and country, and transport them by and by to some foreign land. But I understand it now. I have had my three sons in your school steadily since they entered it, and no harm has happened to them. The eldest has qualified for the public service as an interpreter. The other two have learned nothing bad. The religion you have taught them, of which I was so much afraid, has made them better. I myself believe its truth, though the customs of my country forbid my embracing it. I have no longer any fears; you labor for others' good, not your own. I understand it now.[7]

The oldest of the three brothers, Tong Mow-chee, was enrolled in the school under the name A-chick, aged 11, on 4 November 1839. He was received along with four other boys on this date as the first students on the school roll. On 1 November 1841, A-chick's brother, Tong King-sing, was enrolled as Akü, aged 10, a member of the second class, and on 7 April 1843, their youngest brother, Tong Ting-keng, entered the third class as Afu, aged 8.

The first class has attracted the most attention, especially as one of its members was Yung Wing, who proposed the Chinese Educational Mission for training Chinese students abroad in the 1870s. After an initial weeding out of those not considered suitable, the class consisted of only six students, who appear to have been exceptionally clever; at least, their future careers indicate that they were especially gifted.[8] This conclusion is also supported by their rapid acquisition of English. After only six months' instruction, the boys were able to write letters to their principal's former pupils at the New York Institution for the Deaf and Dumb. Unfortunately, only two of these letters were published, but for students who had been studying English for only six months they indicate rapid progress in the language. Undoubtedly, they were written with considerable tutorial supervision and suggestion, but they provide information on Tong A-chick's schoolboy routine and reflect the impact of the missionary emphasis of the school upon the students.[9] One of the youngsters wrote:

I am glad in this school. Every morning get up at 5 o'clock, wash body, and face and hands, and go to the garden to walk and pick flowers. At 7 come to school in library, learn Chinese books, at 12 go to play. At 7 o'clock go to parlor to pray to God every morning and evening ... After dinner we go to the garden, hops and play. 9 o'clock to bed. On Sabbath day we read the Bible. God made the world, and heavens and the sun and moon, and the stars and things. Made heaven in six days, only one day did not make because it is Sabbath day.[10]

A letter written by Tong A-chick was published after he had been in the school for a little more than two years. The Revd S.R. Brown commented that since the boys had been under his instruction their manners and habits were much changed and 'their convictions of what is right and wrong are clear and manifest'. He looked forward to their eventual conversion, but with much concern. 'Poor boys! they will have such difficulties to contend with if they become disciples of Christ, as might shake the faith of many a profession of religion in a land where Christianity is popular. Here everything from every quarter is against them.' We shall note later that Tong A-chick was baptized and for a short while was active in the cause of Christianity, but his interest did not last and there is no evidence that he was an active Christian in later life.

A-chick's letter, dated Macau, 14 January 1842, expressed the high regard he felt for his school and reflected a developing sense of Christian morality.

Mr. Brown is the best teacher that I know in my life, and his school too. In this part of the country I think there is no such school as his.

Hear there is a school for Deaf and Dumb in New York. But if Chinese were so, he would not learn any thing, neither how to read or write, until he died.

When school formed had five boys—after about nine months some went home, because English were at war with China. Afterwards eldest of them whose name was Aling went home, because he did a very bad thing and committed a great sin against God, as in the law of Moses and the prophets.

Atseuk was taken home by his father. One day, as the English were fighting with the Chinese, his father came to Mr. Brown's school and wanted to take Atseuk home. On the same day Mr. Brown was not at home. Then he wished to take him back without asking Mr. Brown. But Atseuk wouldn't go, and his father gave him a flogging and he cried, and after about an hour they went. Next morning father came and wanted to take his things home, when Mr. Brown saw him he rebuked him and he went home.

Now in this school our teacher has appointed a monitor to keep the boys still when the teacher is out, and the school in order, and they ring the bell to call the boys into study their lessons and say them to the teacher.[11]

A year and a half after writing this letter, Tong A-chick's schooling was interrupted by a term of service as interpreter in Shanghai.

In 1842, the Treaty of Nanking was signed and the British were granted the right to trade at the five treaty ports. This privilege meant the opening of a consular establishment in the ports and the need arose for a competent staff of translators and interpreters. As always, very few qualified personnel were available. A request was made to Mr Brown to supply interpreters from his students for Shanghai, the first consulate to be opened. He was reluctant to interrupt the education of his students, but official pressure, reinforced by reference to the yearly government grant the school received, was strong, and Brown agreed to send two of his students for a limited period. Tong A-chick, the student who had been longest in the school, was chosen, along with T'in Sau. The latter had only been in the school for a few months, but was an advanced-transfer pupil from Singapore.[12] They were to serve for six months and then be replaced.

The difficulty of finding capable interpreters was a constant problem.[13] The authorities looked to the English-language schools conducted under missionary auspices as a source of supply. The East India Company had assisted in the support of the Anglo-Chinese College at Malacca and, after the revocation of its charter, the Company's annual grants had been continued by the British Plenipotentiary in China. At the time of the opium war, there was a desperate need for interpreters. An appeal was made to the Government of the Straits Settlements for the services of students educated at the Anglo-Chinese College, but none could be found who were willing to come to China. This soured Sir Henry Pottinger and gave him cause to doubt the effectiveness of the College, and when it moved to Hong Kong in 1843, he abruptly terminated the annual grant and transferred it to the Morrison Education Society. It was natural, therefore, that his successor, Sir John Davis, should make a demand upon that school for interpreters, and it was difficult for Brown to resist the request. He comments on the problem in his report to the Directors in 1844:

It is the desire of the Society, and must naturally be of all friends of the pupils, to see them fill stations of usefulness with honor to themselves and their patrons; but as the Trustees in taking these lads entirely away from parental influence, have taken upon themselves those duties, they consider that they and the instructors are bound to make the best arrangement possible for the real welfare of the lads. In choosing or refusing situations for them, they feel that regard should be paid to the moral and social position of the boys, selecting, as much as can be, those possessing freedom from great temptation, and not exposed to those vicious influences under which even persons trained under Christian parentage and influence make shipwreck of reputation, health, prospects, and life itself here and hereafter.[14]

True to his trust, Mr Brown kept a close check on the two boys he had sent to Shanghai. The British Consul, Mr Balfour, reported to him that he was quite pleased with both the ability and the conduct of the boys. He had found them so useful that he was not willing to send them back after the agreed six months' term, and in addition made a request for more boys to replace his entire group of Chinese linguists, whom he found 'useless and troublesome'. One of the boys sent Brown a diary relating what he had been doing, and the other wrote frequent letters. Both indicated that 'they were grateful for the benefits they have received and are attached to their benefactors'.[15]

When A-chick finally returned after a year and a half's service in Shanghai, he brought a note from the Consul giving a favourable account of his conduct while he had been in the public service and expressing the Consul's obligation to the Morrison Education Society for providing the assistance of its pupils. A-chick's fellow-student remained behind in Shanghai and entered the Chinese customs service.

Returning to Hong Kong in 1845, Tong A-chick resumed his studies at the Morrison Education Society School after the Chinese New Year holiday. Essays written by the six members of the senior class were published in November 1845. One of these, entitled 'Chinese Government', appears to reflect the impressions gained by A-chick in his post as consular interpreter at Shanghai. The essay points out the injustice and corruption of the Chinese Government. While very critical of malpractice in the Government, the author was quite conversant with its administrative structure and practices. There is no definite statement as to the authors of the various essays, but internal evidence would indicate that this was probably the one written by A-chick.[16]

The Morrison Education Society School was closed in the spring of 1849. The students were distributed among three schools: the Presbyterian Mission School at Canton under the supervision of Dr A.P. Happer, the London Missionary Society School at Hong Kong under the supervision of the Revd Dr James Legge, and the Church of England Anglo-Chinese School at Hong Kong under the supervision of the Colonial Chaplain, the Revd Vincent Stanton. Along with seven of his schoolmates, Tong A-chick continued his studies under Mr Stanton. In March 1850, upon the arrival of the first Bishop of Victoria, the Right Revd George Smith, Stanton handed his school over to him and the Bishop reorganized it as St. Paul's College. The Bishop took a particular interest in Tong A-chick and mentions him in several of his official reports.

A-chick's brothers, Akü and Afu, entered Dr Legge's school. In his *Report of the Preparatory School and the Theological Seminary in Hongkong of the London Missionary Society for the year 1850*, published in Hong Kong, Dr Legge lists T'ong A-foo (唐亞扶) as one of the six members of the first or senior class. He also states: 'T'ong A-kü, who was received into the school in 1849 when the Morrison Education Society ceased and had been a pupil there between seven and eight years, remained here until the month of the vacation in August last, after which he entered the service of a Commission Agent and Auctioneer. He is a clever lad, but has made no profession of Christianity, though he continues to attend English services at the Union Church'. Tong Afu had left Dr Legge's school by October 1856, for, at that time, as a clerk of the solicitor, George Cooper Turner, he witnessed a land transfer document. His last signature as a witness is on a document dated 23 December 1856. At some time between that date and 6 July 1857, when Chan Quan-ee was the Chinese clerk for Mr Turner, Tong A-foo must have left Turner's employment.[17]

The three boys expressed their appreciation of the advantages

their education had given them by making generous contributions
to causes sponsored by their former schools. In 1861–2 there were
five life subscriptions to the Morrison Education Society belonging
to former students and in 1862–3 there were seven; of these Tong
A-chick and Tong Akü each contributed $35 and Tong Afu contri-
buted $30. In 1856, Dr Legge received contributions from seven of
his former students for work among the Chinese in Hong Kong.
Tong Akü, government interpreter, contributed $30 and Fong
(*sic*) A-foo, in a lawyer's office, $15. A note dated Canton, 8 April
1872, written by Tong Afu in response to an appeal by Dr Legge
for contributions towards the building of a chapel at a mission hospital in Canton suggests that Afu had not mastered his English as
well as his elder brothers. He also apologized for not accepting
Christianity. 'It is true that I owe much to the Church and to my
teacher, too, it is bad I know to forget the Gospel you taught me.
But I feel ashamed and pain to come to the subject more nearer.
Your pardon I must crave.'[18]

Interpreters for the Hong Kong Government

In the autumn of 1847, Tong A-chick was appointed to the position of interpreter in the Magistrate's Court at an annual salary of
£125. The former interpreter, Daniel Richard Caldwell, had had
to declare bankruptcy and resign as Assistant Police Magistrate
and Interpreter. As usual, a qualified replacement was hard to find
and the Government again turned to the Morrison Education Society to acquire the services of A-chick.[19]

Not everyone, however, was confident of A-chick's trustworthiness as an interpreter. In reporting a court case, the *China Mail*
noted that the foreman of the jury objected to having A-chick
serve as interpreter. He refused, however, to state the grounds for
his objection and the judge compromised by ordering another interpreter to check on the accuracy of A-chick's interpretation.[20]
The suspicions of the jury foreman appear to have had some
foundation, for, in the summer of 1851, A-chick was charged with
being in league with pirates. A pirate ship had been seized and
documents were found on board which implicated A-chick. In particular, there was a letter in which he was thanked by 'his brethren
of the sea', as they called themselves, for getting one of their number cleared of the charge of piracy by means of false interpretation
in court. In July 1851, a commission composed of three Justices of

the Peace investigated the charges against A-chick as well as other abuses in the Police Court. A-chick, however, had influential supporters. A newspaper account says that 'both His Excellency the Governor and his Worship the Chief Magistrate of Police were determinedly opposed to Tong A-chick's dismissal; and although Tong A-chick applied for his discharge from public service, Mr. Hillier would not grant it to him'.[21] However, the investigating commission threatened to resign if their recommendation for dismissal was not put into effect, and as soon as Mr Hillier left the colony about the beginning of September 1851, A-chick was replaced by another former student of the Morrison Education Society.

At about the same time, Tong A-chick became involved in a court case which reflected one of the less favourable aspects of social conditions in Hong Kong. The case involved a 16-year-old girl. Her mother had been connected with a brothel. She needed money and, having no security but the good looks and body of her daughter, then only 9 years old and already a singer in the brothel, she had pledged 'the body' of the girl to a brothel-keeper willing to advance the money. The mother subsequently died, leaving the note unpaid and her daughter in the service of the woman to whom she owed the money. The brothel-mistress also served as middleman and security for obtaining a loan to cover the burial expenses of the girl's mother, thus further obligating the girl to her. The brothel in which she was employed was frequented by Tong A-chick. He took a fancy to her and ran up a large bill with the brothel-mistress. With the promise of marriage, he induced the girl to leave the brothel and live with him, leaving behind her mother's unpaid debt as well as his own unsettled bill.

The brothel-keeper threatened to sue for the recovery of her debts. Tong A-chick tried to settle the two accounts with a token payment, which she refused, though this counter-offer delayed court proceedings. In the meantime, A-chick was dismissed from his government post and the brothel-mistress gained new courage and brought her demands before the court. The girl was imprisoned as a debtor, but when the case was tried in the Court of Summary Jurisdiction, the Magistrate dismissed the claims on the grounds that it had not been proper to secure the original debt by a pledge of 'a body' for what seemed the obvious purposes of prostitution.

With the case decided in favour of A-chick's inamorata, he took out a summons in the name of the girl against the brothel-keeper for certain property she had kept when the girl had left to live with A-chick. Before the case was heard, A-chick's uncle, who had been compradore to a former Sheriff of Hong Kong and was still rendering service to the Government, tried to use his connections to intimidate the brothel-keeper. But in spite of his appearance in court on behalf of the girl, as well as the testimony of others of some standing, she lost the case.[22]

The publicity connected with this sordid affair did not enhance Tong A-chick's reputation in the community, and it seemed better for him to leave Hong Kong and try his fortune in another place. His uncle was planning to go to California so it was natural for A-chick to join him.

When Tong A-chick was dismissed from his post as interpreter in the Magistrate's Court, his brother Akü (Tong King-sing) was appointed on 17 December 1851 to fill A-chick's place at a salary of £100. This was £25 less than the annual salary his brother had been receiving. In 1854, Akü submitted a request for an increase, stating that he found it difficult to meet the expenses of his family, which consisted of six in Hong Kong and others in his home village. He was granted the substantial increase of £50, but in January 1856, he resigned his post as interpreter.[23]

Several charges of irregularities had been brought against him. None of them were proved, but they were aired in the local press and his reputation was under a cloud. He then became caught up in the charges and countercharges of the Caldwell–Ma Chow Wong affair.[24] However, Tong Akü had influential defenders. The Assistant Police Magistrate, in submitting testimony in the libel trial of the editor of a local newspaper, spoke strongly on Akü's behalf and recommended that he should be recalled as a government interpreter. The Attorney-General also gave him a strong recommendation: 'Tong Akü was the ablest interpreter amongst the European and Chinese, not even excepting Mr. Caldwell, whom I have known, during the two and half years I have filled the office of Attorney General. As to his good faith and trust-worthiness, I hold him not inferior to any. I believe him to have been sacrificed to Mr. Caldwell and Ma Chow Wing.'[25]

In the list of pawnbrokers' licences for Hong Kong, Tong Akü is registered as the proprietor of the Quin Sing shop on Queen's Road for the years 1857 and 1858. He may also have been a silent partner in the shop in the Lower Bazaar registered in the name of

Tong Hop Sing in 1855 and 1856.[26] In a court case in 1856 regarding goods looted from a pawnshop during a fire, the charge was made that Akü had an interest in the shop, but he denied it, though the ground on which it was built was affirmed to be his. The news-writer claimed that the Chinese maintained that he held two out of the four shares in the shop. The reporter suggested that, in view of the fact that there had been cases of alleged oppression in the Magistrate's Court arising out of his co-partnership, the matter should be investigated by the Police Commission.[27] These shops were profitable ventures for, in a letter Tong King-sing wrote to William Keswick of Jardine, Matheson and Company, dated 1866, he stated that from two pawnshops he had owned for four years in Hong Kong he made 25 to 45 per cent annually on his investment.[28]

At the same time that Tong Akü was under fire as interpreter, a relative, Tong Sing-po, was accused of misappropriating funds as the Treasurer of the Committee for the Celebration of the Festival of the Hungry Ghosts. The *China Mail* of 4 September 1856 remarked that 'members of the Tong family connected with the Hongkong Government ... have an unfortunate knack of getting themselves into scrapes, for we are told that A-chick ... has latterly been rendering himself obnoxious to his countrymen in California as head of one of the *hwuy*, and that his life even is in danger. We have heard that it is A-chick's intention to return to Hongkong'.

Tong Mow-chee (A-chick) in California

The years spent by Tong Mow-chee (A-chick) in California provided the first opportunity for the Tong brothers to serve the special interests of their countrymen. Although only 24 years of age, A-chick soon became an important leader and spokesman for the Chinese community in California. His English-language education and his intimate knowledge of Western ways qualified him for this position.

After A-chick's dismissal from his post as interpreter in the Hong Kong Government in 1851, he prepared to leave Hong Kong and join the Chinese exodus to California. He left about the middle of January 1852. The departure had been delayed because of difficulties resulting from the disastrous Bazaar fire at the close of 1851. In the four hundred odd buildings destroyed at that time were most of the provisions, clothing, and necessities the emigrants had accumulated for their voyage to San Francisco, along with their written contract in Chinese with the Captain and charterers of the ship on which they were to sail. This loss resulted in a dispute with the Captain and an appeal was made to the Revd S.W. Bonney at Whampoa, where the arrangements for the charter had been made originally. Bonney came down to Hong Kong and quickly sorted things out, so that the ship could leave with its load of emigrants.[29]

A-chick left well supplied with letters of introduction to church people in San Francisco. On 29 June 1851, along with two of his fellow-students at St. Paul's College, he had been baptized by the Bishop of Victoria.[30] Strangely enough, his dismissal from government service and his connection with the young prostitute did not seem to put him out of favour with the Christian community. Bonney had recommended him to Mr Buel, agent of the American Bible Society, the Revd T.D. Hunt, a Congregational minister, and Mr Bokee, a business man formerly in the employment of the China-trade firm of Olyphant and Company. From his patron, the Bishop of Victoria, A-chick received a general letter of introduction 'to any Christian minister he might meet'.

Upon arrival in San Francisco, A-chick presented his general letter of introduction from the Bishop to the Revd Dr Van Mehr, rector of Grace Church Episcopal, who wrote to the Bishop:

It was with no ordinary degree of pleasure that I made the acquaintance of a young Chinese convert called A-chick, who brought an excellent letter of introduction from you. And I presume you feel deeply interested in his welfare ... He came to see me as soon as he had arrived and has visited me almost daily. Knowing the spiritual temptation of this life killing place, the very seat of Mammon, I have advised him to prepare for communion. I have read with him a part of Bishop Wilson's preparatory to the Holy Communion, and conversed much with him on the nature and design of the Sacraments. What strikes me most is the depth of his heart and the consciousness he has that it is the hardness of heart of his countrymen which prevents them becoming Christians. It is unfortunate that he has to live altogether in continual companionship with them. As far as I can see, he is a converted man and promises to remain faithful. I shall do what I can to fulfill God's design with this redeemed soul, until he returns under your immediate care.[31]

A-chick attracted the interest not only of the Revd Dr Van Mehr, but also of several other churchmen interested in the evangelization of the Chinese. Albert Williams, founder of the First Presbyterian Church in San Francisco, reported that he met A-chick and that 'his answer to questions touching matters of Christian doctrine are intelligent and satisfactory. He is associated with his uncle, accompanying him in a mercantile venture, and will remain in this city. I have much hope, that through his instrumentality we may bring the gospel more directly to bear upon his interesting country'.[32]

Soon after A-chick's arrival, a Bible class for Chinese was organized by a Presbyterian elder, Thomas C. Hambly. Its first members were A-chick 'and his companions'. It was realized that if the Chinese in San Francisco were to be reached by the Church, it was not enough to have classes for them in English. Hence the Session of the Presbyterian Church requested their board of foreign missions to send a Chinese-speaking missionary to San Francisco. In response to this request, the board sent a returned missionary from China, the Revd William Speer. Speer arrived at San Francisco in October 1852 and met A-chick the following month. He gives a somewhat detailed account of A-chick's activities and prospects in California and remarks:

Song [sic] Achick is regarded by the American community here as a man of more than common ability. He received us in his office attached to the hall of the company whose chief he is. His dress is the native silk gown, close pants, and embroidered shoes. His address impresses strangers as both dignified and courteous. His education is perhaps defective in the Chinese classics, but he may reach powers under his own government, on the basis of wealth, and hereafter wield an important influence over the undisclosed but portentious [sic] destinies of the vast empire of whose subjects he is begotten.[33]

Speer was not successful, however, in enlisting Tong A-chick as one of the charter members of the first Chinese Christian congregation organized in the United States, which opened in San Francisco on 6 November 1853.

After A-chick's original contact with the Christian community through the Revd Dr Van Mehr's confirmation instruction and through attendance at Elder Hambly's Bible class, his spiritual enthusiasm waned. He was probably too caught up in his business and diplomatic activities. In order to have the full confidence of the general Chinese community it was probably expedient not to have too intimate and open an association with the Christian community.[34] However, the Chinese were not antagonistic towards Christian work among their countrymen. An appeal to the Chinese community was made by Mr Speer for funds for a mission building. Tong A-chick assisted in gathering contributions. Two thousand dollars were raised among the Chinese, and an interested missionary remarked that it was 'not only the first contribution made in this country, but by that people anywhere to any considerable extent, toward the erection of a Christian church'.[35] Tong K. Achick and Company contributed $100.

Soon after A-chick's arrival in the spring of 1852, he had found himself in a position of leadership in the Chinese community for an attack of haemorrhages forced the generally acknowledged representative of the Chinese community to relinquish his position at this time. He was a colourful figure named Norman Asing. An election was held and Tong A-chick was elected as his successor. I am not sure whether the position to which he was elected was that of the head of the Kwong Chau Kung Sz or of the Yeong Wo Wui. The latter was organized by the men of the Heung Shan District in 1852. It is clear that Tong A-chick was the head of the Yeong Wo Association in 1852. He retained this position for several years, probably until his return to China.

The event, however, which made A-chick responsible for representing the Chinese community before the American community was political opposition to a bill to introduce foreign contract labour into California.[36] The merchants were generally in favour of contract labour. The miners were strongly opposed to it; they regarded contract labour as an economic threat. This view appeared to be that of the majority and Governor Bigler addressed the Legislature on 23 April 1852, opposing the legalization of contract labour.

The Governor's message had attracted the attention of the few Chinese who could read English. They, in turn, explained it to the general Chinese community. In response, two of the leaders of the community, Hab Wa of the Sam Wo Company and Tong (in the original account the name appears as Long) A-chick of Tun Wo and Company, published a letter in reply 'for the Chinamen in California'. In it they set forth the significant contribution the commerce of the Chinese merchants had made to the economy of the State and emphasized that the Chinese immigrants were not coolies but free labourers.

Encouraged by the interest aroused by their first letter, the

Chinese sent Tong A-chick as their ambassador to the Governor. 'We charged him to see the Governor face to face, and to tell him again the truth about us, and to endeavour, by supplicating words, to induce him to use his powerful influence in persuading the American miners to abide by the law which the Legislature had passed, allowing foreigners, Chinamen as well as others, to work in the mines on the payment of a Tax.'[37]

To create a favourable climate for the presentation of the Chinese position to the Governor, the Chinese community sent with Tong A-chick 'shawls of rarest pattern, rolls of silk of costliest texture, and some seventy handkerchiefs of the choicest description'.[38] Tong A-chick felt that his visit to the Governor had accomplished some good. He had been hospitably received and entertained. Indeed, the Governor had requested that the Chinese present another letter to him stating their case and he promised to answer it by a speech or proclamation on their behalf. 'When we heard this, we were much rejoiced, and believed our sorrows were nearly at an end.'[39] Consequently, they quickly drafted another letter and again sent it with Tong A-chick to the Governor. But soon they received word that the Governor had found the letter unacceptable and had submitted a draft of one that he would consider suitable. They, however, found that 'the words were not our words, and that we cannot say them with the truth of honest men, and that they contradict what we have already said'. So, despairing of the support of the Governor, they proceeded to publish their original letter dated 16 May 1852.

The letter pointed out that mutual interchange would be beneficial for both Americans and Chinese. 'Our intercourse may benefit us both very much, and that will be better than quarreling about our respective merits. Why should East quarrel with the West? God made them both, and placed the day between them, that the nations should use it in doing good works to one another.' This letter was signed by Tong K. Achick of Tun Wo and Company, and also by Chun Aching on behalf of Sam Wo and Company.

When several bills were introduced into the California Legislature in 1853, proposing that 'no Asiatic or person of Asiatic descent or Chinese should be permitted to work in any mines in this state', the matter was referred to the Committee on Mines and Mining Interests. The Committee held hearings in which the heads of the four district houses testified. Tong K. Achick acted as their interpreter and presented the Chinese position.⁴⁰ He also prepared a detailed analysis of the organization and functions of the five district associations with a numerical account of the Chinese belonging to each.

Speer testified to the good work done by A-chick on behalf of the Chinese. 'This is the individual whose efforts last Spring (1852) in behalf of his countrymen, were the chief means in turning the tide of public opinion in their favour, when those unfriendly to them made the attempt to expel them from the country. And if he remains here, there is no man whose influence will be more felt among the large bodies of emigrants of his own race already in the State, or coming in the spring.'⁴¹

Tong A-chick interrupted his stay in California with a visit to Hong Kong for a few months in 1853 or 1854. This is mentioned in a report written by the Bishop of Victoria. The Bishop welcomed him and was pleased with the letter the Revd Dr Van Mehr had sent with A-chick stating that 'it is impossible not to appreciate his sociable disposition, his kindness, his gentlemanly behaviour, his Christian deportment'.⁴² In 1856 or 1857, A-chick returned permanently to China.

A Brief Survey of the Later Careers of the Tong Brothers

This study is intended to illustrate the background of representative members of a new Chinese bourgeoisie by examining the formative factors in their youth which contributed to their success as adults. It is not inappropriate, however, to set forth briefly their adult careers; that of Tong King-sing is well documented, those of his brothers less so.

Not long after Tong King-sing resigned as interpreter in the Hong Kong Government, he joined the Chinese maritime customs service at Shanghai. In 1863, he joined the compradorial staff of Jardine, Matheson and Company, and in 1873 was appointed General Manager of the recently organized China Merchants' Steam Navigation Company. He resigned in 1884 and until his death in 1892 was connected with the Kaiping mines.

Tong Mow-chee, on his return from California in 1857, also joined the staff of the Chinese customs service. In 1871, he was compradore at Tientsin for Jardine, Matheson and Company, and in 1873, when his brother resigned as their Shanghai compradore, he took his place. He held this position until his death in 1895, though for a time he was associated with his brother in the management of the China Merchants' Steam Navigation Company. He was acting manager when Tong King-sing was on a European tour in 1883. To avoid the Company's ships being seized by the French, the property of the Company was transferred to Russell and Company in 1884, and Tong Mow-chee returned to Jardines. He became President of the Canton Guild in Shanghai and of the Hankow Tea Guild. According to a sketch of his life on the occasion of his 61st birthday, 'he had arduous and unpleasant duties to perform in connection with the Great Swatow Guild opium case in the Mixed Courts (of Shanghai) and the farming of the likin on opium in the Settlement. In addition he is director of different native and semi-native companies, and only lately he manifested his progressive spirit by his speeches at the public meeting in furtherance of the opening of Zoological Gardens in Shanghai'.[43]

One of the early business enterprises in which Tong Mow-chee and his brother, Tong King-sing, were interested was the first sugar refinery built in Hong Kong. The sugar company grew out of a business partnership between Tong King-sing, William McGregor Smith and a Mr Dahlbeck. When the Company was formed, Smith was the largest shareholder, contributing 16,000 taels. Tong King-sing put in 3,000 taels. They had intended to conduct business at Kiukiang, but instead transferred to Shanghai, where they operated successfully until 1864. It was arranged that Smith should go to England to purchase machinery for a sugar refinery. But while he was absent, business declined and Dahlbeck absconded, leaving debts of 5,000 taels. Tong King-sing became responsible for these debts. He was already in financial straits as he had encountered other losses and had had to pay some $30,000 to get one of his brothers out of the hands of the mandarins. After Smith returned with the machinery, King-sing transferred his share in the business to his brother, Tong Mow-chee. The refinery was set up at East Point, Hong Kong, under the firm name of Smith, Wahee and Company. Wahee was Wong Yan-ting, also known as Wong Wa-hee. Tong Mow-chee sold out his interests in December 1869.[44] The Company eventually went bankrupt and was taken over by Jardine, Matheson and Company.

The youngest of the brothers, Afu, seems to have been known later as T'ang T'ing-keng. According to Feuerwerker's study on China's early industrialization, Afu was manager of the Canton branch of the China Merchants' Steam Navigation Company. He can probably be identified as the Tong Ying-sing of Canton who, with Cheang Luk-u of Hong Kong, acquired title in 1882 to a part of Marine Lot 225 just west of Western Market, where the China Merchants' Steam Navigation Company established their Hong Kong branch office. In 1884, Tong and Cheang transferred this property to William Howell Forbes, the head partner of Russell and Company.[45] In the same year, Tong King-sing and his brother were charged with irregularities in the handling of the company's finances. They had enough of their shares confiscated to make up for the deficits in their accounts.[46]

In 1883, one of Tong King-sing's brothers bought one of the mansions on the Praia Grande in Macau for 10 million patacas. The purchase was greeted as evidence of the confidence of Chinese capitalists in the future of Macau.[47]

Conclusion

All three brothers made a contribution to China's effort to adjust to the new demands made upon it when China's traditional system proved ineffective in meeting the economic and military imperialism of the West. The comment made about Tong King-sing at the time of his death could apply to each of the brothers: 'From the early days when he was a boy at the once famous Morrison School in Hong Kong, Tong King Shing had been in harness, and actively engaged in important work that has already proved of great and permanent service to his country.'[48] Their English-language education, conducted on Western pedagogical principles, their services as interpreters and clerks for foreigners, and their early business ventures shaped the thought and characters of the Tong brothers and directed them to their life work.

3 Translators, Compradores, and Government Advisers

STUDENTS who had learned English at missionary schools were sought after by government officials to serve as translators and advisers, and by the business community to act as compradores. They became middlemen between things Chinese and things foreign.

Commissioner Lin's Translators

In the several studies of Commissioner Lin and the Opium War the translators he used in his efforts to acquire a more adequate knowledge of the West are mentioned. The first notice of them is given in a postscript to an article, 'Crisis in the Opium Traffic', printed in the June 1839 issue of the *Chinese Repository*:

The commissioner has in his service four natives, all of whom have made some progress in the English tongue. The first is a young man, educated at Penang and Malacca, and for several years employed by the Chinese government at Peking. The second is an old man, educated at Serampore. The third is a young man who was once at the school at Cornwall, Connecticut, U.S.A. The fourth is a young lad, educated in China, who is able to read and translate papers on common subjects, with much ease, correctness, and facility.

A more exact identification of the four translators is given in the semi-annual report of the Canton mission of the American Board dated 4 July 1839, to be found in the archives of the Board on deposit at Houghton Library, Harvard University.

Four Chinese: Aman, who was with Dr. Marshman at Serampore, Shaou Tih, who was educated at Malacca and since employed as Latin translator of the Russian commission at Peking, Alum, who was at Cornwall, Connecticut, U.S.A., and last but not least, Atih, the son of Afat—he is decidedly the best English-Chinese scholar in China—all acquainted with English are in his pay.

The four translators shared one common element: they all had acquired their knowledge of English under missionary sponsorship. The official 'linguists' of the Co-hong system at Canton could not be used for general translations. Their abilities were confined to a limited commercial field and they had little or no understanding of the broader aspects of Western thought and literature. Hence, when Commissioner Lin wished to have the mysteries of the West unlocked, he had to find Chinese with a broader and more adequate understanding of the English language and of foreign ways of thought and action. He found four who met these requirements among the small group of Chinese who had been educated by the missionaries.

When Lin was sent to Canton by the Imperial Government of China to suppress the opium trade, he was as ill-informed of the ways of Westerners as any other member of the official class. After six months in Canton, in answer to an enquiry from Peking about the supposed custom of foreigners on ships buying Chinese children, he stated that, in some cases, as many as a thousand or more were bought at a time.[1] But already his programme was under way to provide him with more accurate information. He realized that if he was to deal effectively with foreigners, who generally acted in a manner far removed from the customary polite Chinese pattern, he must know more about them and their countries. Since his contact with them was limited to infrequent formal interviews circumscribed by official etiquette, he sought information concerning foreign ways from his translators. A programme of translating Western writings was instituted.

Outside the foreign business houses there was little Western literature available in Canton. Lin's translator, however, had easy access to the weekly issues of the English newspapers published in Canton. From the Revd Samuel R. Brown, principal of the Morrison Education Society School in Macau, the *Encyrcropania* was bought. And when the Spanish ship *Bilbiano* was seized and burned by the Chinese in September 1839, its library was sent to the Commissioner.[2] He also requisitioned all the globes, charts, atlases, geographies, encyclopaedias, and dictionaries he could find in Canton.[3]

The two major problems Lin had to deal with were the opium trade and a general embargo on trade at Canton. Naturally, he felt a special need for information on these matters. In July 1839, he sent some quotations from Vattel's *Law of Nations* referring to war, blockades, and embargoes to the hospital of Dr Peter Parker in Canton and requested a translation. He also desired a medical opinion about opium and a general prescription for the cure of its smokers. In reply,

An explanation was written in Chinese, to the effect that opium was classed among the poisons by scientific men of the West, but at the same time [it was] a valuable medicine in the hands of the skillful physician—that, when taken in excessive doses, it is capable of producing death ... Some explanation was also afforded, of the manner in which by its gradual influence, the use of opium undermines the whole constitution. And it was then pointed out, that the treatment for the recovery of those suffering under its use must vary.[4]

Lin also had available for translation Thelwall's *The Iniquities of the Opium Trade*.

Lin was only too well acquainted with the attitude of the opium merchants regarding the trade. Their reluctance to co-operate with him in the suppression of the trade was quite evident. He turned to a Western doctor for information about the scientific nature of opium. In Thelwall, he read the views of an enlightened minority of the British public who deplored their nation's involvement in the trade.

In a comment Lin wrote on translations of correspondence between the British and the Governor of Macau, which he forwarded to Peking, he justifies his policy of seeking information concerning the foreign powers:

At this crucial phase of our effort to ward off the foreigners, we must constantly find out all we can about them. Only by knowing their strength and weakness can we find the right means to restrain them. For that reason I have got hold of six letters that passed between the Portuguese and English and have secretly had them translated by people who can read foreign languages.[5]

Of the 'people who can read foreign languages', Aman was an old man educated at Serampore. According to the Revd Elijah Bridgman, a missionary of the American Board of Commissioners for Foreign Missions, Aman's ability to speak and write English was 'rather indifferent'. Soon after Bridgman's arrival in China in 1830, a Mr H. visited him and told him about

a man born in Serampore. His father was a Chinese, his mother a native of Bengal. For more than ten years he was in one of the Mission schools, and enjoyed tuition of Mr. Marshman. It is now eight or ten years since he came to Canton. He continues to speak and write the English language, though rather indifferently. He is poor and low.[6]

Bridgman's informant, 'the young Mr H.', was undoubtedly a fellow American, William C. Hunter, who had studied Chinese at the Anglo-Chinese College at Malacca. Hunter also gives us interesting information about another of Lin's interpreters, Yuan Te-hui, more commonly known in contemporary records as Shaou Tih. Shaou Tih had received a Latin education at the Roman Catholic School at Penang. In William C. Hunter's reminiscences of his schoolmates at the college at Malacca published in his *Bits of Old China*,[7] he states that Shaou Tih was reported to have been a convert to the Roman Catholic faith, 'evidences of which, however, we never saw'. About the year 1825, Shaou Tih and a companion, Antonio Frederico Moor, entered the Anglo-Chinese College. Both were in their early twenties. Hunter describes Shaou Tih as fearfully pockmocked, but,

it soon became evident that he was no ordinary person. He was familiar with Latin, and our Chinese teachers were one and all struck with his superior attainments in their own language ... He was from the province of Sze-Chuen, and about twenty-five years of age. He spoke a robust Mandarin dialect, and made himself of great use in preparing copy for wooden blocks for the Chinese printing establishment, as he wrote a beautiful hand. In manner he was rough and abrupt, and his small twinkling eyes, keen and penetrating. During about sixteen months that Moore, myself, and Shaow-Tih were at the College together, the latter applied himself to the study of the English language, not lightly but profoundly, and when I left for Canton he had made wonderful progress. Everyone in the College referred to him as 'the reader', from the attention he gave to his studies.

In addition to his diligent application to the mastery of English, Shaou Tih wrote a book for the use of the students in the college entitled *English and Students Assistant, or Colloquial Phrases*. It was published by the Malacca Mission Press in 1826. He also translated into Chinese Keith's *Treatise on the Globes* and Stocki's *Clavis*. In 1827, Shaou Tih and his Chinese companion were forced to leave Malacca because of the activities of the triad societies.[8] He returned to Canton and remained there until 1829. In that year, his former Malacca schoolmate, William C. Hunter, recommended him to Howqua, the hong merchant, who in turn endorsed his application for the post of interpreter at the Imperial Foreign Office in Peking. Howqua had been requested by the Governor of Kwangtung to recommend a suitable person for the office. To test the applicant's ability to translate, the Peking Office had sent to

Canton a set of Russian papers in Latin of which they had a previous translation. The performance of Shaou Tih was satisfactory and he was interviewed by the Governor, 'provided with a boat and an official flag, and sent off to the Court of the Celestial Empire'.[9]

Shaou Tih's connection with triad societies may be the source of the comment in a newspaper notice that he 'is a pretender to the throne of the last dynasty, but this is probably mere play'. In the summer of 1830, he returned to Canton in an official capacity to procure foreign books to take to Peking. In 1838, he again returned to Canton for more books. The following year, he became one of Lin's translators. The *Chinese Repository*, in July 1839, printed one of his translations, labelling it as 'the first document which ever came from the Chinese in the English language'.[10] The English was in Chinese idiomatic style and, following the Chinese pattern, was without punctuation. It was an invitation to the British to reopen trade, but under the condition laid down by Commissioner Lin that none of it be in opium. Shaou Tih also translated Lin's letter to Queen Victoria. He continued working for Lin until 1840 and then returned to Peking. From that time the Western world lost sight of him.

Alum, the third of Lin's interpreters mentioned in 1839, was a former student at the Mission School of the American Board of Commissioners for Foreign Missions at Cornwall, Connecticut, from 1823 to 1825. The school was opened in 1817. At various times, young men from the islands of the Pacific came to the ports of New England. An interest in their spiritual welfare resulted in the organization of the foreign mission school at Cornwall. The founders hoped that the school would provide an atmosphere conducive to the conversion of its students to Christianity and that their academic training would 'qualify them to become useful Missionaries, Physicians, Surgeons, School Masters or Interpreters: and to communicate to the Heathen Nations such knowledge of agriculture and the arts, as may prove the means of promoting Christianity and civilization'.[11] The novelty of the school and its pious objectives attracted a great deal of attention. However, the school was not a total success. The boys aroused not only the interest of the religious and the curious but also the romantic interest of the village girls at Cornwall. Two of the daughters of the local leading families married students. This and other factors led to the closure of the school in 1825. During its brief history, there are records of five Chinese who studied there.

In 1824, William Alum and a companion, Henry Martyn Alan, were sent to the school under the sponsorship of the Female Society of Philadelphia for the Education of Heathen Youth. Thomas La Fargue, in an article on 'Some Early Chinese Visitors to the United States' refers to the two boys as 'two Chinese, evidently brothers, Ah Lan and Ah Lum'.[12] This relationship is not supported by the statement in the *New York Observer* of 3 July 1824 that a letter had been received 'from the father of one of these youths'. The father could not comprehend the idea of disinterested charity. To him it was incredible that his son should be the recipient of so much expenditure of funds and of such kindness on the part of the sponsoring society. He asked, 'Who shall pay the debt?'.

Shortly after their arrival at the school the principal reported that 'they were promising as to abilities and native education; but they have been used to a good living and an easy life ... and what is more, they are frequently disagreeing between themselves'. Not long before the closing of the school in 1825, the boys ran away. They eventually returned to Canton. In 1834, one of them was teaching English to servants in the foreign factories as an 'outside shopman not connected with the Hong merchants'.[13] Henry Martyn Alan died in January 1836, 'a besotted heathen'.[14] In 1839, his companion, William Alum, was one of the four interpreters employed by Commissioner Lin.

According to the estimate of his English teacher, Liang Tsen Teh was the best qualified of Lin's translators. A-teh (or Atih), as he was commonly called, was the son of Liang A-fa, the first ordained Chinese Protestant minister. When the boy was about 3 years old, his father brought him to Canton to be baptized. Dr Robert Morrison notes this event in his journal in the entry for 20 November 1823:

Today Leang A-fa, our Chinese fellow-disciple, brought his son Leang Tsen-teh, and had him baptized in the name of God the Father, Son and Spirit. Oh! that this small Christian family may be the means of spreading the truth around them in this pagan land.[15]

Shortly after the arrival of the Revd E. Bridgman at Canton in 1830, A-fa entrusted his 10-year-old son to Bridgman's care so that the boy might learn the English language 'and be familiar with Scriptures in that tongue, that he may, by and by, assist in a revision of the Chinese version'.[16] Bridgman, of course, was also concerned about the boy's spiritual welfare. In May 1832, Bridgman reports that 'the spirit of God has most manifestly been striving' with the lad, 'convicting him of sin. He is a child of many prayers'.[17] A-teh continued his studies in English, Hebrew and general subjects under Bridgman at Canton until the autumn of 1834, when the activity of a handful of Chinese Christians at Canton attracted the attention of officials. They arrested several and seized the printing blocks on which A-fa and his colleagues had been working. A-fa was forced to flee to Singapore, taking his son with him. At Singapore, A-teh's education was supervised by the American Board missionaries. His expenses were paid by the Morrison Education Society. In 1837, he returned to Canton to resume his studies under Bridgman.

When Lin ordered all the Chinese employed by foreigners to leave the foreign factories in March 1839, A-teh left Canton to live at Macau with the servants of Mr Charles W. King, an American merchant. However, agents of Commissioner Lin sought him out and offered him the lucrative position of interpreter. Towards the end of May he left Macau for his new position in Canton. At first, the missionaries were very apprehensive about this move. They were afraid that it would endanger his piety and weaken his former close attachment to the missionary enterprise. But when they began to hear reports of the important service he was rendering in interpreting the West to Commissioner Lin and, through letters and visits, were assured that he was still loyal to the Christian religion, they began to take a more positive attitude towards his new role.

The third annual report of the Morrison Education Society, dated 29 September 1841, notes that one of the students who had been under the patronage of the Society before 1839,

having been sought out while residing in Macao, in the spring of 1839, was with the strongest persuasions and promises induced to enter the service of his imperial majesty's high commissioner, who employed him as English interpreter and translator, and through him obtained translations of many extracts from the newspapers of the day, from Murray's *Cyclopedia of Geography*, and other foreign works, some of them relating to China. The efforts made to secure the services of this youth, while yet his education was but half-completed, are good evidences that the Chinese, even in the highest stations, appreciate the value of an acquaintance with foreign languages and literature. The youth was kindly treated by the commissioner, well remembered, and enjoyed good opportunities for improving his knowledge of his own language. He was kept thus employed till Lin's removal from office ... Many items of information obtained through this medium were sent up to the imperial court; and it was the intention of the commissioner to publish to his own countrymen the results of his inquiries concerning foreign nations. He is understood to have taken all his papers with him on leaving Canton, and he may perhaps, ere long, arrange and prepare his materials for publication.

With the demotion of Lin by the Emperor, the team of translators was disbanded. However, the court instructed Lin to remain in Canton after his dismissal in order to offer assistance to his successor, Ch'i-shan. One of the missionaries of the London Missionary Society reports, in December 1840, several months after Lin's removal from office, that A-teh 'is not now nominally in the pay of local government, but Lin prefers to detain him in his private capacity, designing to introduce him to Keahin, who has been appointed to take the seals of government over the two Kwangs'.[18]

After a year's separation, Bridgman noted a new maturity in his protégé. In a letter dated 29 November 1840, he states that he 'recently had a visit from my dear boy Atih, who has become a man. During his time of service in the office of Lin, he has continued to improve in knowledge, and I trust in piety. He is a very amiable, intelligent, and promising youth, and is (or seems to be) more anxious than ever to prosecute his studies'.[19] He had married in the spring of 1840 and so had a wife to provide for. There was some discussion between Bridgman and Liang A-fa about the young man's future before satisfactory arrangements were made for him to continue his studies.

At Lin's degradation, Atih returned to his home, the house of his father, where his wife is living. Being thus out of employment and fearing at once to return to his foreign friends, his father proposed that he should seek some commercial business for a season in order to gain a livelihood. To this line of business I felt unwilling the boy should be given up even for a short season. From the Government he had been receiving something like ten or twelve dollars a month, and this amount was necessary for his support and that of his family. This I could not well pay, Mr. (John Robert) Morrison has agreed therefore to join me, for the present in giving Atih support; we pay him twelve dollars a month, being six dollars from each, and have secured for him a quiet retreat in the country, away from for-

eigners and government, under the tuition of a maternal uncle. The boy
has a good supply of books in English and Hebrew, and we trust he is
doing well.[20]

Before A-teh had actually retired to his country retreat, Chinese
officials, appreciating the value of his services, had made several
efforts to persuade him to re-enter their service.[21]

When some of the bitter feelings of the Chinese against foreigners had abated, A-teh returned to Macau to study with Bridgman. He was only with Bridgman for a few months in 1842. In July
of that year, he was already in Hong Kong, serving as an interpreter for the Police Magistrate at a salary of $50 a month. The
position was considered to be only temporary, but his new affluence
prompted him to invest in a marine lot in the Lower Bazaar in
Hong Kong. He purchased it at public auction in October 1842 for
$115. In 1844, his father bought the adjoining lot. But neither
father nor son felt at home in Hong Kong. For a time after A-teh
had left his position in the Magistrate's Office, he remained in
Hong Kong, supported by Bridgman. Bridgman was still expressing grave concern over his spiritual state: 'Enticed away by Lin, he
was well-nigh ruined, even now, I am afraid to speak confidently
of him'.[22] Bridgman was appointed a Secretary of the American
Legation to China, under the direction of the Hon. Caleb Cushing,
in the spring and summer of 1844. A-teh assisted Bridgman in his
new duties. Soon after the treaty between the United States and
China was signed on 3 July 1844, A-teh left for Canton to enter the
employ of a salt merchant, P'an Shih-ch'eng, a wealthy descendant
of one of the former Co-hong merchants who was actively promoting the adoption by the Chinese of Western scientific techniques.
A-teh's father also left Hong Kong about this time, disillusioned
with life in the British colony. The two disposed of their Hong
Kong property by selling the two marine lots to Bridgman to be
used as chapel, dispensary, and book deposit.[23]

Bridgman regretted that A-teh had been weaned away from his
immediate influence by the attraction of high pay as an interpreter
for the Chinese and British authorities.

He has suffered much by these connections, and this is one reason why I
so much deprecate them. The young man has probably a better knowledge of Christianity than any other Chinese living. He has an enlightened
and tender, but much abused conscience. He daily reads his Bible and
maintains secret prayer and knows well the necessity of being born again.

I cannot tell you the deep anxiety I have had, and still have, on his account. I have watched for him, and prayed with and for him, even as for a son. And I indulge a hope that the Spirit of God is still strong within him. I write him long letters every week, and shall try to bring him to make a full surrender of himself to his Savior.[24]

But after Bridgman moved from Hong Kong to Canton in July 1845, he had more opportunity to see his protégé and he expressed more confidence in A-teh's spiritual state.

From all that I can learn, he maintains his Christian character, carefully abstains from idolatry, keeps the Sabbath day, is honest and faithful in his intercourse with all men and anxious to know more of the truth of God. He has two children, a daughter and a son, and these with his wife he desires to have consecrated to God, and has asked to have them baptized.[25]

While previously the Americans had benefited indirectly from A-teh's services through Bridgman's use of him during the Sino-American treaty deliberations, now A-teh's linguistic ability and understanding of Western knowledge were available to Ch'i-ying, the Chinese Commissioner, by being channelled through A-teh's employer, P'an Shih-ch'eng, an important member of Ch'i-ying's staff. A-teh, however, left the services of his Chinese employer in 1846 and resumed his studies under Bridgman.

George H. McNeur, in his biography of Liang A-fa, states that after A-teh entered the service of P'an Shih-ch'eng 'he never afterwards took part in mission work'.[26] This statement is not strictly accurate as Bridgman acknowledges the assistance of A-teh in 1847 and 1848. In a letter dated Canton, 18 March 1847, he writes that 'Leang Tsen Teh (A-fa's son) is now investigating the religions of the Chinese and proposes to write a treatise to show to the Churches what the religions of the Chinese are'.[27] In 1848, Bridgman moved to Shanghai and became a member of the Revision Committee of the Chinese Scriptures. He was accompanied by A-teh. He describes the procedure he followed in his Bible revision: 'I have Leang Tsen Teh who prepares a draft from the English version, this he reads to me while I follow and correct him from the Greek text. This then goes to Kiu Taijen and he makes the best Chinese of it he can, and a fair copy is prepared.'[28] Not only did A-teh render scholarly assistance to the missionaries, but he finally declared his Christian faith in 1859 and was received by Bridgman into Church fellowship.[29] This was only a few years

before Bridgman's death and it must have given him much joy to
see this result of his many years of prayer, concern, spiritual nur-
ture, and guidance of his student, protégé, and foster-son.

Towards the end of his life, A-teh assisted Mr H.N. Lay in
opening various Chinese maritime customs stations. For five years,
he was head clerk and deputy commissioner at the customs office
at Chaochow, Kwangtung. He continued with the customs until
1862 when, at the age of 42 years, his health failed and he returned
to Canton, where he died.

Lin's interpreters were a varied group with diverse backgrounds
and qualifications but they shared a missionary-sponsored education. The missionaries were interested in educating a group of
Chinese who, through their training in Western literature and
thought, could produce a body of Christian literature for use in the
China mission, could collaborate in providing a more adequate
version of the Scriptures, and would serve as a corps of educated
evangelists and teachers for the Christian Church. In general,
those who received a missionary education in English did not fulfil
the hopes of their teachers. Most of them were attracted by the
high pay they could command in business or government service
because of their abilities in English. It was from this group, however, that Chinese officials recruited the translators and interpreters they needed when they became convinced of the necessity
of acquiring reliable information concerning the West and its
ways. Coming from a marginal group of Chinese who had relations with foreigners, they served as an important medium in
opening China to the West.

Commissioner Lin was one of the first of the official class to
realize the importance of a knowledge of the West if China was to
meet the challenge of foreign military power and commercial
aggressiveness. Unfortunately, his efforts to handle foreign problems were not successful and resulted in armed conflict and
China's defeat by the British. But his intentions were enlightened,
and his use of a corps of translators was a pioneer attempt to solve
the problem of China's ignorance of the world of the West.

Wei Akwong, Compradore

The career of the first student on the rolls of the Morrison Education Society illustrates the role that English education played in
the social mobility of the marginal Chinese community in the

treaty-port cities in the nineteenth century. The education of this student enabled him to enter into that group of Chinese known as 'the compradore class'. The compradores were influential in proposing, capitalizing, and managing the modernization and industrialization of China in the latter half of the century. They had received their business training and acquired their capital by functioning as 'middlemen' between the European merchant and the Chinese employees and business contacts of the foreign firm. It was a strategic position which called for a foot in two worlds. A background of ability in the English language and an understanding of European thought and manners usually ensured a rapid rise as a compradore. Wei Akwong, under the care of the missionaries, was provided with such a background.

Wei Akwong, who had the additional names of La-yam (魯欽), Ying-wa (應華), and Ting-po (廷甫), was of the twentieth generation of a family that had settled in the village of Tsoi Mei in Chung Shan District, Kwangtung Province, in the Sung dynasty. He was from a branch that had moved to Tsin Shan, a village about half-way between Tsoi Mei and Macau. His father was a compradore to two American merchants, Benjamin Chew Wilcocks, resident in China from 1813 to 1833, and Oliver H. Gorden, who was in China from 1826 to 1837. Akwong was the youngest of ten sons and his father died while he was still a child. His patron, the Revd E.C. Bridgman states that Akwong was forsaken by his parents and elder brothers and had to resort to begging on the streets of Macau. As an adult, he liked to contrast his affluence with the hard times of his youth.

As a leading member of the Chinese community in Hong Kong, Wei Akwong was consulted by Governor Hennessy about Chinese affairs. When asked to give his opinion on the treatment of criminals, he could not support the liberal views of the Governor. In his reply, Akwong looks back on his life and attributes his strength of character and material success to the hard life and discipline of his youth.

At the age of ten I left my native place came to Macao, seeking employment. First turn a beggar boy, afterwards get employment in a Portuguese firm Mano and Co. [perhaps De Mello and Company] Opium dealer, for bad treatment I left my employer and carried food for soldiers. I became sick and was sent by the British Consul 1838 to hospital stayed two weeks and was sent by Rev. Dr. Bridgman to Singapore as the first scholar of the Morrison Education board.

His story, as he recounts it, throws light on the treatment of child servants in some foreign households:

I said bad treatment from employer when I was a boy, at their service. Was in this way I was sent to market to buy the daily requisite of the servants cook and anything forgot to buy would be pinched by the servants cook and in night time while attending the night meals of my Mr. and Mrs. I used to be very sleepy and after time was beaten and made to stand for one or two hours with a plate of cold water upon my head during winter time. In summer had to stand with both hands stretched out for half or one hour or put the two hands to hold my ears stoop up and down from two or three hundred times, that was the way I was treated and brought up to be a good boy to this present. Often time go to bed at 12 o'clock and get up before 5 a.m. fetched large jars of fresh fountain water before 6 then to clean and sweep the house, draw and filled the two casks of water from the well, then received the market cash and buy fish, etc. for the meal when I had bought any stale fish made to go and change for good kind. Such treatment would not endure longer. I took the French leave without saying good buy [sic], had I been treated kindly with indulgence, I perhaps would be a bad boy same as those been turned away.[30]

Those 'turned away' were criminals who had been banished from the colony after receiving a flogging. Wei Akwong was a firm believer in the old adage, 'Spare the rod, spoil the child'.

His humble, but somewhat dramatic origins are presented in the report read by the Revd Elijah Bridgman to the first annual meeting of the Morrison Education Society, held at Canton on 27 September 1837.

The first child whose name was entered on our list was a beggar. Forsaken by his parents and elder brothers, the poor boy was left to wander in the streets, unprovided with food, clothing, or shelter. In this forlorn state, he had become so emaciated and weak, that recourse to medical aid was necessary for his recovery. Even now he suffers from what he endured while a beggar. In this part of China, there are many such children, who must, unless relieved by charity, grow up in ignorance, or what has often happened, pine and die before reaching the age of manhood.[31]

The beggar boy was picked up on the streets of Macau, taken under Mr Bridgman's wing, and enrolled as a student of the Morrison Education Society. As a student of the Society, he was sent to Singapore by Bridgman, where he was placed under the care of the mission of the American Board of Commissioners for Foreign Missions. John Robert Morrison, son of the Revd Robert Morrison, mentions in a letter dated 24 July 1837 that the Society had sent two children to Singapore 'to be educated in the family of one of the missionaries'.[32] One of these students was Liang Tsen Teh, the 17-year-old son of the ordained Chinese evangelist, Liang A-fa.[33] That the other student was Akwong is confirmed by the Minutes of the Singapore mission of the American Board for 28 November 1837, when the school committee was instructed to correspond with Mr Bridgman 'in the case of A-Kwong'.[34] His name is on the roll of the American Board mission school dated 1 February 1840.[35] 'No. 5. A-Kwang, entered 1 February 1837, birth place Macao, age 12 years, sent from China by Mr. Bridgman and supported by Morrison Education Society'. He was one of the first twelve boys enrolled in the school in February 1837 and received an education in both English and Chinese there.

The school taught the boys to read and write Chinese, but great importance was attached to English. The headmaster reported in 1838:

If we hope to train them for teachers of their own people and preachers, if converted, we must, of course, carry them on in science and knowledge of all kinds, far beyond anything existing at present. We suppose it is now granted that those who are to receive anything like an education must be taught English. This being settled, the natural course of things will make the English Department the most important of the establishment.[36]

As in all the missionary schools, the main objective was the conversion of the students, but for this the missionary had to wait for the evidence of 'pious conviction' and the work of the Spirit. Therefore, they set out to 'discipline the mind and give them a knowledge of English, as the medium through which they should acquire knowledge'.[37]

The school was closed at the end of 1842 and Akwong returned to China. During his five years at school he had become competent in English, but his exposure to the Christian faith had not resulted in his conversion. In later life, Akwong expressed his appreciation to the Morrison Education Society for the opportunity it had provided him to acquire an education by becoming a member of the Society with an annual subscription of $75.[38]

When Akwong returned from Singapore, he joined the household of the Revd E. Bridgman in Hong Kong, who continued his education. Bridgman states, in his semi-annual report to the mission board dated 20 July 1843, that 'Akwong, once a beggar, but who is now able to read the English Bible, is also under instruction'.[39] Bridgman was supporting both Akwong and Liang Tsen Teh, with his young family. When A-Teh and his father, Liang A-fa, sold two marine lots in the Lower Bazaar in Hong Kong to Bridgman in December 1844, one of the witnesses to the Memorial was 'Wei Akwong, clerk to Dr. Bridgman'.[40] In July 1845, Bridgman moved from Hong Kong to Canton. Wei Akwong remained behind in Hong Kong. The next notice of him is in 1852.

In that year, Dr Henry Julius Hirschberg, a missionary of the London Missionary Society, solicited contributions from the Chinese community in Hong Kong for the rebuilding of his dispensary and hospital, which had been burnt down in December 1851 in the disastrous fire which destroyed the Lower Bazaar. The response by the compradores of the leading firms and several of the most prominent Chinese merchants was gratifying to the foreign community, as it was the first instance in Hong Kong of the general Chinese population supporting a missionary enterprise.[41] The list of contributors was printed in the *China Mail* and among the largest contributions was that of 'Wai Ah-kwong, Bowra and Company's compradore, $15'.[42] Bowra and Company was the most prominent of the ship chandleries of that period in Hong Kong.

In April 1853, Wei Akwong's employer assigned him Inland Lot 187 A for the nominal consideration of $5. At the same time, the adjoining lot to the west, No. 200, was granted by C.W. Bowra to Ho A-seck, compradore of Lyall, Still and Company. In December 1853, Wei Akwong and Ho A-seck, as tenants in common, bought Inland Lot 187, and in February 1854, when the Government put up for sale several forfeited lots, Wei Akwong bought Inland Lot 192 for himself and acted as agent for Ho A-seck for No. 196.[43] These land transactions completed the proprietorship of Akwong and A-seck of the square bounded by Hollywood Road to the south, Gage Street to the north, Graham Street to the east, and Peel Street to the west, with the exception of Inland Lot 188, situated at the south-west corner of Graham and Gage Streets. Later, in 1862, Akwong bought a section of this lot as well.[44]

Wei Akwong left the employ of Bowra and Company in 1855 and in March was appointed Supreme Court Interpreter in Chinese and Malay at a monthly salary of $60. He found himself under pressure during the period of hostility between China and Britain provoked by the *Arrow* lorcha incident. The Chinese authorities issued an edict ordering all the Chinese in Hong Kong to return to their native places on the mainland. Many of them obeyed the order and left, but others were willing to identify themselves with the future of Hong Kong in spite of official Chinese pressure and chose to remain. The *China Mail* of 30 April 1857 reports that Fuk, the sub-prefect of Caza Branca near Macau, issued warrants against natives of the district of Heung Shan: 'Cheong Achew, the well known carpenter, Tsun Atow, Messrs. Augustine Heard and Company's compradore, Lum Ayow, owner of the Lorcha "Good Chance" and Wei Akwong, formerly compradore of Bowra and Company and more lately Interpreter in the Supreme Court'.[45]

In spite of his refusal to leave Hong Kong, in time Wei Akwong re-established good relations with his home village. A garden which he built there is noted by a traveller in 1875. Leaving Macau and proceeding west past Green Island, he mentions that 'the right or northern shore of the river is lined with a succession of pretty villages, prominent among them may be mentioned that of Tsin Shan, the native place of Mr. Wai Kwong, well known in Hong Kong as a wealthy and liberal minded Chinaman. A very handsome garden which he has built outside the walls of the town forms a prominent feature'.[46]

In 1857, the Mercantile Bank of India, London and China, with headquarters in Bombay, established a branch in Hong Kong. Their need for a competent compradore opened the way for Wei Akwong's further advancement. He faithfully served the bank until his death. Then, his eldest son, Wei Ayuk, who had been acting as assistant compradore, took over his father's position.

As the years passed and Akwong acquired capital, he invested in real estate.[47] When he died, he left these properties in trust. It was not until 1957, more than a century after he had acquired his first property in Hong Kong, that the trust was dissolved.

The fact that Wei Akwong sent his eldest son to England for his education is evidence of the value he placed upon the opportunities provided through his own missionary education. He, Wong Shing, also a former student of the Morrison Education Society School, and Ho A-seck were the first Chinese to finance the education of their children abroad independently. In 1867, each sent a son to study at the Stoneygate School at Leicester. After a year they transferred to Dollar Academy in Scotland. In 1869, Wong Shing forwarded £100 to Dr James Legge to pay for the expenses of his son. In a covering letter he mentioned that 'the boy

Ho Asee is the son of a Chinese opium merchant here. His object in going to England is to be educated in English, as his parents are heathen, they care not anything about religion, and I hope you will do him much good in trying to teach him the truth as it is in Jesus'.[48] The boys returned to Hong Kong in 1872 after completing a tour of Europe. Shortly afterwards, Wei Ayuk, the son of Wei Akwong, married the sister of his former schoolmate, Wong Yung-tsing. Her father, Wong Shing, was the second Chinese member of the Legislative Council, and her husband, Wei Ayuk, succeeded to this position in 1897. He served until 1914, and 'while not noted for long speeches, is regarded as an invaluable adviser in connection with all legislation in any way touching the interests of his fellow countryman'.[49]

The Wei family genealogy contains a laudatory biography of Wei Akwong.[50] It states that, while a student at Singapore, he became well versed in Western knowledge, especially the law. After returning to Hong Kong, 'where East and West meet', trials concerning Chinese litigants were referred to him. 'Many cases were dependent on the statements of Mr. Wei when judgment was passed. He tried to uphold justice, suppress the rascals and protect the innocent and upright.' This may refer partly to his work as interpreter in the Supreme Court and partly to his role as an unofficial adviser to the Government. His biographical notice also extolled his fame as a shrewd and successful business man and praised him for his philanthropy.

Wei Akwong died in Hong Kong on 12 May 1878. The *Daily Press* carried a notice of his death on the following day.

We regret to have to announce the death on Saturday afternoon about five o'clock of Mr. Wai Kwong, compradore of the Chartered Mercantile Bank of India, London and China. Deceased, who had been more than 20 years in the employ of the Bank, was a leading member of the Tung Wah Hospital Committee, was on the Jury list, and always took a prominent part in any matter affecting the Chinese community. He was reputed to be one of the wealthiest of the Chinese residents in this colony.

Wei Akwong wrote his will in 1866.[51] He prefaced it with a brief account of his life, particularly mentioning that he was the first student of the Morrison Education Society and that, since 1843, when he first came to Hong Kong, he had 'ever since lived under the just and equitable rule of the British Government'. He owned shares in a shop in Hong Kong and one in Macau. He instructed his sons to be obedient to the wishes and directions of their mother and that 'they shall always conduct themselves with propriety, leading a steadfast and honest life'.

As executors of his will he appointed his wife, Ow Shee-ayoon, his clerk, Ho A-chee, and his friend, Cheong Tscheng-sai. Conditions changed and he wrote a codicil to his will in 1873. He stated that his wife had died in 1868, his clerk, A-chee, was in Shanghai as compradore of the Chartered Mercantile Bank, and his friend, Cheong, had moved to Macau. In their place he appointed his second wife, Ng She Yook-heng, 'a lady of Canton', his eldest son, Wei Wah-yuk, 'now returned from England', his third son, Wei Wah-sang, acting compradore of the Chartered Mercantile Bank in Shanghai, and his fourth son, Wei Wah-leen. He had a large family of fifteen sons, ten daughters and five concubines as well as his wives Ow and Ng. His eldest son was knighted in 1919 as Sir Poshan Wei. Two sons, Wei On and Wei Pui, practised law in Hong Kong. Several other sons were compradores.

Wei Akwong's fortunes had led him from the compassionate concern of a missionary for an emaciated beggar boy on the streets of Macau to wealth and leadership in the Chinese community of Hong Kong.

Tsang Lai-sun

Professor John K. Fairbank of the Harvard-Yenching Institute, in an address to the Royal Asiatic Society during his visit to Hong Kong in 1976, referred to the importance of the study of what he termed 'China coast culture', by which he meant the type of social groups, values, and institutions that emerged from the commingling of diverse traditions in the port cities of China. He suggested that an understanding of the forces that created this social milieu and an analysis of its structure and operation might provide models for life as it is developing in an age of rapid cultural interchange.[52]

This study of one family which formed a part of the China coast culture illustrates some strands in its creation and emergence as a distinct way of life, with its own values and manners. This new life-style is seen in the family of Tsang Lai-sun in such features as the intermingling of Chinese and foreign home decoration; changed attitudes towards certain Chinese practices, such as the social mingling of sexes, foot-binding, dress, and the wearing of the queue; the employment in a Chinese setting of language, educational, and scientific skills acquired as a result of a Western-style training; and marriage across racial boundaries.

The careers of Tsang (or Chan) Lai-sun[53] and his children illustrate the role marginal Chinese played in the Westernization of China. Chan's mother was probably Malay. His wife, Ruth A-tik, was born in Indonesia and was not of pure Chinese ancestry. In a list of members of the Presbyterian Mission Church at Ningpo for 1850, she is described as 'Indo-Chinese'. Both, as children, came under the patronage of foreigners and both received an English-language education. Miss Aldersey, the patron of Ruth A-tik, first in Batavia and then in Ningpo, mentions Ruth and her friend, Christiana A-kit, in the annual report of the London Tract Society for 1847:

I have two young women Indo-Chinese converts, who, fleeing from persecution, joined me in this country [China]. They have applied themselves to the study of the English language since their arrival in the north, and one of them in particular is thirsty for the intelligence which that language opens out to her. Her desire for information has reference especially to religious subjects.

As we shall note, A-tik's home after her marriage to Lai-sun was what nineteenth-century missionaries called 'pious', but piety was connected with a concern for a modern education for Chinese girls and for some years she taught in a missionary school in Shanghai.

Tsang Lai-sun was the son of a poor gardener in Singapore. He attracted the attention of a missionary of the American Board of Commissioners for Foreign Missions while serving at the table of the American Consul in Singapore. He was enrolled in their school and was baptized. His parents died, leaving him an orphan. When the school was disbanded at the end of 1842, he was taken to the United States by Mr Morrison, a Presbyterian missionary. He was put into Mr Rendall's school in East Bloomfield, New Jersey. He studied there until 1846. Mr Morrison was about to return to Asia and wished to see him settled with definite arrangements for his further education in America. Samuel Wells Williams of the American Board, who was in the United States at the time, arranged for him to receive free instruction at Hamilton College in Utica, New York, for two years. His support was provided by the ladies of the First Presbyterian Church of Utica and his clothes by the ladies of a church in Brooklyn. His college term ended in June 1848 and he returned to China with Mr Williams. Upon his return, he was engaged as an assistant with the American Board mission in Canton. His mother tongue was Malay, though his father was from the Chiu Chow area of Kwangtung Province. He had lost almost all knowledge of the Chinese he had known and had to engage a language teacher to relearn it. In July 1850, he married one of the two girls Miss Aldersey had brought with her from Java to Ningpo in 1843. In 1853, dissatisfied with the wages of a missionary assistant, he withdrew from the service of the American Board at Canton and went to Shanghai where he became quite successful in business.

He first entered the firm of Messrs Bower, Hanbury and Company, where he became a close friend of Mr Thomas Hanbury, one of the partners. He then set up his own business in partnership with Mr H.E. Clapp of the firm Clapp and Company, but the venture was not a success, so Lai-sun joined the staff of Viceroy Tso Tsung-t'ang at Foochow, where he was appointed instructor and subsequently superintendent of the Foochow Naval School. He left the school to become a member of the Chinese Educational Mission in 1872.

He was acquainted with Yung Wing, a graduate of the Morrison Education Society School in Hong Kong and of Yale University. Yung Wing engaged Lai-sun's co-operation in promoting the Chinese Educational Mission in 1872. Tsang Lai-sun was placed in charge of the school established at Shanghai to prepare the students for their journey to America. He accompanied the Chinese Educational Mission to America in 1872, together with his wife and six children. His old teacher, Mr Tracy, relates in 1873 that Lai-sun's two eldest sons would enter college in two more years, and his two daughters, who had been educated partly in England, were to become members of Dr Buckingham's Church at Springfield, Massachusetts. While living in Springfield, he became a member of the Hampden Lodge of Freemasons of that city.[54]

Returning to China in 1874, Lai-sun joined the staff of Viceroy Li Hung-chang as an interpreter. He served as chief secretary at the Chefoo Convention in 1876 and until the time of his death assisted at the many transactions Viceroy Li carried out with foreign powers. He was to have joined Li in his mission to Japan after the Sino-Japanese War, but Li excused him saying, 'You are old and so am I; but I have to go because there is no help for it.'

A missionary educator visited their home at Shanghai. Her account, published in 1857, shows how Tsang Lai-sun and his wife combined their Western-type education with the life-style of the Chinese community in which they lived.[55]

At the time of the visit, Yung Wing was a guest in the home. The missionary visitor noted that Yung Wing greeted her 'with quite an American air', though he had to admit he had forgotten her name. When Yung Wing, even then interested in education, asked if he could visit the girl's school under the missionary's charge, she politely turned him down as she felt that, since the girls were so modest and unaccustomed to a male presence at the school, it would unduly upset them, but she turned to Mrs Tsang and her friend, Christiana A-Kit, wife of Kew Teen-shang, and asked their opinion on the matter. They said they never objected to associating on social and friendly terms with Christian gentlemen. 'But,' said Kit, 'when merchants or other heathen men call to see Attee's husband, she always retires.' Yung Wing remarked, 'When I was in the United States as a student, I often visited young ladies' seminaries and they never objected, in fact, I think they rather liked it.'

The missionary lady took the occasion to probe a little deeper into the attitudes of American-educated Chinese, posing the question,

'And you liked the manners and customs of the women in the United States?'

'Oh, yes.'

'And having returned to China, how is it? Are you diligently seeking for a young lady with bound feet for a wife?—one who must stay at home because she can't walk?'

'No, indeed', Yung Wing said, adding with a touch of humour that he wished for a wife who would be able to run with him should ever the need arise.

The conversation had struck a sensitive issue for these Chinese who had been trained in values very different from those of their contemporaries. With some feeling, Lai-sun's wife spoke out:

'How can this cruel custom be abolished, when Christian women, by binding their own and their children's feet, are handing it down to future generations?'

'Aside from religion,' remarked Yung Wing, 'the practice is barbarous, cruel and atrocious.'

Their changed attitudes towards certain aspects of Chinese life were reflected not only in their conversation but also in the furnishing of their home. The missionary lady commented on the 'nice parlor' fitted out with both foreign and Chinese furniture. 'Most conspicuous was a very nice organ, with which the good man accompanies himself in singing the songs of Zion.'

Tsang Lai-sun died on 2 June 1895 in Tientsin. His obituary was published in the *North China Daily News*, on which his son, Spencer, was a reporter, and republished in Hong Kong in the *Daily Press* on 12 June 1895.

At the time of his death, Tsang Lai-sun was survived by his widow, two sons and two daughters. He was predeceased by his son, William, and a daughter. The death notice of his widow, who died at the age of 92 on 17 January 1917, was published in the *Chinese Recorder*.[56] Her son, Spencer T. Lai-sun, had died only thirteen days before.

Spencer had been educated at Queen's College, Hong Kong, before being taken to the United States by his father at the inauguration of the Chinese Educational Mission in 1872. He and his elder brother, Elijah, attended Yale University. According to his obituary,[57] Spencer had an 'extra-ordinary command of English' and was remarkably well informed on Chinese affairs, being one of the first to forecast the gravity of the Boxer Uprising. He was simultaneously on the staff of a Chinese-language newspaper, the *Hu Pao*, and of an English-language newspaper, the *North China Daily News*, both published at Shanghai. In 1911, he abandoned his newspaper career and as an expectant *taotai* joined the staff of Viceroy Tuan Fang at Nanking. Early in his career, in 1885, he undertook a special mission to India. When a reporter on the *Times of India* interviewed him, he was impressed with Spencer's European-style clothing and the absence of a queue; he was said to have been given special permission for the latter by the Chinese authorities.

During his school-days in Hong Kong, Spencer had become acquainted with the family of the Revd Ho Fuk-tong, most probably because he was a regular attender of the Chinese congregation which met in the afternoons at Union Church. He married Ho Man-kwai, the daughter of the pastor. She died in Shanghai in 1894 at the early age of 28, leaving a young daughter, Daisy.

The other two daughters of Tsang Lai-sun married Europeans. The husband of the eldest daughter was a Danish ship's captain, N.P. Andersen. He had seen service in the Taiping revolution and had had a long career on the staff of the coastal Chinese customs. He was somewhat older than his wife and married in middle age. Mrs Andersen was one of the founders of the Chinese Red Cross Society, serving as its first Vice-President. In recognition of her services, the Chinese Emperor granted her a large honorary board. Their only daughter, K. Ruth Andersen, married Donald R. McEuen, son of a former captain superintendent of police at Shanghai in 1905.

A younger daughter of Tsang Lai-sun married a business man, Mr W. Buchanan, presumably the same as the Buchanan listed in the 1884 *Chronicle and Directory of China* as a land agent and broker with J.P. Bisset and Company of Shanghai.

This, then, is a record of a Chinese family living in a marginal situation. Both Lai-sun and his wife were born in South-east Asian overseas Chinese communities. Both in childhood became caught up in English-language missionary education, which served to alienate them further from Chinese tradition. Lai-sun started his career as a missionary assistant, but to make better provision for his growing family he turned to business, associating himself with foreign business men, not as compradore but as assistant and partner. However, the very fact of his marginal background qualified him, as a member of Li Hung-chang's staff, to make a particular contribution to China's developing relations with foreign powers. His children received a solid Western-style education. Of the two sons who grew to maturity, one was an engineer, the other a journalist, and both for a part of their career served the Chinese Government. His daughters left the Chinese community, but the eldest took her place in public life as a founder of the Chinese Red Cross.

This partial reconstruction of the life history of one China coast family is perhaps more than a mere exercise in reconstructing a family history from scattered sources. It can also be viewed as an illustration of the social processes at work in creating a distinctive culture in the port cities of China, including Hong Kong.

Whether as translators, advisers to Government or compradores, the students of the first mission schools became a new type of middleman, assisting Chinese and foreigners to relate to each other both in confrontation and in adaptation.

4 Friends and Relatives of Taiping Leaders

THE Christian element in the Taiping rebellion has been of special interest to interpreters of the movement. It was this non-Chinese factor which made the rebellion different from all previous Chinese rebel movements. Through its Christian elements, the rebels were expressing one aspect of the effect of increasing Western influence on Chinese national life.

The precise relationship between Christianity and the origin and development of the movement has been a matter of debate. One aspect of the problem is the relationship established between family members and friends of the originators of the movement and the missionaries. On the one hand, there was a tendency for these relations and friends to seek out the missionary in the course of the disruption to their lives caused by their connection with the rebel leaders. They especially looked to the missionaries for financial assistance in their efforts to join the movement once it had been successfully established at Nanking. On the other hand, the missionary vision and hope had been stimulated by the early, but confusing, reports of the Christian nature of the rebel movement. The missionaries welcomed the opportunity to learn more about the movement from first-hand accounts. It was a small book written by the Revd Theodore Hamberg in Hong Kong on the visions of Hung Hsiu-ch'uan which first gave the outside world detailed knowledge of the Christian influence upon the rebels. Most of the subsequent accounts of the movement draw heavily upon the material recorded by Hamberg, who received it through Hung Hsiu-ch'uan's cousin, Hung Jen-kan.

The missionaries were eager to use the refugees, who were physically cut off from the movement by the troops of the Imperial Government, for they hoped that through these converts, whom they financed in their efforts to reach the areas controlled by the Taiping Government, they might influence the movement. Since they believed that those converts who had been under their instruction were better grounded in the fundamentals of the Christian faith than the Taiping leaders at Nanking, the missionaries expected their converts to strengthen the Christian element in the movement and correct some of its reported misconceptions in doctrine and aberrations in practice. They also hoped that, through the good offices of these converts, once they had established themselves at Nanking, the missionary would, in time, be able to join them.

The most prominent of these individuals was Hung Jen-kan, a distant cousin of the Taiping leader, Hung Hsiu-ch'uan. He became the *kan wang* (shield king) in the Taiping Government at Nanking in 1859 and was executed in November 1864, after the fall of Nanking.

Hung Jen-kan accompanied Hung Hsiu-ch'uan to Canton for Christian instruction under the Revd Issachar Roberts in 1847.[1] After a month's instruction, they were sent out on a preaching tour in the course of which they returned to their home district, Hua-hsien, Kwangtung. Jen-kan did not return to Canton with Hsiu-ch'uan for further studies but remained at home to study medicine.

While Hung Hsiu-ch'uan had been preaching near his home in Kwangtung and studying with Roberts at Canton, Feng Yun-shan, a friend of his who had also been influenced by Christian ideas, had been gathering a group of followers in Kwangsi. They adopted the name 'The Society of God Worshippers' and were the nucleus from which the Taiping movement developed. The usual accounts of the movement attribute its origins to the activity of Hung Hsiu-ch'uan. This interpretation rests heavily on the account given in Theodore Hamberg's booklet, *The Visions of Hung Siu-Tschuen and Origin of the Kwangsi Insurrection*, published in Hong Kong in 1854, and on various documents of the movement which were written after the death of Feng Yun-shan. There are several contemporary references which point to Feng as the more active leader in the movement's initial phases. An account given of him by a deserter from the Taiping army and a former member of Gutzlaff's Chinese Christian Union, published in *The Hong Kong Register* on 27 September 1853, states that, when he met Feng in Kwangsi, they recognized each other as fellow-members of the Union. According to the account, Feng had studied under Gutzlaff. I have carefully gone over the rather detailed reports Gutzlaff sent back to Germany reporting the activities of the Chinese Christian Union, hoping that he might have mentioned Feng, but I was unable to find him named. Gutzlaff, however, does report trips made by his workers into Kwangsi, where they preached and distributed tracts. These reports were published in the *Calwer Missionsblatt* and Gaihan's *Chinesische Berichte*.

When Hung Hsiu-ch'uan left Roberts and Canton in the late spring of 1847, he travelled to Kwangsi in search of Feng, arriving there in August. In Roberts' journal, in the entry for 25 June 1847, he states that two of his followers were appointed to visit the inquirer, Hung, in a different province.[2]

Several efforts were initiated to take the families and followers of the Taiping leaders to Kwangsi from Kwangtung, but the plans were frustrated by the authorities. Some were caught and imprisoned, others scattered and fled. The friends and relatives of the leaders of the Taipings were rooted out of their native districts and at the same time cut off from the troops of the rebellion as it advanced from Kwangsi to Nanking. Branches of some clans appear to have settled in Hsin-an District, adjacent to Hong Kong. Many of the people moved in and out of Hong Kong. These movements left traces in the reports and records of the missions, but they are not complete enough to provide a comprehensive account.

The various adventures and travels of Hung Jen-kan before he reached Nanking in 1856 are documented in the writings of Jen Yu-wen.[3] A few additional details are provided by missionary archival sources.

In 1852, Hung Jen-kan was brought to Hong Kong by a young tailor from Lilong (Li-lang (李朗)) in Hsin-an District. He was the grandson of a clansman of Hung, who had befriended Jen-kan during his wanderings. The grandson, Fung (Hung?) Sen,[4] had been under the instruction of the Revd Theodore Hamberg before being baptized. On 26 April 1852, Fung Sen introduced Hung Jen-kan to Hamberg. Two days later, Fung was baptized with ten others in the small chapel belonging to the Basel Missionary Society in Hong Kong. The entry in Hamberg's report lists him as 'Fung Asen, aged 21 years, from Lilong, tailor's worker.' When Hamberg left Hong Kong at the end of March 1853 to establish a station at Pukak (Pu-kit (布吉), Hsin-an District), Fung Sen accompanied him. He was employed by the mission as a watchman.

A biographical notice of one of the Taiping refugees, Li Tsin-kau (李正高), which was published in the missionary magazine of the Basel Missionary Society, *Die Evangelischen Heidenboten*, in June 1868, provides interesting sidelights on Hung Jen-kan's unsuccessful effort to reach Nanking in 1854. It also illustrates the connections established between missionaries and those who had been influenced by personal association with Hung Hsiu-ch'uan before he became the Taiping *wang*.

Li Tsin-kau was a native of Wo Kuk Lyang, in Ch'ing-yuan District, Kwangtung. Hung Hsiu-ch'uan had been a teacher in the household of the maternal grandfather of Li Tsin-kau, and Tsin-kau's father was a good friend of Hsiu-ch'uan. He had often heard his father tell of Hung and his visions. Was the father the Li Ching-fan who drew the attention of Hung to Liang A-fa's Christian tract? Hung himself often visited Wo Kuk Lyang. During these visits there would be discussions about the moral and political conditions of China and hopes expressed that these could be improved and the rule of Heaven (*t'ien-kuo*) established. Hung Hsiu-ch'uan and Li Tsin-kau discussed especially the benefits of fasting and abstaining from meats and the worship of idols. Tsin-kau remembered that Hung spoke often of the power of God to conquer the demons. He also spoke of Jesus as 'our Heavenly Brother who forgave men's sins', but this was not the main theme of Hung's thoughts, 'It was as though it had not much touched his heart (*Wenigstens sei es ihm nicht sehr zu Herzen gegangen*)'.

Li Tsin-kau was caught up in the displacement of former friends and relatives of the Taiping leaders. When the authorities frustrated the plan to join the Taiping movement in Kwangsi, he fled to Macau. He lost track of his brothers and father, and later believed that they were imprisoned. His mother was taken in and cared for by friends of the family, and his wife and children fled to her parents' home. Tsin-kau tried to make a living by travelling about the area between Macau and Canton offering his services as a *feng-shui* expert. After a time, he moved east to the districts of Kuei-shan and Po-lo. After more than a year, he ventured to return to his home district. Here he met up with Hung Jen-kan. The two of them, accompanied perhaps by other friends and relatives, came to Hong Kong, hoping that they could from there find a way to join Hung Hsiu-ch'uan at Nanking, the capital of the Taiping kingdom. As Hakkas, they sought out the missionaries of the Basel Missionary Society, which had devoted itself to work among this dialect group. Jen-kan met the Revd Theodore Hamberg for a second time at Pu-kit in Hsin-an District. There he received further instruction in preparation for baptism and was baptized on 20 September 1853. Hamberg reports six baptisms on this date. The first was 'Fung or Hung, from Faheen, aged 31 years, teacher and doctor', of whom he remarks that he was a relative and youthful friend of Hung Hsiu-ch'uan, the Taiping *wang*. Four others were members of the Kong family of Lilong, and the sixth was 'Fung Tet-schin, from Thatipun, aged 31 years, schoolteacher'.

Li Tsin-kau did not remain at Pu-kit with Jen-kan but continued on to Hong Kong with two friends, Khi-sem and A-kap. They were welcomed by the missionaries and taken on as inquirers to receive instruction. The Revd Rudolph Lechler had returned from his station in the country to await the arrival of his fiancée from Germany. He assisted Hamberg in the instruction of the new arrivals. The basis of the instruction was the Lutheran catechism. In the light of it, Li Tsin-kau confessed that previously he had held a distorted view of the Christian faith. He had understood, under the influence of Hung Hsiu-ch'uan, 'the discourses concerning the power of God and false idols, but had no understanding of sin and forgiveness through Christ'. His prayer had been patterned after a form taught by Hsiu-ch'uan. After three months' instruction, he was baptized by Hamberg, although he had some years previously been baptized by Hung Hsiu-ch'uan at the urging of Hung Jen-kan. The daybook of the Revd R. Lechler in the Archives of the Basel Missionary Society for 28 February 1854 has an entry of the baptism of four men who were instructed by Hamberg at Hong Kong: 'Li Khi Lim, from Tseang ye, Li Hin Long, from Tseang ye, Li Chin Kau, from Tseang ye, and Fun Shen Fong from Tung Kwun.' In September there is an entry for 'Li Khi Sen, from Tseang ye'. This is probably the friend, Khi-sem, who was one of Tsin-kau's travelling companions.

The Hong Kong missionaries were delighted with the arrival of these refugees who were willing to receive Christian instruction and baptism. They seized upon their desire to join their relatives and friends in Nanking as a God-given opportunity to give the Taiping movement a more solid Christian foundation. There had been much discussion about the type of religious belief held by the Taiping leaders, and serious doubt had arisen regarding their interpretation of Christianity. Hamberg hoped to raise sufficient funds through his publication of *The Visions of Hung Siu-Tschuen and Origin of the Kwangsi Insurrection* to finance Hung Jen-kan's trip to Nanking. In reporting to the Basel Missionary Society, he states:

I have spent much on Fung [the Hakka version of the surname Hung] and his friends, and in order not to put a burden on the Mission have translated into English the account of the first [i.e. Hung Jen-kan] and written a small book which is now ready to be printed. Fung and his two friends left today for Shanghai. I have furnished them with the three different translations of the Old and New Testaments, Barth's Biblical History, Genahr's Catechism, a calendar and other writings, also a map in Chinese of the world, a map of China and one of Palestine, a model of a steel punch, copper matrizes and the usual types, in order to show how Chinese characters can be printed in the European manner. In addition a few trifles, such as telescope, compass, thermometer, knives, etc. I am often asked if I will go to Nan-King, however I have decided, and will not change my mind, that I will not go until I have received a regular and definite invitation to go. I have sought to establish what my obligations and duties are in this matter. The people who were brought to me I have baptized, instructed and assisted them on the way insofar as I was able. I believe that Fung respected me and would like to see me in Nanking, as he so often said. However, we cannot be definite about it, because we do not yet know if he will be successful in arriving at Nanking, and further, we cannot be sure that his friend there will welcome the idea, or that no obstacle will be placed in the way of foreigners, or that they have a real desire to be led deeper into the truths of God's words. In a word, everything is very uncertain. We must lay the future of the whole mission, even as our own, into the hands of God.[5]

Hamberg's earthly future was quite short for he died nine days after writing the above.

Hung Jen-kan and Li Tsin-kau encountered misfortunes in their efforts to reach Nanking by way of Shanghai. Hamberg had given them a letter of recommendation to the London Missionary Society agent at Shanghai, the Revd W.H. Medhurst. Medhurst housed them on their arrival in the mission hospital. In Shanghai, they met a friend from Canton whom they invited to share these quarters. This friend smoked opium, and when Medhurst happened to come into the room and saw his opium pipe on the bed, they were all told to leave. A dispute arose between Jen-kan and Tsin-kau, with Jen-kan charging Tsin-kau with carelessness and sensuality. Tsin-kau remarks:

At that time, I was truly in distress, for I had no friend in the world and no money with which to return to Hong Kong. I felt I must certainly come to misfortune. But this was the point when a change occurred in my heart. I was altogether fallen into the depth, then God took me in judgment of my sins, and the Spirit of God did its powerful work in me. The Shepherd of my life took over and from now on I gave my life to him. The Lord changed Medhurst's heart and he gave me money to return to Hong Kong.[6]

Jen-kan also returned to Hong Kong, as he was not able to pass through the Imperial lines to reach Nanking.

When Li Tsin-kau arrived back in Hong Kong, he immediately sought out the Revd R. Lechler, who gave him $2 to return to his home up-country. After visiting his family, he went to the mission station at Pu-kit and was taken on as a helper. When hostilities broke out in 1856 over the *Arrow* lorcha incident, Lechler had to leave Pu-kit and retire to Hong Kong. He took with him Li Tsin-kau, whom he placed in the newly opened hospital of the Berlin Missionary Society operated by Dr Heinrich Gocking. Li served as an overseer and doctor's assistant until the hospital was forced to close for lack of funds in 1859.

Meanwhile, his former travelling companion, Hung Jen-kan, had made a second and successful effort to reach Nanking. Established there in a responsible position, he wrote to Li Tsin-kau, inviting him to join him. Tsin-kau set off for Nanking but turned back before arriving there, because, as he claimed, he had heard alarming accounts of the religious and moral aberrations of Hung Hsiu-ch'uan. On his return to Hong Kong, he was taken on by Lechler as a helper in his ministry to the Hakka population in Hong Kong.

Li Tsin-kau continued as a valuable assistant in the Basel mission in Hong Kong, serving as a catechist until his death in 1885. For some years in the 1860s he was a travelling preacher, using Hong Kong as his home base. His mother, wife and children, and a younger brother joined him in Hong Kong and all of them became members of the Basel Missionary Society congregation on High Street, Sai Ying Pun. In 1858, he mentions a brother, Schiu-siu, in California. The eighth report of the Berlin Society, for the years 1861 and 1862, mentions A-tat, the unbaptized brother of the Basel mission helper Lichenko.

Li Tsin-kau,[7] after his initial efforts to join the Taiping forces, spent the remainder of his life serving the Church in Hong Kong. However, his friend, Hung Jen-kan, became an important figure in the Taiping Government under the title *kan wang*. Before assuming this political role, he was a valued assistant in the Protestant mission work in Hong Kong. While Li Tsin-kau worked among the Hakkas under the direction of the Revd Rudolph Lechler, of the Basel Missionary Society, Hung Jen-kan worked with the Revd Dr James Legge, of the London Missionary Society, among the Cantonese-speaking population.

Dr Legge took an interest in the Taiping movement and saw within it potential for providing a turning-point in the relation of the Christian Church with the whole of China. In the summer of 1853, he sent two of his assistants to Shanghai to open communication with the Taiping Government so as to prepare the way for a missionary to enter Nanking. The delegation consisted of a long-time assistant in the London Missionary Society, Keuh A-gong, alias Wat Ngong (屈亞昂), and a young theological student of Dr Legge's school, Ng Mun-sow (吳文秀). Their efforts were unsuccessful, so after spending six months in Shanghai, they returned to Hong Kong.[8]

We have already noted the unsuccessful effort of Hung Jen-kan and Li Tsin-kau to reach Nanking by way of Shanghai in 1854. Upon returning to Hong Kong, Jen-kan became a language teacher for the Revd John Chalmers of the London Missionary Society, but soon began to be used extensively in the various activities of the mission, preaching in their Lower Bazaar Chapel, visiting prisoners in the gaol, and serving as an evangelist to the sick in the dispensary recently opened by Dr Julius Hirschberg on Queen's Road West. Legge characterized him as 'a man who has won my affection and esteem as few of his countrymen have done', and he impressed Dr Wong Fun, who had recently returned from Medical School at Edinburgh and was associated with Dr Hirschberg in the dispensary, as 'a man of great intelligence and considerable fluency of speech'.[9]

In 1858, with the blessing of the mission, Hung Jen-kan, with a companion, made another effort to reach Nanking, but this time travelling up through Canton and Kwangsi. In a letter dated 5 June 1858, the Revd John Chalmers remarks on his and Jen-kan's hopes:

He has had a desire for a long time to reach his friends at Nanking and endeavour to impart to them the superior knowledge he has acquired, and I doubt not the fact that the present government is so hardly pressed from without had induced him to adventure upon the long and dangerous journey across the country from Canton in hopes that the Nanking party may be persuaded to seek an alliance with foreigners before it is too late. Of course his religious zeal is associated with patriotic feelings. We have always thought that if he could get among the Taiping people he might be the means of correcting many of their errors with regard to Christianity and to foreigners, from whom they have received it.[10]

The London Missionary Society at Hong Kong financed the trip and agreed to grant a monthly allowance of $7 for his family for ten months or until Jen-kan himself was able to provide for them.

In the course of his journey, Jen-kan wrote five letters to the Society at Hong Kong, but only three were received. One written from Hupei states that:

Unexpectantly on 16th October, I was seized and searched by Imperialist guards. They only found some medical books and money. On the 19th I made my escape to Yaou Chow and on the 14th of November eight officers who wished to leave the Imperial service took me to Lung Ping in the province of Hoo Peh. I am safely lodged with two men of my own province Soo [Loo?] Keen and Seu [Leu?] Yuen, who are disgusted with the monstrous behavior of the Imperial soldiers and have been the means of saving a few long haired men from their hands. Some members of their family being in the Provincial city of Yean King (held by the rebels) they wished to give me several hundred thousand cash to take there for the purposes of trade. But just as I was about hiring a junk to go, the long haired men arrived at Hwang Mei (in Hoo Peh) so I stayed a short time here to see whether I could go to Hwang Mei or not. However on the first of December, four steamers made their appearance, I was told they were English, French and American, I embrace this opportunity of writing to you.[11]

After he arrived at Nanking there was little communication between Jen-kan and his former patrons. The monthly allowance for his family guaranteed by the Society ceased in September 1859, but Legge and Chalmers agreed to continue the support on their own to the end of the year, when Jen-kan's wife returned with her children to her home village in Fu-yuan, Kwangtung.

Although Hung Jen-kan did try to interpret the West to the Taiping movement, he soon became caught up in its internal power struggle and found that it was not expedient to push the missionary interests. This added to the growing disillusionment of the missionaries, who had seen the rebel movement as the golden opportunity for the Christianization of China. In August 1860, Legge commented, with regard to Hung Jen-kan, that he was 'sorry to see that he has given up his principles on the subject of polygamy. It does not appear whether he has become a polygamist himself, but he keeps silence among the other chiefs on the subject', and again in January 1861, Legge states that the Revd Dr Griffith John had had an interview with Hung Jen-kan which led him to conclude that 'he is sacrificing what he knows to be right and true to a miserable expediency'. Legge comments, 'my own disappointment is great.'[12]

A brother of Hung Jen-kan named Sy-poe (世甫) was baptized by Legge in Hong Kong at the beginning of 1859.[13] In August 1860, Sy-poe went to Canton to bring his own family and that of his brother to Hong Kong. They had a difficult time maintaining themselves in Hong Kong until Hung Jen-kan sent them $5,000 from Nanking. This enabled them to rent a house and live more in a style befitting relatives of one of the Taiping kings. To celebrate his second marriage, Dr Legge and his new wife entertained their Chinese friends and associates at a feast of twelve tables with some thirty courses. Mrs Legge remarks, in a letter dated 24 August 1860, that 'Sy-poe seemed very desirous I should honour his table ... We had a letter from the Rebel King, he congratulates Dr. Legge on his marriage'. Sy-poe is not mentioned again by the missionaries, but in 1871, Dr Legge states that his son came to the mission house requesting a recommendation for the position of watchman. Legge states, 'He is an honest-looking lad—but alas, that the glory of the Taiping's should thus have passed away'.[14]

Reports in the Archives of the Basel Missionary Society mention Fung Khui-syu, born in 1848, 'son of a Taiping King'. He must be Hung K'uei-yuan (洪葵元) alias K'uei-hsiu (葵秀), the son of Hung Jen-kan.[15] He was employed by the Society as a teacher, first on the mainland, but then, because of the danger to himself and his family created by his former association with the rebellion, he was removed to Hong Kong to teach in the mission's girls' school at Sai Ying Pun.[16] In 1873, a marriage was arranged by Mrs Lechler between Fung Khui-syu, then teaching at Tshong-hang-kang (樟坑逕) in Hsin-an District, and one of the older girls in the Society's boarding-school at Hong Kong. The bride, Tsen A-lin, alias En-min, was an orphan. As a young girl, she had been sold by her mother in Shanghai and brought to Hong Kong to work in a brothel; but she had been found wandering in the streets by a member of the Basel Missionary Society congregation and was taken to the mission house. In 1865, at the age of 12, she was enrolled as a student, and was baptized in 1870, when she received the name Lin (憐), meaning 'compassion', in place of Tchuy-khuyk (Ch'iu-chu (秋菊)), meaning 'autumn chrysanthemum'.[17]

In 1878, a large part of the congregation of the Basel Mission Church at Shau Kei Wan, Hong Kong, emigrated to Demerara,

British Guiana. Fung Khui-syu went with them. The 1885 yearly report of the Revd R. Lechler states:

In Georgetown is a Chinese Church and one of our emigrants has been placed there as Pastor. He is the relative of the former rebel king Fung Syu-tshen, and himself, at the time of the Government of Taipings in Nanking, was made king. He found his way to Hong Kong and was received at our table. I sent him later to Lilong, where he served under Brother Bellon in the boy's school. Because of his relation to the Rebel King, it was difficult on the mainland so he came to Hongkong until 1878, when he emigrated with those of Shaukiwan.[18]

A search of the records of British Guiana might provide details of his later career.

Lechler's daybook in the entry for 12 January 1871 mentions a visit from Tsau-phoi, a member of the Fung family of Tsim Sha Tsui, and on 18 February 1871 he notes that Fung A-lin from Tsim Sha Tsui returned to the girls' school at Sai Ying Pun. It is probable that Fung Tsau-phoi and Fung A-lin were the son and daughter of 'a former Rebel King', who is referred to in the records of the girls' boarding-school of the Basel mission at Sai Ying Pun. A report dated 10 July 1866 lists as a student, Lyu Tsya, aged 18 years, 'betrothed to a son of a former Rebel King, who long has put away the crown, baptized by the Berlin Missionary Hanspach in her home'. Also listed is Fung A-lin, the small sister of the young man. She had been enrolled in 1865, aged 7 years. Her mother was a widow and a Christian.

Keeping in mind that the Hakka version of the surname Hung was written Fung and that the entries in Lechler's daybook were written in an illegible script, it may be that Fung Tsau-phoi is the same as the Hung Tsun Fooi mentioned in T'ai-p'ing t'ien-kuo shih-shih jih-chih (太平天國史事日誌)[19] as being present in Hong Kong after the fall of the Taiping Government.

Two relatives of Feng Yun-shan, a 21-year-old nephew, A-sou (亞樹), and his 14-year-old cousin, accompanied the Revd Issachar J. Roberts to Shanghai in 1853, in an attempt to reach Nanking. A-sou was baptized by Roberts at Shanghai. The Baptist missionary, the Revd Matthew T. Yates, became acquainted with the two boys, but in his book *The Tai Ping Rebellion*, he mistakenly states that they were brothers of Feng Yun-shan.

Fung A-sou found it impossible to reach Nanking, so he came to Hong Kong. From there he went to Canton, where he became a teacher to an American missionary. But he became ill and returned to Hong Kong, where he died on 21 August 1855.

These accounts of some of the events in the lives of friends and relatives of Taiping leaders and their association with the missionary movement in China illustrate the impact that the Christian aspect of the Taiping ideology had on individuals connected with it in a peripheral way. The Taiping rebellion upset the even tenor of their former village life. They became refugees. However, most had an objective: they wished to join their former village clansmen and neighbours at the Taiping capital, Nanking. A few were successful; more, perhaps, were not.

Having been influenced previously by the confused Christian ideas promulgated by Hung Hsiu-ch'uan and Feng Yun-shan during the period before the outbreak of open hostilities between the Imperial forces and the Taiping revolutionaries, they naturally sought out the missionaries for assistance and employment and were also receptive to more thorough training in the Christian faith. The missionaries welcomed them as a means of relating to the Taiping movement with its promise of the establishment of a new dynasty on Christian principles. The promise was never realized and the missionaries eventually were disillusioned, but not before they had formed close relations with these refugees, some of whom became valuable assistants and contributed to the growth of the Chinese Christian Church.

The Taiping kingdom had within it, from the Christian point of view, the seeds of a transformation of China, but the end result was largely disastrous for China, and its fall left behind those who had dreamed of a glory that had passed them by. Some, as this article suggests, adjusted to a life devoted to the Christian Church, while others went their own ways. But the missionaries maintained a nostalgic interest in those who had been closely connected with the leaders of the Taiping movement.

5 Sun Yat-sen's Baptism and Some Christian Connections

A significant event for Sun Yat-sen during his middle school-days in Hong Kong was his baptism by the American missionary, the Revd Charles R. Hager. This event influenced his future life and relationships. Immediately, it provided him with a surrogate family during his several years as a school-boy in Hong Kong. He entered an intimate fellowship bound together by a new commitment for, as a very small, new Christian congregation, its fellowship was close and binding. This congregation was the result of the missionary concern of overseas Chinese. The connection with overseas Christian communities was later used by Sun Yat-sen in his journeys to raise funds and enlist support for his revolutionary cause. His acceptance of Christianity linked him with a distinct group of interconnected families on the China coast and overseas. It was through this group that Sun met his one-time secretary and second wife, Soong Ching-ling. These three different aspects of Sun's baptism will be considered in turn.

The Establishment of the American Board Mission in Hong Kong

In 1873, at the age of 14, Sun Yat-sen left his home village near Macau to join an older brother in Hawaii. There he entered the Iolani School, which was conducted by churchmen. They aroused in Sun a desire to accept the Christian faith publicly. This was vigorously opposed by his older brother, who was supporting him and paying the school fees. To remove the boy from Christian influence, his brother sent him back to his home village in the Hsiang-shan (now Chung-shan) District of Kwangtung.

This move, from the brother's view, was not altogether successful. Sun's attraction to Christianity and rejection of traditional Chinese religious practices were reinforced upon his return by a fellow village youth who had recently come back from Shanghai with similar attitudes. The two offended village opinion by a minor mutilation of an image in the local temple.

Out of favour in their home village, Sun Yat-sen and his accom-

plice in the escapade, Lu Hao-tung, found their way to Hong
Kong. There they met the Revd Charles R. Hager, who recalls in
'Some Personal Reminiscences' published in the *Missionary
Herald* of 12 April 1912 the result of a meeting with the young Sun:
'Of course, I could not help asking him whether he was a Chris-
tian, to which he replied that he believed the doctrine of Christ.
"Then why do you not become baptized?" "I am ready to be bap-
tized at any time", he replied; and so after some months of waiting
he received the ordinance in a Chinese school room where a few
Chinese were wont to meet with me every Sunday.'

Sun Yat-sen was baptized either at the close of 1883 or early in
1884. As a professed Christian, Sun entered into his new life with
enthusiasm. Hager said that, 'After Sun became a Christian he
immediately began to witness for Christ, and such was his earnest-
ness that in a short time two of his friends accepted Christianity.
This was at a time when few converts were made and when many
feared to identify themselves with Christians. But so great was the
influence of Sun that he won these men to the truth. It was the
same power that he always had of making men accept his opinion'.
The two friends were Lu Hao-tung and Tong Phong. Tong had
been a friend and fellow-student of Sun's in Hawaii.[1]

The first name on the register of the Revd Charles Hager's new
congregation was Sung Yuk-lam (宋毓林). This baptism took place
in September 1883. Hager describes how he first met Sung in an
article in *The Pacific* (a weekly paper for California Congrega-
tionalists), published on 31 October 1883, under the title 'How a
Sunday School was Organized in Hong Kong, September 3, 1883'.

Over a week since, a Chinese came to me and said he would like to join
our Church and be baptized; we have no church. I had little idea what led
the young man to change in belief. I sat down with him, commenced to
ask him through an interpreter a series of questions which savored a little
of theology. I tried to be very plain with him and find out his reasons why
he had come to believe in the Lord Jesus. He told me that it was through
the study of the Bible and hearing the Gospel preached that he had determined to become a Christian. His brother and sisters were all Christians,
and he felt that he could no longer worship idols. I did not tell him that I
should baptize him, for I thought I should like to learn a little more about
him.

Mr Hager's investigation showed that the young man, with his elder brother, Sung Chi-yau, was teaching in a government-aided school under the auspices of the American Presbyterian Church. The school-room was in an upper room on a lane near Queen's Road West in Sai Ying Pun. The elder brother was in charge of the school from 1883 to 1894. His nephew, Sung Hok-pang, succeeded him. Hager's American Board mission took over sponsorship of the school from the Presbyterians in 1887.

Hager had been thinking about establishing another Sunday school in addition to the small one held in the mission house. The two teachers brought him the opportunity. Consequently, as Hager relates: 'I told this young man about it, and he promised to ask his brother, and in a few days he came and asked me if I could help him open a Sunday School on the Sunday following at 10:30. I promised gladly.'

As preparation he gave Sung Yuk-lam twenty copies of St. Matthew's Gospel in Chinese for distribution to the children. On Sunday, Hager set out for the school. He took with him literature to distribute at the civil hospital, which was on his route between the mission house on Bridges Street and Sai Ying Pun. When the missionary finally arrived at the school-room, he found there the two brothers, a colporteur of the Bible Society and some forty young scholars.

Hager found himself in a difficult situation as the helper he had been depending upon to assist him did not arrive. Hager was not yet proficient in Cantonese and needed assistance. He was rescued from his dilemma, however, by the providential arrival of Mr Noyes, a Presbyterian missionary who was visiting Hong Kong from his station in Canton. Hager described the situation thus:

There were ten singing books and they could sing a few hymns. We opened with 'Jesus, Lover of my Soul', but I did not recognize it by the tune, much less by the words. Then I asked the principal teacher to pray. All remained standing in a reverent attitude, you could have heard a pin drop. I was perplexed as to what to do next. We sang, while I whispered to go and ask Fung Foo to come as he had promised to be there. But in a few minutes Mr. Noyes ... appeared. Greatly relieved, I asked him to take charge ... He read part of the 19th Chapter of Matthew, where it speaks of little children being brought to Jesus. One boy was asked to read a verse, and then Mr. Noyes would ask them questions and explain it ... We then sang, 'There is a happy land, far, far away, where saints in glory stand, bright, bright as day' ... Mr. Noyes then spoke at some length on the Saviour's love for the sa man tra [sic—should read Sai-mun-tsai or children] at the conclusion of which we sang again. An earnest prayer from Mr. Noyes closed the meeting.

Hager then distributed some children's literature and was introduced to the Chinese mode of receiving gifts: 'No one thanked me, but after the group was dismissed, each came before my desk, put their hands together and bowed in a reverent manner.' He was much impressed: 'I thought I wished American children would be as polite to their superiors as these Chinese children today.'

With the Sunday school launched, Hager soon afterwards baptized Sung Yuk-lam, his first convert. With the addition of Sun and his two friends after a few months, and a servant woman, along with Chinese helpers from California, a small congregation was organized.

The congregation met at the mission house at No. 2, Bridges Street. Hager described the building as 'a humble building.... During the week a Chinese boy's school was taught there, while our young friend [Sun] lived in the second story with some other Chinese, and an American Bible Society's colporteur and I lived on the third story'.[2]

Sung Yuk-lam, the new convert, was placed in charge of the school, which met on the ground floor. He remained there until 1899.[3]

An event much talked about by Sun Yat-sen and the other residents of 2 Bridges Street was an unpleasant encounter with European prejudice experienced by Sung Yuk-lam and a cook who lived there. A report of it is given in the *China Mail* of 28 July 1884, in the police news under the title 'Insolent Chinese':

Cho Kwok-in, a cook, No. 2 Bridges Street, charged by use of threatening and abusive language to Charles Bond, a bill collector, while sitting with wife and daughter listening to the Band at Murray Barracks. He sat on a seat on which two Chinese sat. The defendant ... began using disgusting language. The complainant remonstrated. Defendant said in English, 'You no belong mandarin, what for you sit down by me, you god-damned son of ...' The complainant's wife walked away and defendant assumed a fighting attitude. The complainant told him to go away or he would give him in charge. The defendant said he was sitting on the bench when the complainant came up, raised his stick and told him to go away, which he refused to do. Sung Yuk-lam, defendant's friend, said he was sitting down when complainant and two ladies came up. He got up from the seat but the defendant did not.

The defendant, Cho Kwok-in, was fined $3. Apparently, public benches were considered to be for the use of Europeans and were not to be shared with Chinese, even though the latter might have a prior claim to occupancy.

Even before Hager had organized his Sunday schools, he had opened an evening school to teach English. He began with only four or five pupils, but soon there was an average attendance of between thirty and forty. There was some waning of enthusiasm among the students after the initial novelty had worn off. Some found there was too much use of the Bible in the teaching. Many of those who came were students during the day at the Government Central School. Some of these found the burden of both day- and night-school too onerous and dropped out.

Inasmuch as Yat-sen was living in the same house as Mr Hager, it is likely that he attended these sessions; Hager's description of the class is therefore of interest. He wrote of it in an article entitled 'Three Months on Chinese Soil', which appeared in *The Pacific* on 15 August 1883:

We usually begin with singing some Moody and Sankey hymns, followed by the English Lord's Prayer recited in concert. I tried to have the scholars kneel at the first, but I find they are much stiller when standing, so we all rise and repeat the prayer with bowed heads. After this is the lesson of reading either in their school books or New Testament ... It is my custom to explain the chapter, and at the close to speak a few pointed words upon some particular verse. Then we have a general exercise, in which we read some text of scripture and I explain it and let someone interpret it for those who cannot understand. Most of the advanced can speak English quite well, and interpret it. Some do this perhaps better than some of our Chinese in California. For our closing exercise we usually have singing and then repeat the Lord's Prayer in Chinese.

Indeed, it seems that these evening English classes were almost prayer meetings. It is no wonder that some may have felt they were learning more religion than English. This venture in providing English-language education in the hope that it would promote evangelization was not successful and was abandoned after a year's trial. It was, however, later revived.

Any disappointment over the abandonment of an English night-school was compensated for by the Revd Charles Hager's success in gathering a small worshipping congregation during his first year as a missionary in Hong Kong.

Overseas Chinese Christians and the Hong Kong American Board Mission

An important aspect of the new fellowship in which Sun Yat-sen found himself after his baptism was its close connection with overseas Chinese Christians. As a boy, Sun Yat-sen had himself spent a number of years in the overseas Chinese community of the Hawaiian islands. His experience there gave him an understanding of the peculiar situation of these Chinese expatriates. When promoting his revolutionary cause, he travelled extensively among the various groups of Chinese in other countries. It is not strange that he should associate himself in Hong Kong with a Christian mission that had been established through the efforts of overseas Chinese Christians.

As far as Sun Yat-sen was concerned, the Revd Charles R. Hager was the key figure in this early indirect tie with an American Chinese group.

Hager had been sent to Hong Kong by the Congregational Chinese Mission in San Francisco. His salary was supplied by the American Board of Commissioners for Foreign Missions, a missionary agency of the Congregational Church in the United States. The Chinese mission in San Francisco was the result of work begun by the American Missionary Association in 1870. The Association was also supported by Congregational churches and had been established to provide education for emancipated slaves after the American Civil War. Though the Association's principal work was in the southern states among blacks, it also sponsored schools for Chinese on the west coast.

As the converts of this work had partaken of missionary zeal, they became imbued with the desire to have their new faith preached to friends and relatives in China. Some of them returned to China and wished to have a community of Christians of like mind where they were living. The California converts naturally turned first to the American Missionary Association for help, but this society had neither the money nor the experience needed to extend its work into foreign lands. However, the American Board of Commissioners for Foreign Missions had been working in China since 1835 and thus was much better suited to meet the request of the California Chinese Christians. Consequently, the American Missionary Association referred the request to its sister agency.

After numerous delays, a decision was made in 1881 to establish a mission in Hong Kong.

Some ten years after a plan for a mission was first conceived, the Revd Charles R. Hager was ordained as a missionary to China in the Bethany Congregational Church, San Francisco, California, on 16 February 1883. The remarks made by a Chinese member of the Congregational mission of the American Missionary Association illustrate the close links which were to be established between Chinese Christians in the United States and Hager's mission in Hong Kong.

The Chinese spokesman was Mr Jee Gam,[4] an assistant in the Congregational mission in San Francisco. In his remarks he expressed the concerns, dreams and hopes of his Chinese colleagues for their motherland:

It was ten years ago when our Chinese brethren first felt the need of a mission in China at or near the districts from which most of our brethren came ... The first three years we often expressed our great desire among ourselves for this mission, but never thought of telling our superintendent, Rev. W.C. Pond. Not a word was said to him until at our usual Wednesday evening Bible class, about seven years ago, when the subject of foreign missions was accidentally mentioned. We then told Rev. W.C. Pond what we so much desired. He at once approved it.

He offered some practical advice, hoping to bring their dreams to fulfilment: 'Hong Kong was chosen for the seat of this mission, and Mr. Pond requested that those who were able to write a letter do so, explaining why this mission was so much needed. He accordingly forwarded these letters to the American Missionary Association.'

Fulfilment, however, demanded persistent patience and prayer: 'Though the Association sympathized with our want, yet how this mission could be established looked very doubtful. The matter was left to stand; but we remembered that James tells us to ask in faith, nothing wavering, and we knew that God was able to supply all our need, so we kept praying.'

An unexpected opportunity allowed Mr Jee Gam to share the dreams and prayers of his fellow-Christians with a larger circle. He recounted the train of events which led to this:

In the first part of October, 1879, I was greatly surprised by the very generous invitation which the American Missionary Association tendered to me to attend its Annual Meeting at Chicago. I shall always feel thankful for this great opportunity, and under much obligation to the Association for this kind offer, when I could press the needs of our Chinese to our Eastern friends. I started for the East, but thought nothing of this Hong Kong mission until at the end of the Annual Meeting, when I felt moved by the Holy Spirit to make an earnest plea for this Hong Kong mission. I also spoke of this mission at all the meetings I attended while East. After each meeting my hope was made stronger by the kind words of many Christian friends and for the many promises of help. In fact, many of these promises have been made good.

Three years later, word of a definite decision on the matter was received: 'On the evening of 4th of August, 1882 (the same day the Chinese Restriction Bill went into effect), the good news came through our superintendent that the American Board [of Commissioners for Foreign Missions] had consented to establish the Hong Kong Mission.'

Jee Gam expressed the great joy he felt when the decision was made known: 'Oh, how my heart filled to overflowing, went out to God in thanks-giving and in praise! Immediately we called the brethren to tell them the good news. Christ has told us to ask and we shall receive; yet, when this ten years' prayer was answered, it seemed almost too much to believe, and we are here this evening to praise God once more for His love to us and our benighted countrymen in China.'

The speaker explained the source of the missionary zeal of the Chinese converts and the reason for the mission being in Hong Kong:

And now, why we so earnestly desired this mission, and why Hong Kong is chosen rather than any other city? In reply to this question, let me tell you that a true Chinese Christian has the same desire as any other Christian. As soon as he is enlightened by the light of the blessed gospel, he wishes others to have the peace which Jesus alone can give. He looks at the wide field before him, and feels as so many have felt, that 'the harvest truly is plenteous, but the labourers are few'. Naturally his heart goes out to China, his native land, and he thinks of his own dear relations and friends, without Christ and without hope in this world. Do you then wonder why we so earnestly yearn for this mission?

Hong Kong as a base for the mission had several advantages:

Having Hong Kong for headquarters, missionaries and teachers can be sent from there to preach and teach in the villages from which our young men come. Besides this the English language is used more in Hong Kong than in any other part of China, and the Chinese living there, or those visiting that place, could not be reached in a more efficient manner than by opening the same kind of free schools for them that you have opened for us here. They feel that they need to know the English languages. Of course, there are public schools, where both the English and Chinese language are taught by the British Government, but all have their sessions in the daytime; consequently, the children are the only ones benefitted by these schools. There remains the laboring class unreached. If a free evening school is opened, I have no doubt that much good could be done among them.

One of the first things the Revd Charles Hager did after arriving in Hong Kong was to open and support schools.

Hong Kong had its advantages as a gateway for Chinese migration:

Moreover, Hong Kong is a great highway to all foreign ports, especially San Francisco. Through Hong Kong nearly all the Chinese in the United States have come and will return. If a general mission could be established at this port much co-operating work could be accomplished between our mission here and that at Hong Kong. Christian Chinese returning home, would receive letters of introduction to the superintendent of the Hong Kong Missions. This superintendent would have pastoral care over them, and be a very great help in time of persecution. Converts would be made firmer in faith, and more earnest in leading others to Christ.

The Chinese Christians in California longed for changes in China. Their hopes were for religious conversion. Their mission in Hong Kong brought into their fellowship the man who was to become the father of a great political change in China. Jee Gam expressed considerable expectations: 'We are not only anxious to have these few districts filled with Christianity. That would be selfish. We are working, and praying, and expecting, with God's help to be an important factor in leavening the Chinese empire. 'China for Christ' is our motto, and this has been our aim for the past ten years, and will ever be so. We will endeavour to help with our prayers, and as far as we possibly can with money.'[5]

Jee Gam's remarks forecast the close links forged between the Hong Kong mission and Chinese Christians in America. Jee Gam expressed the hopes, the prayers, and the vision of the Chinese Christians for the new mission. Extracts from a letter written by the Revd Charles Hager before he left for Hong Kong reflect his thoughts regarding the task he was undertaking: 'My dear Christian Chinese Brethren: I take the opportunity to communicate to

you a few of the many things that are weighing upon my heart ...
I accepted the responsible position of going as your representative
from this land, with a feeling a heavy burden was resting upon me.
I do not know as I shall be equal to this task. I do not know as I
shall meet your expectations. Of this I am assured, that without
your prayers and full co-operation and the blessing of God, I shall
utterly fail.'

He reminded his friends that, along with their enthusiasm at the
realization of their dreams for a mission in China, continuing
patience was needed:

Your motto 'China for Christ' is still unfulfilled and you need now, as
never before, to pray and labor for this mission. If you have waited ten
years until God heard your prayers for this new mission, then it becomes
you once more to pray for ten years that God will send the gospel to the
millions of your own number with a converting power ... Let me beseech
you not to think that the work is already done. Let not the ardor of your
love for your countrymen be cooled, but rather intensified. The work,
more than ever before, demands our best prayers, our best labors, and
our best gifts. We have just commenced to labor. We have only just entered the battle, the struggle is still to follow. God grant that we may meet
it like brave men, with loving hearts, faithful endeavors, and generous
gifts. Make and observe these things.[6]

His thoughts expressed a sober realism. He entered into his new
work with devotion and enthusiasm. Within a year of his arrival in
Hong Kong, he had gathered a small group of some half dozen or
more into a small congregation. Among them was the youthful
Sun Yat-sen.

The Christian Élite of the China Coast

Sun Yat-sen's baptism brought him into a distinct circle of China
coast Christians. This group was composed principally of those
who had received an English-language education. It was an élite
circle of the Chinese Protestant Church. As the years passed, Dr
Sun found supporters for his revolutionary cause within the group.

The seeds out of which the élite China coast Christian community grew were the schools established during the opening years of
the Protestant mission to the Chinese. Through the years, a group
of educated men emerged who had accepted or been influenced by
Christianity. They lived and worked in the China coast cities. Not
all the students who entered the English-language missionary

schools became Christian. Others, who accepted Christianity when young, in maturity allowed their connection with the Church to become tenuous. This was true of Sun Yat-sen. His marriage to Soong Ching-ling, while he was still legally married to his first wife, was not in conformity with Christian moral standards and was not approved in strict circles of the Church.

The first generation of missionary-school students were of humble origins, but owing to their facility in English and knowledge of Western ways, they were often able to accumulate wealth and climb to positions of leadership. They sought marriage partners for their sons and daughters among other Christian families. Thus, a complex of interlocking family relationships was formed.[7]

English-language education and the profession of Christianity set the group apart. Its members did not fit into the traditional Chinese social structure. Their missionary mentors did not encourage them to follow traditional Chinese practices or thought systems. Those who accepted the missionaries' view tended to become a separate and distinct group within Chinese society. Because they had had a Western type of education and because of the political views of their teachers, the students of missionary schools were sympathetic to a constitutional form of government. They were critical of the corruption within the Government of China and of its conservative withdrawal at increasing pressure from the West.[8]

The special situation of young men who had been educated in America is a topic in Hager's article 'Three Months on Chinese Soil':

I think I have met some seven or eight of the returned students [of the Chinese Educational Mission] who were recalled some two years ago. Intellectually every one of these students is persuaded of the truth of Christianity, but I am afraid there is lacking that yielding of the heart which is the essential thing ... Everyone of these students is intensely American in their feelings, illustrating over and over again the truth that as a child is educated into manhood, so will he be, think and feel afterwards. They would welcome anything to their country that would revolutionize the whole system of education, thought and government. Quite frequently I press upon them the claims of the Gospel ministry, but their eyes are not turned in that direction. I think that some feel there is an impassable gulf between them and their countrymen, nothing but self-denial, persecution, and perhaps even death to them. It means something to be a Christian here—not less than the whole heart consecrated to God. No weak and vacillating Christian does remain firm here. It means the sacrifice of home, friends and relatives.

This was the situation and atmosphere of the times, as understood by the Revd Charles Hager, in which Sun Yat-sen found himself upon his baptism. It produced a small interconnected group on the China coast. Because of the connection of Dr Sun's second wife with the Wan family of Hong Kong, this is of special interest and illustrates the complexity of ties that were created.

Hager spent his first Sunday in Hong Kong with this family. It was not fortuitous that he should have done so. Five years previously, Wan Ching-kai had been in correspondence with the Chinese in California in regard to their establishing a mission in Hong Kong. His enthusiasm for evangelism is mentioned in a report published by the Revd W.C. Pond, of the California Chinese mission:

Wan Ching Kai ... has suggested that, in that English city of Hong Kong, mission work among the Chinese could be conducted most successfully, upon the very plan which we use here [in California]; and is very desirous himself to send native preachers into the neglected interior districts, asking whether our Chinese brethren here could not help him to do so ... The emphatic testimony which these bear to his good judgment and general efficiency, as well as his Christian character, makes both the work he has done and the work he wants to do, confirm my confidence in the suggestion I have made.[9]

Fung Foo,[10] a member of the California mission who visited Hong Kong in 1878, reported that Wan Tsing-kai, 'the most active deacon of the London Missionary Society congregation in Hong Kong', told him that the Chinese of Hong Kong felt that there was a great need for them to learn the English language. He urged Fung to remain in Hong Kong and establish a night-school to teach English similar to those successfully conducted in California.

Immediately after Hager's arrival in Hong Kong, he wrote an account for *The Pacific* of his first Sunday in Hong Kong. He related how he visited the Wan family: 'After breakfast I went to the house of Mr. Wang [sic] Ching Kai and found Lee Sam[11] there. The family were all gathered together for morning worship, and though the place was far from being anything like our own, it was quite comfortable and pleasant. The family consisted of the father and his two sons, a nephew, and the wife of the eldest son. Two other sons belong to the family, but they were not present.'

The members of the family mentioned can be identified from the register of the London Missionary Society congregation and other sources. The father, Wan Kam-tseung (溫金聰), also known as Wan Tsing-kai (溫清溪) (1813–1915), had come to Hong Kong in 1854 from the San Ning (Toi Shan) District of Kwangtung. By trade, he was a carpenter. Over the years he acquired property, mostly shops in the Chinese business section. He was baptized in Hong Kong on 3 April 1864. In 1900, he was naturalized as a British subject. Hager did not mention his wife, Wan Yan-shi (溫甄氏), but she was living at the time of Hager's visit. Perhaps she was in the country. According to the church records there were six sons, and a nephew's name was also mentioned.

Hager gave some details about the elder son: 'The married son is one of the returned Chinese American students who have engaged in teaching in the Government school,[12] but he leaves soon for Shanghai, to engage in mechanics there. His wife is a pupil of Miss Noyer [sic][13] from Canton and appears to be a very pleasant lady, though she cannot talk a word of English. Her husband speaks English quite distinctly.'

Kwan Yuet-ping (關月平), the wife of this elder son, Ping-chung, the returned student from America, was a daughter of Kwan Yan-cheung. Her brother was a fellow-student and friend of Sun Yat-sen in medical school. The gravestone of Mrs Wan, née Kwan, in the Colonial Cemetery, Happy Valley, Hong Kong, describes her as 'an exemplary Christian, eleven years the president of the Women's Christian Temperance Union, translator of Christian Temperance Literature'. In view of her work as a translator, Hager's statement that 'she cannot talk a word of English' may be questioned. She may well have been shy or remained quietly in the background during his visit as was proper for young Chinese ladies in mixed company. Her mother at one time had conducted a school where she taught Chinese girls English. It would have been strange if her own daughter had not learned the language.

It was through Wan Ping-chung, the returned student and husband of Kwan Yuet-ping, that Sun Yat-sen was connected to the Soong family, from which his second wife came. But before discussing this connection, let us continue Hager's description of his first Sunday in Hong Kong: 'I was asked to unite in prayer with the family and after we had listened to an exposition of 2 Timothy 2:1 (Now therefore, my son, take strength from the grace of God which is ours in Christ Jesus), then we sang 'Gates Ajar' in Chinese as well as we could, after which we were led in prayer by Lee Sam.'

In the afternoon, Hager also attended the Chinese service at Union Church. He remarked, 'I was pleasantly surprised to see the house well-filled, and most of them participating in the sacrament. It seemed such a pleasant contrast to the few who had gathered in the morning. Rev. E.C. Edge conducted the exercise, while his wife led the singing, beating time with her fan, in a vigorous manner.'

Following the Chinese service there was a Sunday school, though Hager thought 'It hardly deserves the name', as there were only thirty or forty present, mostly soldiers and sailors. There was only one Chinese class. The poor state of the school gave the new missionary ideas: 'I pondered how I might open a Sunday school especially for Chinese.'

In the evening he attended a service of the Hong Kong Christian Association at the Temperance Hall, where 'the preaching was not metaphysical, but pure gospel'. The preacher was the Revd D.D. Jones, an independent, who later worked for a time with Hager.

Hager mentioned that the eldest son of the Wan family was a returned student from America. Wan Ping-chung had gone to America in 1873 at the age of 12, as a member of the second group of students sent by the Chinese Government to study in the United States under the auspices of the Chinese Educational Mission. It was while he was a student in America that he met the father of Soong Ching-ling.

Emily Hahn, in a book on the Soong sisters, writes about the meeting of two of the students of the Chinese Educational Mission with Charlie Soong. Charlie, or perhaps it would be better to call him Soong Yau-ju (宋耀如), as he used the name Charlie only after he left Boston, had been adopted by a childless brother of his mother. His surname was thus changed from Han to Soong. The uncle operated a silk and tea store in Boston, assisted by his young nephew, who was learning the business.

The story of the meeting as told by Emily Hahn is interesting, but the reader is not sure on what it has been based: a documentary source, an oral tradition, or the imagination of the author. Miss Hahn links the meeting of the students with the shop-boy to the latter's running away from Boston and striking out on his own. She describes the stirring-up of the boy in this fashion:

'The two young students talked to the wistful little boy behind the counter, telling him of their life at school and of the camp where they were sent each summer.... They visited the shop frequently and kept criticizing young Soon ... that is, how he spelled his name in those days for remaining behind the counter and being satisfied with night school, in America, where a first-class education was so easy to obtain ... Yan-ju listened, his mouth watered for a similar chance.'[14]

When he asked his uncle for permission to attend school full-time, he was turned down. Taking the matter into his own hands, he ran away. He went to sea[15] and ended up at Wilmington, South Carolina. Here he found interested patrons and was sent to Methodist Trinity College in South Carolina, but after two years he transferred to Vanderbilt University in Tennessee to study theology. After his return to China, he was for a time a Methodist preacher in Shanghai.

The two students who stirred up the shop-boy in the tea and silk store in Boston were Wan Ping-chung, son of a deacon in a Hong Kong congregation, and Niu Shang-chou, from Shanghai, who was a member of the first group of students in the Chinese Educational Mission.

The boys from the Chinese Educational Mission were recalled to China in 1882. Charlie Soong returned in 1886. In the course of time, each married a daughter of the Ni family of Yuyao, Chekiang. The family was Protestant although earlier generations, on the female side of the family, had been Roman Catholic. Charlie, shortly after his return, married Ni Kwei-tseng. Niu Shang-chou married Ni Kuei-chin. Wan Ping-chung married Kwan Yuet-ping in Hong Kong. After her death, he married Ni Sieu-tsang, the third of the sisters.

Thus it was that three adolescents in Boston, two of them students, one a clerk in a shop, married three sisters. One of the sisters was the mother of the second wife of Dr Sun Yat-sen. It was in this way that interlocking relationships were forged between China coast Christian families.

The Penang-born medical doctor, Wu Lien-teh, in his autobiography, *Plague Fighter*, speaks of Wan Ping-chung and his connections with the Soong family:

About the year 1901, I meet Mr. Wen Ping-chung, most jolly of all the early returned students from America, then serving as English Secretary to the Viceroy's Yamen. Wen had accompanied the two Imperial Commissioners Tuan Fang and Tai Hung-chi during their tour around the world to study the constitutions of advanced countries, and I had met him in Penang. He was a Christian of the American Methodist Church and had married a Christian lady, whose sister was the wife of Pastor Soong, father ·of the three noted Soong sisters ... At my friend Wen's house I first met Soong Ching-ling, a charming and vivacious girl, just returned from her college training in America, and soon to find an occupation as private secretary to Dr. Sun and some years afterwards became the great man's wife.[16]

Many years before this marriage, Sun Yat-sen, while a middle-school student in Hong Kong, had met Wan Ping-chung through the Revd Charles R. Hager. His baptism made him a part of a special group of China coast Christians.

PART II
THE CHURCH, MIDDLEMEN, AND THE HONG KONG SETTING

6 The Emergence of a Chinese Élite in Hong Kong

THE opening of the Tung Wah Hospital in 1872[1] marks the terminal date for this study of the emergence of a Chinese élite in Hong Kong. We are concerned, therefore, with the first thirty years of the colony's history, from 1841 to 1872.

The first decade was characterized by economic and social problems partially created by a shifting and generally irresponsible population. During this period there were, however, a small number of settlers who were establishing themselves and their families with the purpose of making Hong Kong their permanent home, of acquiring capital, and of investing in real estate. As the colony entered the 1850s, this group increasingly assumed a position of leadership. It was composed of a few successful contractors and builders, several government servants, compradores of foreign firms, and Chinese Christians attached to missionary groups.

The second decade was marked by an influx of population and capital caused by disturbed conditions in southern China created by the Taiping rebellion. This influx turned into an exodus when hostilities began between the British and the Chinese in 1857. But war brought more compradores to Hong Kong as foreign firms moved down from Canton.

In the third decade there was a revival of trade, and a growing merchant class provided its share of élite. By the end of the 1860s, a clearly defined élite group had established itself, providing leadership for the Chinese community.

The purpose of this chapter is to document the conditions from which an identifiable élite group arose in Hong Kong and to illustrate this emergence with biographies of some of its members.

Sources for the Study

The most important sources used to determine the Chinese élite for the period covered by this study are the names given on memorials, petitions, and subscription lists. The repetition of a name on subsequent lists, the amount of the contributions, and the position of the name on the document all serve to suggest the relative status of an individual. Proprietorship of land also suggests potential élite status.

(a) The earliest such document is a petition from landowners dated 19 February 1848, in which they asked for the remission of what they considered excessive Crown rent charges. There are twenty-seven signatures of the principal Chinese landowners.[2]

(b) In September 1852, the *China Mail* published the subscription list for the Chinese hospital proposal by Dr Hirschberg of the London Missionary Society. This also contains twenty-seven names. Of these, ten were compradores, seven shopkeepers, three merchants, three contractors, and one 'gentleman'. Only three names from the 1848 list appear on this list: Loo Aqui, gentleman, Tam Achoy, building contractor, and Chow Aqui, merchant.

(c) On 4 November 1856, a memorial concerning a recent piece of legislation was presented to the Government. It contained both European and Chinese names. Nineteen Chinese signed.[3]

(d) In 1859, the *Government Gazette* published a 'list of Chinese Voluntary Contributions to a Fund for purchasing books, etc., for the Government Schools in the Colony'. Most of the contributions were made in the name of business firms, but all the largest amounts were contributed by individuals. The two largest contributors were both contractors: Tang Luk gave $60 and Tam Tso (Achoy) gave $50. Then there are thirteen contributions of $10 each. Of these, six were from compradores and an equal number from merchants. The remaining contributor in this particular group was a government servant, the overseer of the coolie gangs of the Surveyor-General's Department.

(e) In April 1861, the *Friend of China* published a list entitled 'A Public Declaration of the Shop Keepers of Hong Kong, stating that when Mr. Caldwell managed the Proprietorship of the Chinese here, the people of Hong Kong were at rest, but he resigned his office. They now present their petition to the Governor asking him to retain Mr. Caldwell'. It has sixteen names of firms as the chief petitioners. Beside seven of them are given the names of the head of the firm. Five of these can be found on the 1859 list.

(f) In January 1868, the Hong Kong *Daily Press* published forty-two names of individuals and firms who had submitted a petition to the House of Commons to protest against the imposition of a military contribution upon Hong Kong.

(g) In 1872, the *Chinese Chronicle and Directory* gives the names of the eleven members of the Kai Fong or 'Joss House' Committee, as well as the thirteen members of the Tung Wah Hospital Committee. This was the organizing committee of 1869, which remained in office until the hospital was formally opened in 1872, when a new committee was elected. The Directory also lists a General Committee for the Hospital. This too had thirteen members.

(h) On 1 April 1871, a memorial presented to Henry Charles Caldwell upon his departure from the colony by the Chinese community, which was published in the Chinese section of the *China Mail* and signed by thirty-two of the most prominent Chinese, serves as a check against the Tung Wah and Kai Fong directors.

(i) In May 1872, the *China Mail* listed the names of thirty Chinese who called upon the Governor on behalf of the Chinese community. This delegation was composed of seven compradores, fourteen merchants, two journalists, one contractor, and two government servants.

(j) The relationship between land ownership and élite status can be judged by a list of the twenty highest ratepayers in 1876 and 1881, published in the *Government Gazette*. The list includes both Europeans and Chinese. In 1876, European ownership outranked Chinese by twelve to eight; but in 1881, ownership had changed so that there were seventeen Chinese among the twenty highest ratepayers. In the 1881 list, seven of the top twenty were from compradore families, six were merchants, one was a contractor, and the list also included the widow of the Revd Ho Fuk-tong, ordained minister of the London Missionary Society's Chinese congregation.

After the opening of the Tung Wah Hospital in 1872, the names of the directors of the hospital published in the *Development of the Tung Wah Hospital 1870–1960* are an excellent criterion for determining élite status. After 1872 there is also an ever-increasing number of subscriptions, memorials, committees, delegations, and so on, which serve as counterchecks to the Tung Wah directorships.

For a study of an élite based on such lists, it is necessary to give identity to the names by a biographical sketch. These sketches indicate the manner by which the individual arrived at élite status.

Reconstructing the biographies of these early residents of Hong Kong is not an easy task. Only documentary sources have been used for the reconstruction. No information has been sought from present-day descendants of these individuals. I have relied upon such material as newspapers, Land Registry Office records, the police and lighting rates for 1860, 1868, and 1872, the *Government Gazette* and Blue Books, the published *Calendar of Probates* and *Administrations*, the Colonial Office Records in the Public Record Office, London, and the archives of several missionary societies. The Chinese practice of using various aliases complicates identification. In one instance, for example, an individual used at various times and in various relationships ten different aliases. The varying Romanization for Chinese names constitutes another problem for the researcher who uses Western sources. The contemporary English, Portuguese, Germans, and French each had a different system for Romanizing Chinese characters. For instance, in one place there is a reference to Tso Aon's brother, Chow Yik-cheong. The Chinese character for the surname is 曹; the English in Hong Kong spelled it Tso, while the Portuguese in Macau used Chow. Thus, in Hong Kong records, a name is likely to appear spelled in one way and in Macau in another. For the period covered in this study, there was no officially approved system of Romanization in Hong Kong. Romanization was also influenced by the dialect variations in the Chinese language itself: the spelling of a name might vary according to the place of origin of the individual, whether Hakka, Chiu Chow, Fukienese, or Cantonese. The sources often have a number of variations in the Romanized form of a name. I have used the form that occurs most commonly. The Chinese characters have been given wherever they are available, but they are not given on all source documents or other records.

Government and the Élite

In China, there was traditionally a close connection between the Government and the élite group. With the introduction of the imperial examination system, the élite or gentry were recruited from the ranks of the scholars. Success in the examinations, appointment to government office, and the accumulation of capital and economic power were usually concomitant.[4]

Obviously, this relationship could not be duplicated in Hong Kong. In the years following the establishment of the colony, there was a radical gap between the Chinese population and the colonial Government. Their points of contact were few. As long as the Chinese did not create trouble, the Government was content to let the Chinese community manage its own affairs, the hope being, of course, that the management would be in the hands of responsible leaders. However, social and economic conditions within the community, both before and after the British seizure of the island, mitigated against control being exercised by responsible individuals.

Official government structures at the local level were at a minimum before the arrival of the British. Hong Kong was one of many 'barren rocks' on the edge of San On (later called Po On) District, one of the least important in the Kwang Chau Prefecture. Originally, San On had been a part of the Tung Kwun District, but it had been separated from it in 1573. The separation left it small and insignificant. The limited exercise of government authority and its geographical location made it a base for pirates. One of the stories about the origin of the name of the Tai Ping Shan District on Hong Kong Island is that a pirate named Cheung Po-chai used it as his headquarters. He finally went over to the authorities and left the island. In relief, the local population named the mountainside on which he had dwelt 'Great Peace Mountain'.[5] Since it was easy to slip away by boat if government officials came to check on inhabitants, the islands on the edge of San On District were popular haunts for outlaws and the criminal element.

At the time of the establishment of the British claim to the island, the *Canton Register*, for 23 February 1841, predicted that under British jurisdiction the island would become even more popular with these classes: 'Hongkong will be the resort and rendevous of all the Chinese smugglers. Opium smoking shops and gambling-houses will soon spread; to those haunts will flock all the discontented and bad spirits of the empire.' Future developments substantiated this forecast.

Factors which Impeded the Emergence of Responsible Leaders in the Chinese Community

Samuel Fearon, the Census and Registration Officer, in a report dated 24 June 1845, described the origin of the first settlers of Hong Kong:

The arrival of the British fleet in the harbour speedily attracted a considerable boat population, and the profits accruing from the supply of provisions and necessaries at once raised many from poverty and infamy to considerable wealth. The shelter and protection afforded by the presence of the fleet soon made our shores the resort of outlaws, opium smugglers, and indeed, of all persons who had rendered themselves obnoxious to the Chinese laws, and had the means of escaping hither. In course of time the demands for labour, for the public and other works drew some thousands to the island, the majority of whom were Hakkas or gypsies; people whose habits, character and language mark them as a distinct race. Careless of the ties of home and of those moral obligations, the observance of which is deemed absolutely necessary to the preservation of the national integrity; uneasy under the restraint of law and unscrupulous of the means by which they live, they abandon without hesitation their hearths and household gods, their birthright and their father's tombs, to wander, unrespected, whither gain may call them. The unsettled state of the Colony, and the vast amount of crime during its infancy afford abundant proof of the demoralizing effects of their presence ... [More recently] Hong Kong has been invested by numbers of the Triad Society, the members of which under shelter of a political maxim 'outturn the Tsing ... and restore the Ming' perpetuate the grossest enormities. I have satisfied myself that most of the burglaries have been planned and attempted by members of this dangerous association.[6]

Fearon mentions in his report a person named Aqui as the most influential and wealthy of the native residents. He had rapidly risen from the lowly status of a bum-boatman. William Tarrant, a historian of Hong Kong who was well acquainted with the early days, writing in 1861, commented that

there were some curious fish among the earlier native settlers—the leader of them is still living in Victoria, Loo Aqui, alias See Mun King. If all reports be true, Aqui was monarch of all he surveyed on the water about Hong Kong prior to our taking possession—that is to say, he was the Sea King who took toll from all that passed his squadron. This is of course rumour only; and we but mention it to say that the presence of Aqui on the island had much to do in keeping people of better character from settling, or even visiting the place.[7]

George Smith, the future Bishop of Victoria, visited Hong Kong in 1844 and gave an equally critical description of Aqui's activities:

He possesses about fifty houses in the bazaar, and lives on the rent, in a style much above the generality of the Chinese settlers, who are commonly composed of the refuse of the neighbouring mainland. During the war,

Aqui acted as purveyor of provisions to the British armament and acquired some wealth. After the peace he was at first afraid to return to the
mainland, lest he should be seized as a traitor by the Mandarins. In the
end he settled at Hong Kong, where he is said to encourage disreputable
characters by the loan of money, and in various ways to reap the proceeds
of profligacy and crime.[8]

Loo Aqui (盧亞貴) also appears in the records as Lo Aking
(盧亞景) or Sze Mun-king (〔盧〕斯文景) [Lo] (King, the Gentleman). At the time of the Sino-British war, he seems to have played
both sides of the game. The Chinese Government lured him back
to Canton by offering him an official degree of the sixth rank.[9] He
accepted but did not stay long with the Chinese, and as he was
soon back in Hong Kong enjoyed the rewards of his services as
provisioner for the British forces. He seems to have had supporters in Hong Kong government circles for he secured the grant of a
large and valuable section of land behind the marine lots of the
Lower Bazaar. This was the area between Queen's Road and
Jervois Street extending from the vicinity of the junction westward
to Cleverly Street. He and his family also acquired a number of
marine lots by grant or purchase. Of the twenty-seven who signed
the petition of landowners in 1848, about one-fifth were members
of the Loo clan.[10] Soon after the settlement of Hong Kong, Loo
Aqui was operating a gambling establishment and brothels. In
1845, he built a theatre. For a time he held the opium monopoly,
and when the residents of the Middle Bazaar were removed to the
Tai Ping Shan area in 1844, he petitioned the Government for the
privilege of operating a market for the inhabitants, agreeing to
build a substantial markethouse at a cost of $2,500 and to pay a
monthly rental to the Government of $200 for a period of five
years. Loo Aqui and Tam Achoy were recognized as the leaders of
the Chinese community, for according to a Chinese account entitled 'Information as to the period of the formations of Districts in
Hongkong and the alteration of the Character Wan—a bay—to
Wan—a circuit', in 1847 they built the Man-Mo Temple on Hollywood Road and here 'they judged the people in public assembly'
until 1851, when the shopkeepers of the Lower Bazaar 'repaired to
Man-Mo Temple, elected a Committee, and therein decided all
cases of any public interest.'[11]

As well as his income from various business ventures, Aqui had
a steady income from his properties. In 1850, he was collecting
rent on over a hundred shops and houses. But, in 1855, he was

declared bankrupt. He had stood security for the administration of the estate of the Chinese merchant, Chinam; the administrator had misused the property of the estate, and Loo Aqui had to pay up, which threw him into insolvency. However, anticipating this, he had previously transferred most of his property to his relatives. After his bankruptcy, he no longer appears as a public figure, although two near relatives, perhaps his sons, Loo Shing and Loo Chew (or, as he is sometimes called, 'Young Qui') are on several of the later lists used to determine élite status. One of Loo Chew's sons was compradore for David Sassoon, Sons and Company in the 1870s; another son, Loo Kum-chun, was Secretary to the Tung Wah Hospital in 1872.

The family of Loo Aqui was from Whampoa and they were probably Tanka or boat people. The Revd Charles Gutzlaff, Chinese Secretary to the Superintendent of Trade, reports that 'the most numerous class who have, since our arrival, fixed themselves on the island, are from Whampoa; many of them are of the worst characters, and ready to commit any atrocity'.[12] They had defied the mandarins' edicts prohibiting Chinese citizens from supplying provisions or other services to the British forces. However, it is not surprising that they seized the opportunity to make a quick profit by collaborating with the enemy. They were a secondary caste within the Chinese social structure and were deprived of certain rights. As boat people, they had had a long association with foreign shipping. In recognition of their valuable services to the British, they, along with others, were allotted land in the new town. The Tanka, on leaving their boats for land, soon put aside their distinctiveness and merged with the general population, though they long maintained control of trade in cattle, fish, and prostitutes.[13]

Hong Kong government authorities were much concerned in the first ten years of the colony's existence about the type of Chinese who came to the island. Conditions were not conducive to attracting wealthy Chinese of respectable background, who could strengthen Hong Kong's economy by promoting local and Southeast Asian trade in Chinese products. There had been some optimists who believed that the Chinese would welcome the opportunity to live and trade under an 'enlightened, benevolent government', but they had underestimated traditional Chinese xenophobia and inbred loyalty to China as the motherland.

Descriptions of the type of Chinese settler are found in numerous reports that government officials submitted to London. In 1844, the Colonial Treasurer wrote:

It is literally true that after three years and a half's uninterrupted settlement there is not one respectable Chinese inhabitant on the island ... The policy of the mandarins on the adjacent coast being to prevent all respectable Chinese from settling at Hong Kong; and in consequence of the hold they possess on their families and relatives this can be done most effectually. At the same time, I believe that they encourage and promote the deportation of every thief, pirate and idle or worthless vagabond from the mainland to Hongkong ... No Chinese of humbler class will ever bring their wives and children to the colony. The shopkeepers do not remain more than a few months on the island, when another set take their place; there is, in fact, a continual shifting of a Bedouin sort of population, whose migratory, predatory, gambling, and dissolute habits utterly unfit them for continuous industry, and render them not only useless, but highly injurious subjects, in the attempt to form a colony.[14]

In establishing British government at Hong Kong, it was hoped that Hong Kong could lure away from Macau and Canton a great part of the junk trade and thus make Hong Kong a centre of trade for the whole coast of Kwangtung Province. Though a small beginning was made, this trade soon languished. Remarking on the absence of a substantial local trade with Canton, Gutzlaff stated that this was because

there are no Chinese large firms at Victoria to receive goods in charge, and sell them as soon as there is a demand. Attempts to found such establishments have also been made, but have not succeeded from want of encouragement or on account of considerable individual loss. At the present moment (April, 1845) there remains unfortunately not one single large merchant from Canton in the settlement who is able to promote by his capital and influence such a desirable state. The whole business is therefore in the hands of shopkeepers, compradors and pedlars of whom there are many, though their transactions when considered as a whole are but trifling.[15]

In his remarks on native trade, Gutzlaff states that an attempt had been made by a Cantonese capitalist to establish himself in Hong Kong. He is referring to Chinam (齊南), alias Chan Akuen (陳亞權), who with three partners operated under the firm name of Tun Wo (敦和). The Colonial Treasurer, R.M. Martin, also refers to him in his report: 'One man of reputed wealth named Chinam, who had been engaged in the opium trade, came to Hong Kong, built a good house, and freighted a ship. He soon returned to Canton, and died there of a fever and cold contracted in Hong Kong. It was understood, however, that had he lived he would have been prohibited from returning to Hong Kong.'[16]

In June 1843, Chinam bought Marine Lot 54 from Richard Oswald, paying $8,000. At the time it had on it a Singapore-frame house[17] with brick enlargements. On the lot, Chinam proceeded to build a large *hong* in the Chinese style, but before the building was completed, he died in July 1844. With his death, the firm closed down its operations in Hong Kong and much of the *hong* stood unoccupied for a number of years. One of Chinam's partners, Chan Chun-poo, was appointed his administrator, but owing to irregularities in his handling of the estate he was imprisoned in 1854 and remained in prison for two years where he petitioned the Government for his release on the grounds of his advanced age. The property of the firm of Chinam was sold in 1854 to one Ow Yeung-sun, a trader from the district of San Wui in Kwangtung Province.

Another Canton firm that established itself in Hong Kong in the early days was Akow and Company . It was not in the same class as Chinam's Tun Wo firm, but its position was above that of the shopkeepers and tradesmen concentrated in the Bazaar areas. The company was granted Inland Lot 22 at the corner of Queen's Road and Pottinger Street in the European section. The firm consisted of five partners, of whom one, Cheung Kam-cheong (鄭錦祥), was resident in Hong Kong. He began to speculate in real estate and bought several lots at government land auctions. His land investments were not successful and some of his property was sold at the Sheriff's sale in 1847. Akow and Company sold its Queen's Road property in 1850, though Kam-cheong remained in Hong Kong. In 1852, he contributed $5 to Dr Hirschberg's hospital. His last recorded activity in Hong Kong is the sale of two lots in 1855. At this time, Akow and Company was operating a hotel for foreigners in Canton.

After the death of Chinam, the Government still had hopes of attracting wealthy merchants. A group of Fukienese made enquiries regarding conditions for settlement. For several generations, a number of these merchants had operated large *hongs* in Macau, and the Hong Kong Government would therefore have welcomed applications from Fukien merchants for land grants. In the light of the ancient rivalry between Cantonese and Fukienese, it was felt that the allocation of land to this group needed to

1 Buildings of the Basel Missionary Society station at Sai Ying Pun, Hong Kong, viewed from the west. The building with the belfry is the chapel built in 1867; the upper storey contained a large and small classroom. The building in the middle is the mission house (*Evangelische Heidenbote*, June 1870)

2 The Lower Bazaar Chapel of the London Missionary Society on Jervois Street, Hong Kong (*Calwer Missionsblatt*, June 1849)

4 The London Missionary Society house on the north side of Aberdeen Street. It contained classrooms and living quarters for the students of the Anglo-Chinese College. Below it is the Union Church (Legge Collection, Archives of the London Missionary Society, London)

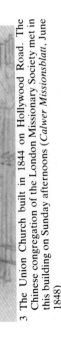

3 The Union Church built in 1844 on Hollywood Road. The Chinese congregation of the London Missionary Society met in this building on Sunday afternoons (*Calwer Missionsblatt*, June 1848)

No. 1. Chinese Printing-Office.　　No. 2. English Printing-Office.　　No. 3. Chinese School,　　No. 4. Western Gate of Malacca.

5 The Anglo-Chinese College at Malacca (*Missionary Sketches*, January 1825)

6 The chapel and mission house of the Basel Missionary Society station at Sai Ying Pun. The photograph was taken from the corner of Third and Western Streets. The 1867 chapel remains, but the mission house has been rebuilt since the drawing of about 1870 shown in Plate 1 (from a booklet published to mark the one-hundredth anniversary of Kau Yan Church in 1967)

7 Buildings of the Basel Missionary Society station at Sai Ying Pun on the north side of High Street (from a booklet published to mark the one-hundredth anniversary of Kau Yan Church in 1967)

8 St. Paul's College, built as a wing of the Bishop's residence, Lower Albert Road (from a booklet published to mark the one-hundred-and-twentieth anniversary of St. Paul's College in 1971)

Patron.

H. E. Sir HENRY POTTINGER, BART. G. C. B. &c. &c.

OFFICERS OF THE SOCIETY, ELECTED SEPT. 29, 1842.

President.

Rev. E. C. BRIDGMAN, D. D.

Vice-President.

W. LESLIE Esq. (Absent) ASSISTANT J. MACVICCAR, (Acting)

Treasurer.

ALEXANDER MATHESON, Esq.

Corresponding Secretary.

S. WELLS WILLIAMS, Esq.

Recording Secretary.

J. R. MORRISON, Esq. (Deceased) A. ANDERSON, Esq. (Acting)

Auditors.

W. H. WOESS, Esq.   D. L. BURN, Esq.

Principal of the Society's School in Hongkong, Rev. S. R. Brown.

Note.—A donation of $25 at one time constitutes a person a member; or an annual Subscription of $10.

9 Officers of the Morrison Education Society from a circular to the friends and patrons of the Society, dated Macau, 20 December 1843 (Sword Family Papers, Manuscript Division, Pennsylvania Historical Society, Philadelphia)

10 To Tsai Church, Hollywood Road. The congregation began under the auspices of the London Missionary Society but became fully independent in 1888 (from a booklet published to mark the fiftieth anniversary of Hop Yat Church in 1976)

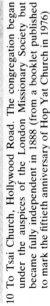

11 Wong Yuk-cho, pastor of To Tsai Church (Legge Collection, Archives of the London Missionary Society, London)

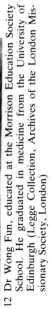

13 Ho Alloy, otherwise known as Ho Shan-chee, a pupil of the Anglo-Chinese College in Hong Kong. He was later on the ambassadorial staff of Chan Lai-tau in Washington and promoted the organization of the Canton and Hong Kong Telegraph Company (Legge Collection, Archives of the London Missionary Society, London)

12 Dr Wong Fun, educated at the Morrison Education Society School. He graduated in medicine from the University of Edinburgh (Legge Collection, Archives of the London Missionary Society, London)

15 Ho Fuk-tong (1818–71), a student at the Anglo-Chinese College, Malacca, ordained as pastor for the Chinese congregation of the London Missionary Society in Hong Kong in 1846 (Lam Chi-kan (1977))

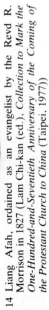

14 Liang Afah, ordained as an evangelist by the Revd R. Morrison in 1827 (Lam Chi-kan (ed.), Collection to Mark the One-Hundred-and-Seventieth Anniversary of the Coming of the Protestant Church to China (Taipei, 1977))

17 Sun Yat-sen aged 18 (Lam Chi-kan (1977))

16 The Revd Charles Gutzlaff (1803–51) dressed as a Chinese sailor (Lam Chi-kan (1977))

林毓宋1	港香		Removed
孫日新2	香山省城	翠亨鄉	Removed
八媽3	省城		Deceased
陸中桂4	香山	翠亨鄉	
唐雄5	〃	〃唐家〃	
任顯德6	香港		Removed Deceased
宋連好7	小	〃 〃	〃
宋江爵8	小	〃 〃	〃
周慈愛9	小	〃 〃	〃
任顯日10	小	〃 〃	
陳神重11	恩平長灣林		

香港基督教會史

孫總理信奉基督教之經過

18 The first page of a record book of the China Congregational Church, Hong Kong, giving baptisms by the Revd C. Hager. No. 2 is Sun Yat-sen, and Nos. 4 and 5 are his friends Lu Hao-tung, given here as Luk Chung-kwei, and Tong Phong (Lam Chi-kan (1977))

19 Wu Ting-fang, Chinese Ambassador to the United States, while on a visit to New Orleans (from a newspaper clipping (undated and the name of the newspaper not included) in the Archives of the Chinese Presbyterian Church, New Orleans)

WU TING FANG WRITING AUTOGRAPH'

20 Dr Morrison and his assistants translating the Bible into Chinese, from a painting by George Chinnery (W.J. Townsend, *Robert Morrison, Pioneer of Missions to China* (London, Pickering and Inglis, no date but *circa* 1860s))

21 The Revd James Legge and his students, Le Kin-lun, Sung Fuh-keen and Woo Wan-sew, otherwise known as Ng Mun-sow, in the Theological Seminary, Hong Kong (H.E. Legge, *James Legge, Missionary and Scholar* (London, The Religious Tract Society, 1905), p. 52)

理教師大人 納鑒
才德兼備
教澤淵深
香港華民拜題

22 Tablet presented by the Chinese community in Hong Kong to Dr James Legge
   (H.E. Legge (1905), p. 203)

23 Miss Harriet Noyes, founder and principal for over fifty years of the True Light School for Girls at Canton. Her school produced doctors, nurses, teachers, and Christian home-makers (*Kowloon True Light Middle School 1872–1970* (Hong Kong, 1970))

24 Medical students from the True Light School for Girls at Canton (Harriet N. Noyes, *A Light in the Land of Sinim*, p. 88)

be handled with care. The Governor explained in his report to England that

These people constitute a very peculiar race, being far more commercial, migratory, and maritime in their habits than any other natives of China. Their spoken language is altogether unintelligible to the people of Canton, between whom and themselves a species of irreconcilable feud has existed from time immemorial. Hence they cannot inhabit the same neighbourhood without quarrels, and occassionally [sic] bloody conflicts. If land is put up by auction the Fokien (or Chinchew men) would in competition with the Cantonese either be excluded altogether, or mingled with the Cantonese be to the prejudice of general peace and order. It is important to secure the settlement of this class of people (in the present instance men of substance). The Council agreed with me to grant them a special location ... placed much to their satisfaction in the neighbourhood of East Point, and they have commenced building on five contiguous lots.[18]

This report was dated July 1845. However, in the Surveyor-General's return of registered allotments of 24 June 1846, he reported that the lots granted to the Chinchew merchants had been rejected by them. So again, the prospect of the settlement of wealthy Chinese merchants was not realized.

The Blue Book reports for both 1845 and 1846 noted some signs of a growing stability in the Chinese population. In 1845, it was stated that 'both in numbers and respectability the Chinese are improving, being accompanied in a greater number of instances by their families', and in 1846, 'the proportion of females increases as a feeling of security induced Chinese settlers to bring over their families'. The settling of families was welcomed because it indicated that the Chinese who did settle were willing to consider Hong Kong a place of permanent residence. Although some progress had been noted in this area, the report for 1848 indicated that it had not been sustained. 'There exists no local attachment, which may be ascribed to the absence of respectable families born on the island, with which the adventurers could contract marriages. The rent of houses and shops is at present low enough to enable any man who has a middling trade to lodge his family, yet very few decent married females reside here. In this respect there has been very little improvement during the past year.' The paucity of Chinese families in Hong Kong is reflected in the annual census of shops and buildings. In 1845, there were as many brothels as families, twenty-five families and twenty-six brothels. Within five years, the number of families had increased to one hundred and forty-one, but there were only six more brothels than in 1845. The 1850s saw a substantial influx of Chinese families escaping from the turbulent conditions in Kwantung Province created by the Taiping rebellion.

This influx changed the characteristics of Hong Kong's Chinese population, which acquired more stability, responsibility, and economic strength. An examination of an emerging élite in this period shows that its members can be divided into five occupational groups: contractors, merchants, compradores, government servants, and Christian employees of missionary groups. The biographies of individuals in each of these groups found on our lists for determining élite status provide the background for élite emergence in the 1850s and 1860s.

The Contractors

When Hong Kong was settled, the immediate need for buildings brought many connected with the building trade to Hong Kong. Only a few were able to survive the perils of the business. They were not accustomed to building in the Western style and therefore often underestimated on contracts, resulting in their bankruptcy. In 1844, the Land Officer commented that 'almost all contracts hitherto entered into with Chinamen have been obliged to be finished by Government, for the works were taken at far too low an estimate, and the consequence was, when the parties found they would become losers, both contractor and security decamped, and in some instances they were imprisoned'.[19]

One of the few contractors who did survive in this early period of Hong Kong's history was Tam Achoy (譚才), alias Tam Samtshoy (譚三才), alias Tam Shek-tsun (譚錫珍), although he too almost went to prison for debt, escaping only through the generosity of his creditor. Achoy was generally recognized as the most prominent leader of the Chinese community when an élite was first beginning to emerge out of the hotchpotch of shopkeepers, craftsmen, and traders. He and Loo Aqui had built the Man-Mo Temple, where they performed in part the traditional role of village elder, and Achoy was also Trustee for the I Ts'z Temple in Tai Ping Shan (1851) and the temple in Queen's Road East at Wan Chai (1869). In 1847, the Colonial Treasury had on deposit £185 16s.8d. from Tam Achoy for erecting a Chinese school in Sheung Wan (Lower Bazaar).[20]

Achoy had come to Hong Kong in 1841 when the British laid claim to the island, having been formerly a foreman in the Government Dockyard at Singapore.[21] He was granted a certificate for the easternmost of the lots in the Lower Bazaar and soon began to buy up the interests of the adjacent property-owners until he had acquired an extensive sea frontage. He built some of Hong Kong's most prestigious early buildings, such as the P. & O. Building and the Exchange Building, which was bought by the Government and used for many years as the Supreme Court Building. With increasing capital, he began to broaden his interests and secured permission from the Government to build and operate a market. This was a most profitable venture and when the Lower Bazaar was destroyed in the Christmas fire of 1852, Achoy soon rebuilt it, operating it under his firm's name, Kwong Yuen. During the period after 1848, when Hong Kong became a port of embarkation for thousands of emigrants, Achoy was one of the leading brokers and charterers of emigrant ships. In front of his lots he erected a wharf, which he leased to the Hong Kong, Canton and Macau Steamboat Company, after its formation in 1865. In 1860, he appeared in the courts on a charge of piracy. In response to a request by the mandarin of his home district in Hoi Ping for assistance in suppressing some Hakka bandits, Achoy had chartered the vessel *Jamsetjee Jeejeebhoy* from Kwok Acheong, the P. & O. Company's compradore. Engaging some Europeans in the colony, he took them up to Hoi Ping, where they attacked some Hakka villages. Achoy pleaded that he had not realized that this would be against British law and therefore threw himself upon the mercy of the court.[22] He again assisted his home district in 1865 by supplying the local militia with Western-made armaments. This earned him official recognition and a biographical notice in the *Hoi Ping Gazetteer*. In later years, his constitution was affected by habitual opium-smoking and he did not participate actively in public affairs. He died in 1871, leaving a large fortune.[23] In 1857, the editor of the *Friend of China* described him as being 'no doubt the most creditable Chinese in the Colony'.

Tang Aluk (鄧亞六), another contractor, though not so much of a community leader as Tam Achoy, was a generous benefactor of worthy projects. He was the largest contributor to the Chinese school-book fund of 1859, contributing $60; Tam Achoy contributed $50, and Kwok Acheong, the P. & O. compradore contributed $20; all other contributions ranged from $10 to 50 cents. The fact that Tang Aluk's name was 'number six' indicates he was of humble origin. He began as a stone-cutter, most of whom were Hakka. It is probable that Aluk belonged to this group. In time, he built up a successful contracting business. At his death in 1887, he left a large estate, much of which was in landed property. The administration of his estate involved many lawsuits among his heirs. A newspaper commentator observed that the estate was a gold mine for the legal profession as suits and appeals dragged through the courts for several decades after his death.[24]

The Merchants

Hong Kong had difficulty attracting merchants with capital. The abortive efforts of Chinam and several Fukienese merchants to settle in Hong Kong have already been mentioned. Several other merchants appear on the earliest of the élite lists, indicating their presence in the first decade of the colony's history.

In 1852, 'Cun-wo A Kwi, merchant' contributed $5 to Dr Hirschberg's hospital. This was Chow Aqui (周亞蔡) of the firm Cong-wo, which had been established in the Lower Bazaar in 1842, with a branch at Canton. In 1849, he bought the lease of the Central Market, holding it until 1857. He became a large investor in real estate, but sold most of his property in 1866 and retired to Macau.

A merchant who survived the pitfalls of commerce in early Hong Kong was Wong Ping (王炳). He is named as a silk merchant on the landowners' petition of 1848, but he was one of Hong Kong's first industrialists in that he owned a rope walk beyond the western end of the Lower Bazaar. He was one of three Trustees to hold Inland Lot 361 in Tai Ping Shan on behalf of the Chinese community. The lot was granted in 1851 and upon it was built a temple 'for the reception of Tablets to the memory of ... deceased countrymen'.[25] The building was used, however, not only for memorial tablets but also as a depository for those who were about to die, following established Chinese custom. The European community was shocked when this use came to its notice. The reaction and public discussion which followed resulted in the Government allocating a grant from the revenues of the gambling monopoly to the Chinese community for the erection of a suitable hospital to be known as the Tung Wah. Wong Ping was not a member of the Organizing Committee of the Hospital, though he was on the Kai Fong Committee for 1872. He died in 1887. Wong Yue-yee, alias Wong Yick-bun, of the Chun Cheong Wing Nam Pak Hong, a director of the Tung Wah in 1872, may have been a relative as Wong Ping is mentioned in 1881 as a managing partner of the Chun Cheung Hong for some twenty years. He was also associated with the Tsui Shing firm and the Tuck Mee Hong.

In the 1850s, the Taiping rebellion upset the social and economic structure of China. The changes in China were reflected in changes in Hong Kong. The Taiping threat upon Canton created a refugee group which sought more stable conditions in Hong Kong. Some were wealthy and brought their capital with them. The Revd Dr James Legge, reflecting upon the colony's progress during his residence there, remarked:

It has always seemed to me that this was the turning point in the progress of Hong Kong. As Canton was threatened, the families of means hastened to leave it, and many of them flocked to this Colony. Houses were in demand; rents rose; the streets that had been comparatively deserted assumed a crowded appearance; new commercial Chinese firms were founded; the native trade received an impetus which it did not lose till it was arrested by the superfluous vigour of some of Sir Richard MacDonnell's early ordinances.[26]

A new category of Fukien brokers and merchants began to appear on the annual censuses. In 1848, two Fukien merchants and five Fukien brokers were reported, but they did not appear the following year. In 1853 there were six Fukien brokers, and within three years the number had increased sixfold. Not all the brokers and merchants were from Fukien. A significant number were Cantonese or Chiu Chow. In 1858, a new category, 'hongs', or large merchant establishments, was introduced into the annual census of Chinese shops and businesses. Thirty-five were listed in 1858, but sixty-five in 1859.

Some of the capital brought to Hong Kong in the 1850s was invested in real estate, and a group of large land-proprietors developed. These investments formed the foundation of the fortunes of several prominent Hong Kong families.

One of these families was the Li from San Wui District of Kwangtung Province who have been among the Chinese élite for well over a century. The family established its interests in Hong Kong in a very modest way in 1854, when two brothers, Li Sing (李昇), alias Li Yuk-hang (李玉衡), and Li Leong (李艮), bought an Upper Bazaar lot. They soon built up a money-changing business and lent money for mortgages. In 1857, they bought half of the lot where Chinam had previously built his large Chinese *hong*.

Here they established the Wo Hang firm, which operated in many different fields.

In 1865, together with two Americans, Lee Sing of the Wo Hang firm and Pang Wah-ping (彭華炳) entered into partnership as the American Trading Company of Borneo, with the intention of developing the concession that the Sultan of Brunei had granted to an American, Charles Lee Moses. The Chinese partners supplied most of the capital. The company established a settlement, but after a few years of shipbuilding, experimental planting, and trade the project was abandoned. The company did not have sufficient capital to finance the undertaking properly.[27] This drain of capital may have been the primary cause of the bankruptcy of Pang Wah-ping in 1866. He had acquired his original capital from profits of trade in unprepared opium, and during his years of prosperity his name appears on the various documents used as criteria for élite status.

The Li family, however, was more firmly established and survived the failure of the American Trading Company of Borneo. Its interests were diversified. It had large real estate holdings in Hong Kong, which brought in regular rental income. It was perhaps the largest broker for coolie labour and charterer of ships for these emigrants. In 1868, gambling was legalized in Hong Kong and the monopoly was bought up by the Li family firm. They also had interests in the opium monopoly.

Their financial investment in Hong Kong appears to have led them to identify their interests with the British at the time of the Second Opium War, and a Chinese source states that they 'gave contributions to foreigners to the extent of over a lakh of ready money and recruited native braves who went to the front at Tientsin. When peace was declared they shared in the War Indemnity as well as in the Imperial effects and curios of the Yuen-ming-yuen (Summer Palaces)'.[28] They were accused of supporting France in its efforts to gain control of Annam. The Chinese authorities of their home district tried to derive some benefit from the fortunes of the family by requesting large contributions for the reclamation of waste land. When the family seemed somewhat hesitant to meet the full demands of the authorities, they sought to provoke generosity by seizing a member of the family who happened to have returned to his home district, imprisoning him, and eventually putting him on trial.

This account of the troubles the family encountered in its relations with Chinese officialdom illustrates the predicament in which wealthy merchants and compradores found themselves when tensions developed between the Western powers and the Imperial Government of China. If they had not cut themselves off entirely from their place of origin but tried to keep up their relations with clan and family, they exposed themselves and their family to the charge of playing traitor to Chinese interests. However, their financial connections with foreigners inclined them to identify with the foreign cause. They usually tried to have it both ways, walking the thin line, but in periods of crisis they were forced into accommodation with the foreigners if they were to protect their financial investments.

Li Leong, one of the brothers, died in 1864, leaving his property in a family trust, which was later divided into five shares. The leadership of the clan then devolved upon Li Sing, although many other members of the family are in the Hong Kong records—so many, in fact, that it is a difficult task to establish exact relationships. But it is the name of Li Sing which appears in the various lists until his death in 1900. He was one of three Trustees who held title to the Queen's Road Temple in Wan Chai in 1869. The same year, he was one of the organizing members of the Tung Wah Hospital. Other members of the family have continued the tradition of Li Sing as community leader to this day.

One of the organizing directors of the Tung Wah Hospital was Ng Yik-wan (吳翼雲), alias Ng Chan-yeung (吳振揚), of the Fuk Lung opium firm. The founder of the family in Hong Kong was Ng Yu, who first appears on the records in 1858 when the Fuk Lung opium shop was the successful bidder for the opium monopoly. He was secured by Loo Aqui who had held the monopoly in an earlier period. The Fuk Lung firm was made up of five members, all from the Tung Kwun District of Kwangtung. One of them was Shi Sing-kai, one of four named in a petition to the Government in 1878, which resulted in the organization of the Po Leung Kuk. Ng Yu, the head of the Fuk Lung firm, died in 1870, leaving his property under the management of his son, Ng Kai-kwong (吳啟光), alias Ng Pat-shan (吳弼臣), alias Ng Po-leung (吳保良), who was the sole beneficiary of his father's estate. Ng Kai-kwong died in 1884, leaving three minor sons to inherit his property.

Another of the founding directors of the Tung Wah was the Chiu Chow merchant, Ko Mun-wo (高滿華), alias Ko Cho-heung (高楚香), of the Yuen Fat Hong. He was the founder of the firm which established itself in Hong Kong about 1858 and developed an extensive business in the importation of rice from Siam. It soon became one of the wealthiest Chinese firms. In 1881, Ko Mun-wo was the sixteenth highest ratepayer, and when he died the following year, the value of his estate was estimated at $163,000. After his death, the business was continued by his four sons.

Tang Pak-yeung (鄧伯庸), alias Tang Kam-chi (鄧鑑之), was the youngest member of the first Tung Wah Hospital Committee. He was a merchant in the chartering firm of Kwong Lei Yuen and had received an English-language education. He was not a large property-owner, nor does his name appear in other lists of the élite.

The Compradores

The compradores were an important new class which arose in the nineteenth century in the port cities of China. A recent study by Yen-p'ing Hao entitled *The Compradore in Nineteenth Century China, Bridge between East and West*[29] shows how influential this group became in providing capital for the introduction of modern forms of communication, industry, mining, banking, and journalism in the later Ch'ing dynasty. The origin of the compradore system lay in the Co-hong organization through which China channelled all trade with foreigners before the opening of the treaty ports in 1843. The compradores were recruited from the Canton and Macau areas. A large majority of the most influential compradore families were from the Heung Shan District near Macau. When foreign firms came to Hong Kong they brought with them their compradores. As trade increased on the China coast, the compradores were provided with an opportunity to accumulate considerable capital. This they invested in real estate and in Chinese commercial firms.

The later Ch'ing dynasty was often in financial difficulties. One method of raising income was through the sale of official degrees. The compradores and merchants of the port cities, who formed a newly created bourgeois *nouveau riche* group within Chinese society, were eager customers. Purchased degrees were an easy way to acquire a social status which had previously been reserved for scholars, government officials, and gentry. The account of the Governor's visit to the Tung Wah Hospital in 1878, published in the *Hongkong Government Gazette*, states that 'there were present nearly three hundred influential Chinese residents from all classes of the community. Of those present some fifty or sixty were in their mandarin costumes'.

When the second Sino-British war broke out in the late 1850s, the foreign firms at Canton moved to Hong Kong, taking their compradores with them. This influx was an impetus to the already significant role that compradores were assuming as leaders in the Chinese community. The compradores of the old-established Hong Kong firms formed the core of this leadership.

In the early days of the colony, the two leading foreign firms were Jardine, Matheson and Company and Dent and Company. One would expect, of course, that their compradores would be among the élite of the Chinese community. The earliest compradore of Jardines that I can definitely identify is Ng Chook (吳祝), alias Ng Choong-foong, alias Sooi Tong. At the time of the opening of the Tung Wah Hospital, the newspaper account states that he was the oldest man on the committee, although his name does not appear on the official list of committee members. He died some months after the opening. His estate was administered by his son Ng Seng-kee (吳成基), who was living in Shanghai. The first date to be found for Ng Chook in Hong Kong is his purchase of the lease of the Central Market in 1848. It is uncertain whether he is connected with Ng Sow and Ng Lok, both compradores originating from Macau, who bought and sold a large amount of real estate from 1842 to 1847; or whether Ng Wei, alias Ng Wing-fui (吳榮魁), alias Ng Ping-un (吳炳垣), who was a compradore for Jardines at Foochow in the 1860s and subsequently at Hong Kong, was a near relative of Ng Chook. Ng Wei was a member of the Tung Wah Hospital Committee in 1883 and died in 1897 at Canton.

In 1861, two of the compradores of Dent and Company, the rival of Jardines, provided capital for a significant real estate development in Hong Kong. The large property where Dent and Company had their stables and residences for their taipans was bought up by Chiu Wing-chuen and Yeong Lan-ko, along with two European partners of the firm, with the intention of building Chinese houses of a better type to accommodate the wives and families of the growing class of well-to-do compradores. Previously, the compradores had not brought their families to Hong Kong; they remained in their home village or in Canton. The editor of the *China Mail* comments that 'Messrs Dent and Company have shown both wisdom and kindness in disposing of their land for such purposes'.[30]

Chiu Wing-tsun (徐榮村), one of the purchasers, and his elder brother, Yuk Ting (玉亭), had both been compradores in Dent and Company. Their nephew, Chiu Yee-chee (徐雨芝), was compradore at Shanghai and became one of the organizers of the China Merchants' Steam Navigation Company in 1872. Chiu Wing-tsun died at Macau in 1873, leaving property in Hong Kong estimated at $111,000.[31] Yeong Lan-ko (楊蘭高), the other Chinese purchaser of the Dent property, had succeeded his relative, Yeong Atai (楊亞帝), alias Yeong Chun-kum, to the position of first compradore of Dents at Hong Kong upon the latter's death in 1870. Yeong Lan-ko, alias Yeong Sun-yow (楊燻餘), also known as Asam (亞三), was one of Hong Kong's largest landowners. In 1876, he was the nineteenth largest ratepayer and, in 1881, had risen to fifth position. He died in 1884 at Pak Shan, the family village in Heung Shan District.

Before the Dents sold their property, the few substantial Chinese who had family residences in Hong Kong were located at the former Middle Bazaar site. When the inhabitants of the Middle Bazaar had been relocated at Tai Ping Shan, the Government replotted the area and set aside new lots which were meant to be bought principally by Europeans for residences or business houses.[32] Two of the more substantial Chinese bought lots at the sale in 1844: Ying Wing-kee (吳永祺), alias Ng Wing-kee (吳永祺), a compradore and merchant who died in 1849, and Tong Kam-sing, a contractor who died in 1845. Other Chinese of this class soon bought lots from European owners so that they might establish family houses in a better part of town. These included Wei Akwong, compradore of Bowra and Company and later of the Chartered Mercantile Bank; Ho Sek, compradore of Lyall, Still and Company; Lee Kip-tye, a Fukien broker, who began his Hong Kong career as a government interpreter; Wong Shing, newspaper editor and manager of the London mission press; and Cheung Achew, a wealthy carpenter.[33] The Revd Ho Fuk-tong and his family lived in the nearby compound of the London Missionary Society. In time, this area around Peel, Graham, and Gage Streets and Hollywood Road became a centre for Parsee and Indian merchants, as well as European brothels. Some of the old families stayed on, but the opening-up of the area bounded by Wyndham, Wellington, and Pottinger Streets by the Dents provided a needed location for the houses of the more well-to-do Chinese. After the Peak was developed in the 1870s and 1880s, the wealthy Chinese moved up to Mid-levels, occupying the mansions of the Europeans who moved to the Peak.

Of the individuals who had their family residence in the former Middle Bazaar area were two who were on the organizing committee of the Tung Wah Hospital, Wong Shing and Ho Asek (何亞錫), alias Ho Fai-yin (何裴然), alias Ho In-kee. Ho Asek first appears in Hong Kong records in 1849, when he purchased a lot in Tai Ping Shan. At the time, he was compradore of the opium firm of Lyall, Still and Company. It failed in 1867 and Ho Asek embarked upon his own business ventures under the firm name of Kin Nam. According to a newspaper account, he was subject to a $2,000 'squeeze' from the mandarins during the second Sino-British war.[34] He traded extensively in opium as well as rice and, in 1871, held the gambling monopoly from which within a year he realized a profit of $28,000. In an action brought against him in 1871, he testified that he operated with a capital of $200,000.[35] In 1868, two of his employees were brought before the court on a charge of extortion. In the evidence presented it was stated that, in about September 1866, some influential Chinese started a system of subscription or unofficial taxation to support district watchmen. The city had been divided into two sections, East and West. The West District was superintended by Tam Achoy and Ho Asek, 'a most respectable and honest trader'. A shopkeeper resisted the pressure put upon him to contribute and brought a charge of extortion against two of Asek's employees who had been collecting for the scheme. The court gave judgment in favour of the defendants.[36] Ho Asek was still a member of the Kai Fong Committee in 1872. He died in Pang Po (probably Ping Po (平步)), Shun Tak District in 1877. His wife was granted letters of administration on his estate, but as she was blind, she gave her power of attorney to Wei Akwong. His estate was held in trust until 1919, when the family property was sold at auction.

Dent and Company (which failed in 1867) and Jardine, Matheson and Company were the leading firms in Hong Kong in the early years; but if we think of the financial giants today, the Hongkong and Shanghai Bank takes its place beside the leading *hongs*. The Bank was organized in 1865, and, as we might expect, its first compradore, Lo Pak-sheung (羅伯常), alias Lo Chungkong (羅振綱), was on the Tung Wah's organizing committee. He died in 1877 and his position as compradore was taken by his son, Lo Hok-pang (羅鶴朋), alias Lo Sau-ko (羅壽嵩). Unfortunately, the son overcommitted himself in several speculative ventures and, not seeing any legitimate way of extricating himself from his financial difficulties, absconded in 1892 with over a million dollars of the Bank's assets; at least, that is the figure reported in the newspaper accounts. An indication of his penchant for unwise investments is the $30,000 he put into the organization of the *Uet Po* newspaper in 1885. Within a year this had been spent and he was forced to sell out to Lo Ping-chi, who was able to operate the paper with an expenditure of only several thousand dollars for a number of years.[37]

In the field of shipping, the P. & O. Steamship Company played an important role in the Hong Kong economy. It established a branch in the colony in 1845. Its compradore was Kwok Acheong (郭亞祥), alias Kwok Kam-cheung (郭甘韋). The newspaper notice of his death states that he 'originally belonged to ... the boat people's clan, but afterwards obtained admission to Tam Achoi's clan, Tam Achoi being a Punti ... '.[38] This substantiates my previous statement that the boat people who settled on land generally wished to lose the peculiarities of their origins. Acheong was one of the first settlers in Hong Kong, having organized a provisioning system for the army and navy at the time of the first Sino-British war. However, he did not receive the extensive land privileges granted to Loo Aqui for his services. When the P. & O. Company disposed of their shipwright and engineering department in 1854, it was taken over by Kwok Acheong. He developed a fleet of steamships in the 1860s which provided keen competition for the European-controlled Hong Kong, Canton and Macau Steamboat Company. In addition to his shipping interests, he operated a bakery, imported cattle into the colony and operated as a general merchant under the firm name of Fat Hing. In 1876, he was the third largest ratepayer in Hong Kong, and the first among the Chinese. He died in 1880, leaving an estate valued at $445,000. He was survived by seven sons. Two of them were listed among the twenty largest ratepayers in 1881, Kwok Ying-kai being eighth and Kwok Ying-shew fourteenth. Both of them became involved in the land speculation mania of 1881 and their property became subject to foreclosure.

The death notice of Kwok Acheong states that he was one of the original directors of the Tung Wah Hospital and the year before his death he was re-elected to that position. As he died in 1880, he must be the same as the Kwok Siu-chung (郭兆春), alias Kwok Ching-san (郭青山), of the Fat Hing firm listed as a director of the hospital in 1879 and in 1873. He was a member of the Kai Fong Committee in 1872 and signed almost all the lists and subscriptions. The Government frequently consulted him about affairs which affected the Chinese community. His death warranted an extensive biographical notice in the English-language papers. It characterized him as 'a man of remarkable intelligence and keenness in business, and of great cheerfulness and urbanity in his social relations. He was a liberal subscriber to all charities and behaved handsomely to those in his employ. His acquaintance with the English language never rose above' respectable "pidgen"; but he agreed well with and was much respected by foreigners, with whom he had constant intercourse and large transactions'.[39] His funeral cortège was one of the largest Hong Kong had witnessed. It took one hour and thirteen minutes to pass one spot. One of its features was four tablets on poles with flowers surrounding the inscriptions of his purchased Chinese ranks.

The Chairman of the organizing committee of the Tung Wah was the compradore of Gibb, Livingston and Company named Leong On (梁安), alias Leung Wan-hon (梁雲漢), alias Leung Hok-chau (梁鶴巢). He would seem to be the same as the Leong Po-wan named as Gibb, Livingston and Company's compradore on the 1852 list of contributions to Dr Hirschberg's hospital. On the 1859 contribution list for Chinese textbooks he appears under his usual name, Leong On.

In 1876, the London Missionary Society wished to raise funds for a proposed school in Wan Chai. Mr Eitel called a meeting of leading Chinese compradores to present his Society's plans to them and to enlist their financial support. However, he encountered the opposition of Leung On at the meeting. Eitel wrote to the mission directors in London:

I explained the whole subject, especially dwelling on the point that as soon as our native church is able to provide for all the expenses connected with the chapel it shall be handed over to the native church, and that I intended to insert the same stipulation in the deed for the school building. Unfortunately there was a very loquacious compradore present, who lately at an interview with the Governor made himself notorious by his narrow selfconceit, a Mr. Leung On, compradore to Gibb, Livingston and Company. He proposed that we should teach the boys no religion but confine ourselves to exclusively secular teachings. When I positively declined doing any such thing, he cooly proposed that I should hand over the piece of ground to him, saying he would build the school himself and keep it going if the Bible and Christian books were excluded. Of course, I declined this proposal, and stuck to my own plans.[40]

It is not surprising that Eitel does not mention Leung On as one of the contributors to the school fund, though he quickly raised $585 from other compradores and felt confident that the amount could be increased to $2,500 with more extensive solicitations.

In 1883, Leung On encountered business reverses and the court appointed Trustees to administer his bankrupt estate. He died in 1890 at Canton, leaving an estate in Hong Kong estimated as being worth $20,000. His son and his grandson succeeded to his position as compradore for Gibb, Livingston and Company, the latter dying in 1962; thus, the Leung family served the company for well over a century.

Fung Ming-shan (馮明珊), alias Fung Po-hai (馮普熙), alias Fung Chew (馮照), another of the founders of the Tung Wah, was compradore to A.H. Hogg and Company in the 1870s, but later became the compradore of the Chartered Mercantile Bank. He had received an English-language education and may have been a classmate of Ng Choy (Wu Ting-fang) at St. Paul's College, as they were partners in several land transactions in Hong Kong. Fung Ming-shan was one of the signatories in 1878 of the petition from natives of Tung Kwun District to the Government concerning the kidnapping and sale of children, which resulted in the organization of the Po Leung Kuk. He was naturalized as a British subject in 1881. He died in 1898, leaving a widow and two sons, one of whom died in 1906.

Another of the organizing directors of the Tung Wah was the compradore of Gilman and Company, Choy Wing-chip (蔡永接), alias Choy Lung-chi (蔡龍之). Along with Choey Teo-soon and Chop Aping, he was a partner in the Wing Cheong Shun firm, which failed in 1873 owing some 160,000 taels. He was probably the brother of Choy Aloy, who was compradore to J.J. dos Remedios and Company in the 1870s; both were in Hong Kong as early as 1865. Choy Achip died in 1874 and the administration of his estate was granted to his eldest son, Choy Afoong.

One compradore family from Macau that appears on a number of lists had by 1881 become the largest ratepayer. It was headed by Ng Acheong (吳亞昌), alias Ng Ying-cheong (吳英昌), who died in

1873. He left an estate worth $260,000. The family were compradores to the firm of Messrs Douglas Lapraik and Company. Lapraik began his career as a jeweller and watchmaker, but by the 1850s had extended his business into commerce, and eventually the firm built up a large shipping concern. His compradore first appears on the Hong Kong records in 1855. After the death of Ng Acheong in 1873, a near relative, Ng Sang (吳生), alias Ng Yingsang, alias Ng Chuk-shau, succeeded as compradore. He fell victim to the fever of land speculation in 1881 and suffered heavy losses. Concern over his strained financial position so affected his health that he died in 1883. Action was brought by his employers against the Ng family property to cover debts he left in his compradore's account.

The Government Servants

A lifelong career by a Chinese in government service usually would not have provided an opportunity for the accumulation of sufficient capital to enable him to enter the élite group. The highest-paid positions were those of interpreter, but a Chinese who had sufficient competence in English to be appointed to this position could earn more as an employee of foreign firms. However, many of the young men who received an English-language education, at first in the mission schools or at the Morrison Education Society School and, after 1860, at the Government Central School (now Queen's College), upon leaving school became interpreters and clerks in the Government. They might stay with the Government for several years but normally did not make a life career of government service. There were, however, two long-serving government employees, Tso Aon and Cheong Assow, who rose to élite status.

When the British established their government offices in Hong Kong, the man who became responsible for all the Chinese staff in government offices, as well as serving as compradore to the Treasury, was Tso Aon (曹亞安), alias Cho Yune-choong, alias Cho Wing-chow. His family had lived in Macau for several generations, and in 1834 he entered the service of the British in the office of the Superintendent of Trade. (With the revocation of the charter of the East India Company at Canton, a Superintendent of Trade was appointed by the British Government.) When he moved to Hong Kong, he had accumulated enough capital to invest in real estate, and when he retired from government service in 1857 without a pension, he lived off the income from his real estate, pawnshops, and other business ventures. He died in 1874 at Macau and was survived by several sons. One of his grandsons was the Revd Tso See-kai (曹思楷), Vicar of St. Paul's (born 1895, died in 1928). Tso Aon's brother, Chow Yik-chong (曹益昌), alias Chow Yin-yin, alias Chow Yau (曹有), alias Chow Kam-ming (曹金明), alias Chow Wai-chun (曹謂泉), was a large landowner and capitalist in Macau. He was knighted by the Portuguese Government, made a member of the Macau Legislative Council, and was a leader of the Chinese community in Macau. He died in 1896. His son, Tso Seen-wan, came to Hong Kong, practised law, and was a member of the Legislative Council from 1929 to 1937.

Another government employee appearing on a number of élite lists, although his family was not as distinguished as that of Tso Aon, was the Overseer of Coolies in the Surveyor-General's Department. Cheong Assow (張亞秀) was appointed to this office in September 1844. He also invested in real estate, which upon his death in 1897 was divided among his seven sons. In 1848, the Surveyor-General suggested that Assow was underpaid, as he found him an invaluable man in his department:

The headman Assow I cannot speak too highly of, he is intelligent, honest, and careful, and displays great zeal for the Department. He understands English perfectly, and I can trust him to make measurements for me upon lines that are clearly defined, which he performs with great accuracy ... His wages are very small for a man of his usefulness, and I should wish much that they were raised as he is one of the most deserving Chinamen I ever met. His education under me (for he has now been in the Department nearly five years) has progressed so satisfactorily that he is of more service than many of the English overseers I have employed, whose wages are never less than $30 per mensem.[41]

Those Employed by Missions

Another group which identified itself with Hong Kong was a small number of Christians who came from Malacca, Singapore, and Macau under the patronage of missionaries. As Christian converts, they had renounced the traditional practices connected with the veneration of ancestors and thus cut themselves off from participation in the ritual observances which bound the Chinese family together. There seemed little chance that they could expect to be welcomed back in their home villages. In a sense, they were as marginal to the social structure of China as were those who had had to flee China because of criminal activities. Unlike the tradesmen and small merchants, they did not view Hong Kong as an opportunity to make a quick fortune which they could take back to their home village and invest in paddy-fields or in shares in local firms and shops, or, if more affluent, endow or build schools or family temples, or contribute to public improvements such as roads and bridges.

Originally, the Christian Chinese were in the employment of the missions, and as most of them remained so, they did not receive high wages. But, as earnest Christians, they did not pass their time in gambling, visiting the sing-song girls, or smoking opium. All of these activities tended to make inroads into the income of many of the other Chinese, particularly those who were in Hong Kong without families. Avoiding the temptations of money-absorbing local high-life, the Christians were able to invest their small savings in real estate. When the London Missionary Society moved to Hong Kong, the Revd James Legge brought with him from Malacca a printer named Ho Asun (何亞信), alias Ho Ye-tong (何義堂), and Ho Tsun-shin (何進善), alias Ho Fuk-tong (何福堂), alias Ho Yeung (何養). They both began to invest in Hong Kong real estate, though Ho Fuk-tong became much the larger proprietor. They made their first investment soon after their arrival, but as income from rents permitted, they continued to purchase property until their deaths. Ho Asun died in 1869 and Ho Fuk-tong in 1871. At the time of their deaths, their property had appreciated greatly in value, so that the value of Ho Fuk-tong's estate was $150,000. It was one of the largest estates appearing on the schedules up to that date.

Although neither of these two Christian converts appear on the lists,[42] their children assumed a place of leadership in the Chinese community. Of the several sons of Ho Asun, Ho Chung-shan (何寵生) was proprietor of the *Wah Tsz Yat Po* from 1886 to 1889; but his brother, Ho Shan-chee (何神芝), or Ho Alloy (何亞來), had a more prominent career. He began as a teacher of English in the Chinese government schools (1855–7) and then became Chief Interpreter in the Police Court (1857–66). He incurred the ill-will of the English section of the community when he accepted charge of the opium tax station that the Viceroy of the Two Kwangs attempted to establish in Hong Kong. In the 1870s, he joined the staff of the provincial government at Fukien, where the *Daily Press* correspondent from Foochow reported that the Governor of Fukien was 'happy in the possession of this peripatetic conglomeration of legal imposture and contemptible impudence'. He later was part of Chan Lai-tau's ambassadorial staff at Washington, and upon his return to China in 1882, promoted the organization of the Canton and Hong Kong Telegraph Company.[43]

Associated with Ho Shan-chee in the Telegraph Company was a kinsman, Ho Kwan-shan (何崑山), alias Ho Amei (何亞美), the Secretary of the On Tai Insurance Company in Hong Kong. Ho Kwan-shan had been educated at Dr Legge's Anglo-Chinese College in Hong Kong and was a schoolmate of the sons of Ho Asun. Upon completing his education, Ho Kwan-shan joined his elder brother, Ho Low-yuk (何流玉), in Australia in 1858. From Australia he went to New Zealand in 1865 to arrange for the importation of the first Chinese labourers to New Zealand. Returning to Australia, he served for a time as interpreter at Ballarat, Victoria. In 1868, he came back to Hong Kong, where he became a clerk in the Registrar-General's Office. Later, he became interested in developing mines on Lantau Island and in Kwangtung Province.[44]

The most prominent of the Ho clan, however, was the family of Ho Tsun-shin (何進善) or, as he was better known in Christian circles, Ho Fuk-tong (何福堂). His father had been a block-cutter for the press of the Anglo-Chinese College at Malacca. Ho Fuk-tong joined him there and became a student at the College. He showed scholastic aptitude and for a time accompanied the son of the senior missionary at the Malacca Station to India for advanced study. Upon the arrival of the Revd James Legge at the mission, a close bond was established between the two young men. Ho Fuk-tong was his junior by three years. When Legge moved to Hong Kong in 1843, Ho Fuk-tong accompanied him and was ordained as the Chinese pastor of the London Missionary Society congregation in 1846. He continued as a faithful minister of the congregation (now Hop Yat Church) until his death in 1871. He was conscientious in his service to the church, but he was also very successful as a financier. After his death, there were numerous court suits over the interpretation of his will and the administration of his estate. Some of the difficulties arose because Ho Fuk-tong held his property under various aliases. In one of the cases, a barrister gave his opinion as to why Ho Fuk-tong followed this procedure:

He was not only perhaps a good preacher but a remarkably good man of business. He undoubtedly made a good use of his time, money and opportunities. He was a man who, from comparatively small beginnings, invested small sums of money in lots of land which he held on to, undoubtedly became in course of some years a man of considerable means and property. ... As a man in this position he took a very sensible view of the character and disposition of the gentleman under who he was working in his special services as a preacher. He came to the conclusion that Dr. Chalmers, the head of the Mission by whom he was employed, would not like a man engaged in such services to have too great an interest in money. It was not wise for him to pose as a man possessing very much property, and if it were known that he did possess so much, more assistance might be looked for from him on behalf of the mission, than he cared to give.[45]

Be that as it may, this wealth did enable his sons to acquire a good education and thus qualify themselves for leadership in the Chinese community.

In 1873, his son, Ho Kai (何啟), went to study in England. He returned with degrees in medicine and law and an English bride. His wife soon died and her bereaved husband endowed the Alice Memorial Hospital in her memory. Ho Kai was said to have been the first Chinese in Hong Kong to wear Western-style clothes. He was a recognized leader of the Chinese. A member of the Legislative Council from 1890 to 1914, he was knighted in 1912.[46]

Another son of the Revd Ho Fuk-tong, Ho Wyson, alias Ho Shan-po (何神保), also studied law in England. He did not have the gifts of leadership of his father and brother. An account of him written in 1891 states that although he 'is a thoroughly well read lawyer, ... [he] is handicapped in court practice by a bashful modesty and a deficiency in what is known as "the gift of gab". He is also handicapped in general business by his phenomenally limited office hours. It is a joke in legal circles that Wyson's hours are from twelve to three, with an interval of one hour for tiffin'.[47] He died in 1891.

Another son of the Revd Ho Fuk-tong, Ho Shan-yow (何神祐), was a student of law. In 1897, he was a member of the ambassadorial staff of his brother-in-law, Wu Ting-fang, and became Consul-General in San Francisco, where he promoted the organization of the Chinese American Commercial Company, which had capital of a million dollars.

The eldest daughter of Ho Fuk-tong, Ho Mui-ling, married Ng Choy (伍才), alias Wu Ting-fang (伍廷芳), a young graduate of St. Paul's College. Ng Choy's father was a business man who had spent some years at Singapore, where he became a Christian and

married a Malay woman. He returned to Canton and put his two
eldest sons, Afat and Akwong, into the boarding-school of the
Presbyterian mission. In 1851, when the California gold-fever was
rampant in Kwangtung, Ng Afat was the ringleader in stirring up
the students of the school to rebel against the hold the school had
over them because of the bonds their parents had signed guaran-
teeing that their sons would stay in the school until their education
had been completed. The students resented being held to this
agreement as they wished to try their fortune in the gold-fields.
The school authorities found it necessary to dismiss Afat. He came
to Hong Kong and was employed as clerk in the Police Magistracy.
His brother, Akwong, was a more tractable student and successfully completed his course of studies. After leaving school, he too
came to Hong Kong and was for a short time an interpreter in the
Harbour Master's Office, but then, in about 1864, became the
General Manager of the Chinese edition (*Chung Ngoi San Po*) of
the *Daily Press*.[48] The Wu family was interested in promoting
Chinese jounalism. In the obituary notice of Mr Chiu Yu-tsun, in
the *Daily Press* of 12 June 1908, the editor of the *Chung Ngoi San
Po* stated that when he joined the staff of the paper in 1873 it was
'under the management of the present Chinese Minister to
Washington H.E. Wu Ting Fan and his brother the late Mr Ng
Chan'. When Ng Chan died about 1890, Mr Chiu succeeded as
sub-lessee and General Manager.

Wu Ting-fang was only 4 years old when the family returned
from Singapore. In time, he became a student of St. Paul's College
in Hong Kong, where he was baptized. Upon graduation, he followed the pattern set by his brothers and entered government service as chief clerk and shroff in the Court of Summary Jurisdiction.
However, with the financial assistance of his wife's share in the
estate of Ho Fuk-tong, he was able to study law in England. He
returned to Hong Kong to practise law and in time was appointed
a Magistrate. In 1880, Governor Hennessy appointed him as the
first Chinese member of the Legislative Council. He served for two
years, but then resigned to join the staff of Viceroy Li Hung-chang
at Tientsin. In 1897, he was appointed the Chinese Ambassador to
the United States and continued serving his country in other posts
of responsibility until his death in 1922.

A classmate and good friend of Wu Ting-fang, named Chan
Ayin (陳亞賢), alias Chan Oi-ting (陳藹亭), was one of thirty representatives of the Chinese community to call on Governor Sir

Arthur Kennedy to welcome him to Hong Kong in 1872. He is also named among fourteen who, dressed in their official robes as mandarins, welcomed the Governor on his visit to the Tung Wah Hospital in 1878. He was baptized while a student at St. Paul's College and, like most of the others whose careers are being considered in this section, entered government service after completing his education. He was connected with the Magistrate's Court, but in 1871 he left to become a reporter for the *China Mail*. When the *China Mail* began publishing the *Wah Tsz Yat Po* in 1872, he was head of this department. In 1877, he surrendered his lease of the paper but continued with the *China Mail* for a short period. He then gave up his career in journalism to join the staff of the newly appointed Chinese Ambassador to the United States. As a member of the staff, he was appointed Consul-General in Havana, Cuba. He continued to serve in the Chinese diplomatic service for ten years, but then returned to China where he became director of the Chinese Engineering and Mining Company and of the Shanghai–Nanking Railway Administration. He died at Shanghai in 1905.[49]

While editor of the *Wah Tsz Yat Po*, Chan Oi-ting was also instrumental in organizing and managing the Chinese Printing and Publishing Company, which bought the press and type of the London mission press in 1872. This company began publishing the *Tsun Wan Yat Po* (*Universal Circulating Herald*) in February 1874. It advertised itself as the 'first daily newspaper ever issued under purely native auspices'. The paper was registered under the name of Wong T'ao (王韜), a scholar of the Chinese classics. Few Chinese in Hong Kong at this period were noted for their literary or scholarly ability. Ho Fuk-tong was a good scholar, but in the area of Christian thought; having mastered Greek and Hebrew, he translated and edited Biblical commentaries in Chinese. Though acquainted with the Chinese classics, he was not an outstanding Chinese scholar. Wong T'ao, who like Ho Fuk-tong was closely associated with the Revd James Legge, was generally recognized as a competent Chinese literatus. He was a baptized Christian and had come to Hong Kong from Shanghai because of suspected connections with the Taiping movement. He was recommended to Legge by the missionaries in Shanghai. Legge, who was involved in translating the Chinese classics, found Wong T'ao to be an invaluable assistant and paid him the following tribute: 'This scholar, far exceeding in classical (knowledge) more than any of his countrymen whom the author had previously known, came to Hong Kong in the end of 1863, and placed at his disposal all the treasures of a large well-selected library. At the same time entering with spirit into his labours, now explaining, now arguing, as the case might be, he has not only helped but enlivened many days of toil'.[50] Wong T'ao continued as editor of the *Tsun Wan Yat Po* until he left Hong Kong to return to Shanghai in 1884. He was largely responsible for the prestige the paper achieved, fulfilling in some measure the hopes of the prospectus for the paper that it 'would eventually become in China what the London Times is in England'.[51] As a mark of his position in the community, his name appears on several memorials and deputations of representatives of the Chinese in Hong Kong in the 1880s.

Another Christian who was instrumental in introducing Western-style journalism in China was Wong Shing (黃勝), alias Wong Ping-po (黃平甫). Like Ho Fuk-tong and Wong T'ao, he was closely associated with Dr Legge for a number of years.

Wong Shing was a native of Heung Shan District near Macau and was in the first class of the Morrison Educational Society School. The school's principal, the Revd Samuel Robbins Brown, took Wong Shing with three other students to the United States in 1846 for advanced study. Wong Shing's health broke down and he had to return to Hong Kong after two years in America. While he was abroad, he had been baptized and, on his return, became a member of the Chinese congregation of the London Missionary Society. One of his benefactors had been Andrew Shortrede, owner and publisher of the *China Mail*, and for about two years after his return from America he worked for the *China Mail*. In 1864, mention is made of a Chinese publication known as Assing's *Daily General Price Current*.[52] This was probably a journalistic venture of Wong Shing. He also served as an interpreter for the Government. In 1853, he was placed in charge of the printing establishment of the Anglo-Chinese College operated by the London mission. He continued as manager for some ten years, when he left to join the staff of the Chinese Government School being established at Shanghai to teach foreign languages to Chinese students. However, he did not find the work there satisfactory, and after a short time returned to Hong Kong and resumed management of the mission press. In 1872, he went to Peking to set up a printing office with moveable type for the Tsungli Yamen. From there he went to the United States with the second group of students in

Yung Wing's Chinese Educational Mission scheme. In 1858, his
was the first Chinese name to appear on the roll of jurors in Hong
Kong. He was a member of the organizing committee for the Tung
Wah Hospital. In 1884, he was the second Chinese to be appointed
to the Legislative Council, serving until 1890. He died in 1902. His
obituary mentioned his frugality and his lack of parsimony: 'His
family was poor and he was taught to be frugal. He could save
about $1,000 and bought land in Hong Kong ... before Hong
Kong business flourished ... It increased ten times in value. He
had the opportunity to raise rent, but he did not do so. Those who
had property and could earn more ridiculed him. He had a family
of children, and his expenditures increased, so that his income did
not take care of his expenditures, but he still held to his idea.'[53]
Realizing the advantages he had derived from a foreign education,
he was among the first Chinese to finance privately the education
of his children abroad.

When the Revd Elijah Bridgman, a missionary of the American
Board of Commissioners for Foreign Missions, moved to Hong
Kong from Macau in 1842, he had under his patronage two young
men who had been his students. They had also been sponsored by
the Morrison Education Society as students at the boarding-school
of the American Board at Singapore. One was Leung Tsun-tak
(梁進德), who was employed as an interpreter at the Hong Kong
Magistracy. He was a son of Leung Afat (梁亞發), an ordained
evangelist of the London Missionary Society.[54] The other was Wei
Akwong (韋亞光), whom Bridgman had picked up sick and starv-
ing on the streets of Macau some years previously. Akwong, unlike the other Chinese mentioned here, never received baptism.
At first, he assisted Bridgman in his missionary work in Hong
Kong, but when Bridgman moved to Canton in 1845 Akwong remained in Hong Kong. He became compradore for the ship chand-
lers and storekeepers Bowra and Company, but in 1855 was
appointed Supreme Court Interpreter in Chinese and Malay. In
1857, when the Mercantile Bank of India, London and China
opened its Hong Kong office, Wei Akwong became the bank's
compradore. He retained this office until his death in 1878 and was
succeeded by his son, Wei Ayuk (韋亞玉), alias Wei Bo-shan
(韋寶臣). Wei Akwong was a recognized leader of the Chinese
community, and his name appears on numerous petitions and
memorials. Like Wong Shing, he sent his sons abroad to study. His
eldest son, Wei Yuk, married a daughter of Wong Shing, and

followed in the footsteps of his father-in-law by serving on the Legislative Council from 1896 to 1917.[55] He was knighted in 1919 and died in 1922.

The Bishop of Victoria had under his patronage upon his arrival in Hong Kong in 1850 a young Chinese whom he had met in England. Chan Tai-kwong (陳大光) was a native of Pun Yu District of Kwangtung, but he turned up in England in 1845 as a young man aged 18. How he got to England and what he was doing there is difficult to determine but in 1849 the newly appointed Bishop of Victoria met him and took him under his patronage, with the hope that he could be trained as an evangelist among the Chinese. Soon after coming to Hong Kong, Tai-kwong was sent to Singapore to marry Gay Eng, also known as Sarah Hughes, a pupil in a school for Chinese girls conducted by Miss Grant. Upon his return to Hong Kong he was placed on three years' probation before ordination, but the Bishop did license him to preach to the prisoners in Victoria Gaol. Chan Tai-kwong, however, had difficulties adjusting to his new position. His experience in England had spoiled him. He had received much attention and had been presented to the Archbishop of Canterbury, who had been impressed enough to make him a gift of theological works to start his library. But the Hong Kong Bishop's hopes of using him as an agent for the Church of England's mission among the Chinese were soon dimmed. He was deficient in Chinese and had to begin a course of study in the Chinese classics. At the same time, the English he had acquired during his stay abroad was not sufficient to write grammatical English. In spite of these deficiencies, he was appointed an assistant tutor in the newly opened St. Paul's College. When the Bishop went to Shanghai in 1853 to investigate rumours concerning the Christian aspect of the Taiping movement, he took Chan Tai-kwong and another prospective evangelist, Lo Sam-yuen, with him. The two Chinese tried to get through the Imperial lines and reach Nanking; but they ran into frequent outbreaks of hostility between the warring groups and were forced to return to Shanghai.

Chan Tai-kwong's interest, however, was neither in being an evangelist nor in being a teacher, or even perhaps an emissary of Christian interests to the Taipings. He was attracted to the business world and the prospect of wealth. The advantages of his connections and his ability to speak English furnished a ready entry into Hong Kong's business world. In 1856, he left St. Paul's College and served for a time as an interpreter in the Government, as well as taking advantage of some business offers. He was also taken on by a group of Chinese engaged in the opium trade.

Financed by Leong Attoy, Li Tuk-cheong and Li Chun—the latter two members of the Li family's Wo Hang firm—Chan Tai-kwong bid for the opium monopoly in 1858. It was granted to him, but his firm soon ran into financial difficulties and he was forced to renege on the contract after several months. The Sheriff foreclosed on the property of Chan Tai-kwong. He then appears to have left the colony, perhaps going to Singapore. However, in December 1867, he was appointed Chinese clerk and shroff to the Hong Kong Court of Summary Jurisdiction. Here he often served as arbitrator in disputes among Chinese. He continued with the Court until his death in 1882. His son-in-law, George Orley, a sanitary inspector, was appointed administrator of his estate, which was valued at $3,000.

Chan Tai-kwong only appears once on our élite lists. In 1872, he was a member of the general committee of the Tung Wah Hospital. He was a member of the Masonic Order in Hong Kong. His first four children, a son and three daughters, were baptized at St. John's Cathedral, but his venture into the opium trade marked his departure from the Christian community. He later took on two concubines and was survived by six sons. His eldest son, George Chan Su-kee, was the first Chinese to be married in a civil ceremony at the Registry Office in Hong Kong.

In this group of Chinese who came under the influence of the missionaries, with the exception of Chan Tai-kwong, certain repeated patterns can be found. They all received an English language education at mission schools and their sons were usually educated abroad. Almost without exception, they served for a time as interpreters in the Hong Kong Government. Most of them were interested in journalism. The first four Chinese appointed to the Legislative Council were from this group, their service covering the years 1882 to 1914. Either they were blood relations or they intermarried, so their family structure forms a complex of interrelationships. Several of them served the Chinese nation in high posts of responsibility. They were the most significant of the several groups that provided a Chinese élite in Hong Kong before the turn of the century.

Conclusion

With the establishment of the Tung Wah Hospital, the Hong Kong Chinese had a structure within which they could handle the problems that were peculiar to the Chinese community. They had also a representative élite leadership through which they could make representation to the Government and to whom the Government could turn for advice on problems affecting its relationship with the Chinese community. Although criticism arose concerning the operation of the hospital committee—it was charged with exercising too much power and in effect forming an unofficial Chinese Legislative Council alongside the British administration—in general both parties, the Chinese community and the Government, found the hospital committee to be representative of responsible leadership and hence a helpful bridge between the two groups. With the appointment of a Chinese member to the Legislative Council in 1880, Chinese leadership was incorporated as a more integral part of Government, and its members may be regarded in many ways as the élite of the élite. But these developments are beyond the time-limit set for this particular study.

7 The English-educated Chinese Élite in Nineteenth-century Hong Kong

THE Chinese élite of nineteenth-century Hong Kong consisted of interpenetrating advisory, financial, and professional groups. Members of this élite played an important role in bridging the social and cultural gaps between the Chinese and the British in the colonial society. In some cases, they played a further important role in the modernization processes of China. Yet they were almost all of humble origin. In this chapter the progress to élite status is examined, and the achievements of a number of members of this élite are recorded.

Ho Ping-ti, in his study of social mobility in China,[1] argues that the most important rung in the ladder to élite status was success in the Chinese civil service examinations. I will show that the first rung in nineteenth-century Hong Kong was education at an English-language school, and further, that people typically progressed after their education, from government servant (usually as interpreter) to compradore, capitalist, and finally appointment to the Legislative Council.

Ruling, Financial, and Professional Groups and the Use of English

The advisory élite of Hong Kong might be narrowly defined as the official and non-official members of the Legislative and Executive Councils, that is to say, these Councils comprised both civil servants and private persons. Competence in the English language has been a requirement for appointment for a Chinese. Until 1973, all business was conducted entirely in English. [As long as the present forms of government structure and government procedures prevail, moreover, it is difficult to conceive of a non-English speaker operating with any effectiveness as a member of the advisory élite.] In the nineteenth century, a few Chinese were members of boards created by the Government: the Sanitary Board, the Medical Board, the Board of Queen's College, and the Board of the Hong Kong Polytechnic Institute. These bodies also conducted their business in English. Other committees created for the management of particular Chinese affairs always had a large number of English-speaking members. The most important was the District Watch Committee, which was reorganized in 1892 with the appointment of members of the recognized Chinese élite.

The Chinese financial élite was not restricted to English-speakers but the compradores of foreign firms constituted perhaps the most significant element in this group. Some knowledge of English was a requirement in this position, as the compradore was the middleman between the foreign firm which employed him and the Chinese staff of the firm, and between that firm and the Chinese merchants and traders with whom it transacted business. Many of the wealthiest of the compradores had received a formal English-language education.

The Chinese professional élite comprised those who had received professional training in Western law, medicine, or dentistry, and who practised in Hong Kong. In the nineteenth century, they amounted to only about two dozen individuals. All had received an English-language education.

A few Chinese who rose to élite status, especially in the professions, and some appointees to the Legislative Council, were second-generation Hong Kong-born individuals, or sons and relatives of English-educated Chinese who had acquired wealth; but, most Chinese rising to élite status had humble origins.

Knowledge and Acquisition of English

When and how did the Chinese learn their English in the nineteenth-century society of Hong Kong? If we classify 'pidgin' as English, the most common way the Chinese acquired English was by association. Those who had frequent contacts with the foreigner as domestic servant, shopkeeper, or business man acquired this distinctive form of communication which had been developing through the years of Sino-Western contact. The phonetics of pidgin were largely based on English, but the sentence structure was predominantly Chinese. It was far enough removed from both languages to make it an unwieldy vehicle for conveying meanings beyond the mundane affairs of the household, shop, or business *hong*. But in these areas it served as a bridge of communication. Because neither side was sure of the precise meaning of the speaker, its use was open to a great deal of misunderstanding, and it could become a cover to hide various kinds of subterfuge between Chinese and foreigners. Dr S.W. Williams suggests in *The Chinese Commercial Guide* that 'the only remedy for those who dislike it is to learn to speak Chinese better than the native speaks English'.[2] But there have always been more Chinese making the effort to learn the language of the foreigner than the reverse.

A special group of English-speaking Chinese throughout the nineteenth century, however, consisted of growing numbers of Chinese who had lived abroad for some years in English-speaking countries and had acquired a competent knowledge of the language. Many of these had had some formal instruction during their overseas residence. In the first half of the nineteenth century, a Chinese was a curiosity in foreign ports. Often, he was taken under the patronage of some interested person who provided him with an opportunity for study. Usually, the motivation for this philanthropic action was the hope that the young Chinese would be converted to Christianity, and that, on his return to his homeland, he would share his new faith with his countrymen. The records of the various missionary societies record the names of several of these young men. Whether the Chinese returning from overseas did so share his faith is one question. But evidence suggests that he sometimes shared his knowledge of English. In 1834, a young man who had studied at the Foreign Mission School at Cornwall, Connecticut, USA, was reported to be teaching English to the servants in the foreign factories at Canton as an 'outside shopman not connected with the Hong merchants'.[3] In 1852, two members of a class of nineteen who left the Presbyterian school for boys in Canton opened classes to teach English. Perhaps it was this type of class that Dr Williams talks about as being attended by Chinese seeking employment in European establishments:

Before they consider themselves qualified to act as servants, they receive what in their opinion is a tolerable English education, which consists in committing to memory a number of words and phrases from Chinese and English vocabularies written in the Chinese character, and with the English phrase constructed according to the Chinese idiom. There are always a few men to be found in Canton who get their living by thus teaching English to lads in the shops about the foreign houses and ships.[4]

Before the establishment of English-language schools for Chinese at Macau and Canton, several of the missionaries in these places, notably Dr Peter Parker and the Revd Elijah Bridgman, took under instruction small groups of Chinese boys. However, the great bulk of the Chinese who learned formal English in the nineteenth century were trained in schools where English was the principal means of instruction, that is to say, they acquired Western-type knowledge along with their English. Most of these schools were conducted by mission societies.

Most members of the English-speaking élite in Hong Kong received their education at one of the following schools:

(a) The Morrison Education Society School, 1839–49: the principal project of the Morrison Education Society; founded at Canton in 1835 in memory of the Revd Robert Morrison; disbanded in 1869. The school opened at Macau in 1839 under the direction of the Revd Samuel R. Brown; moved to Hong Kong in 1842; closed in 1849.

(b) The Anglo-Chinese College, 1819–56: students accepted at Malacca in 1819 by the Revd William Milne, agent of the London Missionary Society; moved to Hong Kong in 1843 by the Revd James Legge; disbanded in 1856.

(c) The American Board School at Singapore, 1835–42.

(d) The Revd Dr Andrew Happer's American Presbyterian Boarding School, 1844–56; opened in Macau in 1844; transferred to Canton in 1847; disbanded in 1856.

(e) St. Paul's College, 1851: Church of England Anglo-Chinese School organized by the Revd Vincent Stanton, Colonial Chaplain of Hong Kong, in 1848; building rebuilt and opened as St. Paul's College in 1851; closed in 1867; reopened in 1872 for a short period; Chinese classes started in 1877; Anglo-Chinese School for Chinese Boys formed in 1884; closed in 1900; re-organized under Church Missionary Society in 1909.

(f) Diocesan Native Female Training School, 1860: opened under the patronage of the wife of Bishop Smith. In 1866, name changed to Diocesan Female School; in 1869, reorganized as Diocesan Home and Orphanage. In 1892, girls transferred to Fairlea Girls' School. Diocesan Boys' School opened in 1869 as part of Diocesan Home and Orphanage. These schools were especially directed towards the education of Eurasian children.

(g) St. Joseph's College, 1876: Roman Catholic English School on Staunton Street, 1860. A commercial course opened at St. Saviour's College in 1864, moved to Caine Road under the new name of St. Joseph's College in 1876.

(h) American Board missionary, the Revd Charles Hager, opened an English evening school in 1883.
(i) St. Andrew's School, 1855–62: a school supported by local private subscription. It was intended mostly for non-Chinese but a few Chinese were enrolled.
(j) Hong Kong Government Central School, 1862: name changed to Victoria College in 1889; in 1894, name changed to Queen's College, its present name.

The Morrison Education Society School, the Anglo-Chinese College, and St. Paul's College educated most of the English-speaking élite who emerged in the 1860s and 1870s. In the last decades of the century, more of the élite were educated at Government Central School and the Diocesan Boys' School.

The various schools opened by the Chinese Government to meet the challenge presented by Western technology recruited scholars from Queen's College. Such schools as the Imperial Arsenal at Foochow, those established by Viceroy Li Hung-chang at Tientsin, and the Naval School of Western Studies at Whampoa, Kwangtung, periodically had contingents of Hong Kong students. Most of the students who completed their course in the Chinese government schools entered the service of the Ch'ing Government. A few rose to high rank. The loss of bright students from Hong Kong to China aroused some local criticism. The Governor, Sir George Ferguson Bowen, however, felt that the expenditure of Hong Kong money on the education of boys who would later serve China was valid because it would provide a nucleus of Chinese officials favourable to British interests.[5]

The Careers of the English-educated Élite

Whether they received their English-language education in China, Hong Kong, or abroad, some moved about after their education. Some educated in Hong Kong went overseas as interpreters or business men. They usually returned to Hong Kong after a time with capital which they used in promoting and financing commercial and industrial enterprises conducted along Western lines. Others left to join the Chinese Imperial Customs service as Chinese clerks, usually remaining in this position until retirement or death.

Examples of positions obtained by school-leavers of English-language schools in Hong Kong are provided by reports written by their headmasters.[6] In 1883, out of a class of forty boys who left St.

Joseph's College, twenty were in good positions: two in government offices; three with solicitors; four with bankers; and eleven in mercantile firms. In the same year, out of one hundred and eighty-one boys leaving Central School (Queen's College), thirty had found very good positions: three were in solicitors' offices; three in government service; two in the Chinese Imperial Customs; and twenty-two in important firms. Between the years 1884 and 1890, thirty-two from Central School had entered government service, one hundred and fifty went to European professional and mercantile firms, and eighty-nine were in the employ of the Chinese Government in customs, medical, diplomatic, or telegraphic departments.

Generally speaking, those students who were at the top of their classes in Hong Kong usually received appointments as government interpreters, clerks, writers, or shroffs (experts in the intricacies of Chinese currency who handled money transactions). Those appointed as interpreters were most likely to reach the highest status eventually. The fact that they were interpreters indicates that their English-speaking ability was probably the best among their classmates. Clerkship in a solicitor's office was an alternative route to the top. Other boys with family connections in the compradore departments of foreign firms began their climb as assistant compradores, thus bypassing the government servant rung of the ladder.

English-speaking Chinese as Interpreters

In the nineteenth century, one of the most difficult problems the colonial Government faced in its administration was the maintenance of law and order. Its population was composed initially of some of the more troublesome elements of southern China. The fact that the Chinese did not understand the nature of the British legal system and that the British did not understand fully the character and customs of the Chinese intensified the problem.

All legal matters were transacted in English. This necessitated the use of interpreters and translators both for the legal profession and for the courts. Thus, there was a demand for those who had a reasonable command of both the Chinese and the English languages. Qualified persons were in relatively short supply. Lack of interpreters as well as inaccurate or poor interpretation impeded the proper operation of justice. The European population of Hong Kong was very conscious of the righteousness and dignity of 'British justice' and was impatient with anything that tarnished its brightness. The problem of the recruitment of properly qualified interpreters and translators was often raised in the press, in the courts, and in the councils of Government.

In general, there were three groups available for recruitment: English-speakers who had learned Chinese; Macanese who had grown up speaking Portuguese, English, and Chinese; and Chinese who had learned English. It is, of course, the latter group that interests us, for the position of interpreter became the first step for the majority of the English-educated Chinese who rose to élite status. It also illustrates the important bridge function of English-speaking Chinese in Hong Kong.

The young Chinese boy in Hong Kong who left school, seeking a position, usually entered government service as an interpreter, clerk, or shroff. The position of interpreter was the best paid post available and only a relatively well-trained and competent English-speaker could successfully fill this position. Therefore, it was the young men who had completed their full term of study who became interpreters.

Until the 1860s, the Hong Kong Government was hard-pressed to secure sufficiently qualified personnel. Only a handful of young men really competent in English were produced by the English-language schools, and those who were employed in the Government did not stay for a long period. Their position was often not a happy one. They had acquired a degree of Western culture but were not accepted as social equals by their foreign co-workers. While their salary was greater than other Chinese employees in the Government, it was below that of the non-Chinese who were serving as interpreters. Several of the interpreters became involved in the web of criminal activity which was an integral part of the structure of Hong Kong. They were frequently exposed to the temptation of bribes for giving false interpretation.

Throughout the nineteenth century, the Supreme Court used non-Chinese principally as interpreters. From its establishment in 1844 and up to 1860, it depended upon Daniel Richard Caldwell, a controversial figure who was in and out of government service several times during the period. Upon Caldwell's final dismissal, a certain Rafael Arcanjo do Rozario was transferred from the interpreter's post in the Police Magistracy to that in the Supreme Court. He died in office in 1881 and James Dyer Ball, who had grown up in China as a son of a missionary, was appointed to the vacancy. He retired in 1908. By 1881, the need was felt for a permanent second interpreter and a Chinese, Li Hong-mi, was transferred from the Police Magistracy to this post. He retired in 1909.

Lee Kip-tye (李傑泰) is designated as an interpreter in the Supreme Court on memorials he signed as a witness between 1849 and 1856. His name does not appear on the civil servant lists in the Hong Kong Blue Books, however, and he probably served as a part-time translator of the Fukien dialect. He was a native of Fukien engaged in a lucrative trade between Hong Kong and Tientsin. He died in 1856 and his estate was administered by Lee Kip-bee (李傑被), presumably his brother.

For a period of less than two months in 1855, Wei Akwong (韋亞光), educated at the American Board school for Chinese at Singapore, filled the office of interpreter in the Supreme Court.[7] He did not like the position and resigned. [In 1857, he became compradore of the Mercantile Bank of India, London and China. His son Wei Yuk (韋亞玉), or Ayuk, alias Wei Bo-shan (寶臣), was a member of the Legislative Council from 1896 to 1917.]

In 1856, during a spell when Daniel Richard Caldwell had resigned from government service, Yung Wing (容閎) was appointed Supreme Court interpreter. He had been a student at the Morrison Education Society School and had been taken to America by the school's principal. He graduated eventually from Yale University and returned to China in 1854. Objection was raised to his holding the appointment of interpreter while being employed in a solicitor's office at the same time. As a result, he offered his resignation soon after his appointment to the interpreter's post.

The Police Magistrate's Court also depended upon Caldwell for interpretation in the period between 1844 and his first resignation in 1847; but after that time it attempted to have a complement of Chinese to serve as interpreters. The first of these was Tong A-chick (唐亞植), alias Tong Mow-chee (茂枝), alias T'ang T'ing-chih (廷植), appointed on 16 October 1847. He had been educated at the Morrison Education Society School. Before his appointment he had had a year and a half's experience as translator and interpreter at the British Consulate in Shanghai. Although Caldwell rejoined government service in December 1847, A-chick was retained. Caldwell was competent only in oral Chinese and the Government found Tong A-chick's ability to translate as well as to interpret too valuable to be dispensed with. He continued to serve until September 1851, when he was dismissed upon the recommendation of a committee of inquiry, which substantiated charges brought against him of having close connections with pirates. In spite of his dismissal and subsequent involvement in legal action over a prostitute, he had a successful career. He became a wealthy San Francisco merchant and was head of one of the district associations there. Later, after his return to China, he was compradore for Jardine, Matheson and Company at Tientsin and Shanghai.

The vacancy caused by Tong A-chick's dismissal was temporarily filled by a European, Horatio N. Lay, who was seconded from the consular service. But, in December 1851, A-chick's brother, Tong Akü (唐亞區), alias Tong King-sing (景星), alias T'ang T'ing-shu (廷樞), was appointed. He had been educated at the Morrison Education Society School, but upon its closure in 1849 was transferred to Dr Legge's Anglo-Chinese College. He resigned his position as interpreter in 1856. Charges were also brought against him but they were never substantiated. Like his brother, he became a member of the business élite. He was Shanghai compradore of Jardine, Matheson and Company, and in 1873 was appointed General Manager of the China Merchants' Steam Navigation Company.[8]

With the opening of a court of small claims in 1850, an additional interpreter was needed. Wong Shing (黃勝), alias Wong Tatkoon (達權), alias Wong Ping-po (平甫), was appointed. He had been a classmate of the Tong brothers at the Morrison Education Society School, and with Yung Wing had been one of the students the principal, Samuel R. Brown, had taken for study in the United States. He did not remain long as interpreter for the Government, but soon assumed responsibility for the management of the printing establishment of the London Missionary Society in Hong Kong. In 1873, he accompanied the second group of boys sent by the Chinese Educational Mission for study in America, a project initiated at the suggestion of Yung Wing. Wong Shing served on the Legislative Council of Hong Kong from 1884 to 1890. He had several offers to serve the Chinese Government. His ability as a translator and writer received the notice of prominent Chinese government officials, who recommended him for an official appointment, but he refused, as he did not wish to become a government official in the Ch'ing regime. He died in 1902.[9]

A permanent second interpreter was appointed to the Magistracy in 1852. The appointee was Ng Afat, who had been dismissed from the Presbyterian school conducted by the Revd Dr Andrew P. Happer at Canton. Influenced by the California gold-fever sweeping the Canton delta, and restive because of the bond his parents had signed ensuring that he would remain in the school until he had completed a five-year course, he had become 'insubordinate and quarrelsome' and was considered by the school principal as the leader of student discontent. In Hong Kong, he held the post of interpreter for three years. Circumstantial evidence points to his being the eldest brother of Ng Achoy (伍亞才), alias Wu Ting-fang (廷芳), the first Chinese member of the Hong Kong Legislative Council and a prominent figure in the Ch'ing and Republican Governments in China. Another brother, Ng Akwong (伍亞光), also a former student of the Canton Presbyterian Boys' School and later pupil with his younger brother Ng Achoy, at St. Paul's College, Hong Kong, was appointed interpreter in the Harbour Master's Department in 1861. He remained there for three years and then became the editor of the Chinese edition of the Hongkong *Daily Press*.

Ng Achoy, after completing his studies at St. Paul's College in 1861, was appointed clerk and student interpreter in the Police Magistracy, holding the office with periodic promotions until 1879, when he left to study law in England.[10] An even younger brother may have been Ng Afoo, who was appointed Clerk of the Court of Summary Jurisdiction in 1866 in place of Ng Achoy, who had been promoted to a higher position. Ng Afoo had been a student at St. Paul's College and for two years previous to his appointment in government service had been clerk to the solicitor, F.I. Hazeland. He is probably the same Ng Afoo who died in 1868 and is listed in the Hong Kong Probate Calendar.

The position of third Chinese interpreter to the Magistracy was created in 1855. Ng Mun-sow (伍文秀), alias Ng Asow (亞秀), was appointed to the position. Ng was born in Malacca. Being an orphan, he had been befriended by the Revd Dr James Legge, who brought him to Hong Kong in 1843 when the Anglo-Chinese College was moved from Malacca. Asow, as he was usually known, was one of the three students Dr Legge took to Scotland in 1845. There he was baptized, along with his two companions, and the three became the nucleus of a theological class upon their return to Hong Kong.

Asow was the most promising of Dr Legge's theological students, but he became involved in a case of lost or stolen bills of

THE ENGLISH-EDUCATED ÉLITE 149

exchange, and, though cleared of the charges, was suspended from the church fellowship. With this check to a career in the Church, he accepted the position of interpreter. Upon the resignation of Ng Afat as second interpreter, Ng Asow took over his post in 1857. However, the following year he was dismissed for his connection with certain criminal elements of Hong Kong, although he had supporters who maintained that the charges against him had been rigged. After his dismissal, he entered the Chinese maritime customs service in 1859.[11] He was stationed at Shanghai and remained in the service until his death in 1881.

In the same year that Ng Mun-sow, or Asow, was dismissed, his brother-in-law, Ho Alloy (何亞來), alias Ho Shan-chee (神芝), was appointed third interpreter. He had been a pupil in Dr Legge's Anglo-Chinese College, and, after leaving, taught English in the Tai Ping Shan and Lower Bazaar government Chinese schools before his appointment as interpreter in 1857. In 1863, he was promoted to first Chinese interpreter. He resigned in 1866 and received an appointment to the staff of the Governor of Fukien, later becoming a member of the Chinese Legation in Washington.[12]

Fan Awing (范亞榮) was appointed third interpreter in 1859. He had first been appointed in 1857 as a messenger and process-server in the Magistracy. The following year, he was promoted to student interpreter. He left the service in 1863 to join the Chinese maritime customs service. He was still in the service in 1880, then stationed at Newchang. He had been a pupil of Dr Legge's school and was probably the son of Fan Kee-chung. According to a report written by Dr Legge in 1850,[13] Fan Kee-chung had been a clerk in a government office for many years. In 1849, he brought his eleventh and twelfth sons to be enrolled in the Anglo-Chinese College. Dr Legge remarks that, in his old age, Fan Kee-chung was being supported by his children. I did not find his name in the civil servant lists in the Hong Kong Blue Books and it may be that he was employed in the office of the Chinese secretary to the British Superintendent of Trade in China.

Fan U-wai (范汝爲), alias Fan Che, and Fan U-k'u (范汝駒) were also students at the Anglo-Chinese College. Both entered government service. On leaving school, Fan U-k'u became an English teacher in the government Chinese schools. After the consolidation of several of these establishments into the Hong Kong Government Central School, he was appointed assistant master in the school. Fan U-wai, who was a native of Tam Pui village, Nam Hoi District, Kwangtung, was sent to Melbourne, Australia, after his studies. On his return to Hong Kong, he was appointed Chinese clerk and interpreter in the Office of the Colonial Secretary in 1862. In 1867, he was transferred to the Registrar-General's Department. He served there until 1873. Fan U-wai invested in a number of farm lots in Kowloon which, upon his death in 1878, he left to his three sons. He appointed his brother, Fan U-hon (范汝漢), his executor. Fan U-wai's youngest son, Fan Hok-to, was educated at Queen's College, leaving in 1891 to become clerk and interpreter in the Botanical and Afforestation Department. He died in 1895.

Another brother may have been Fan Ayow, who was appointed to the newly created office of shroff in the Harbour Master's Department in 1852. He is not listed in this position for the following year. He too had been a student at the Anglo-Chinese College.

In 1861, the Government had the opportunity of reinforcing its depleted interpreters' posts. Upon the handing back of the city of Canton to Chinese control, several of the interpreters in the service of the Allied Commission, which had been administering the city, became redundant. One of these was Bedell Lee Yune who was recommended as 'possessing great capacity as interpreter, which he exercised with zeal and good faith to his employers'.[14] He had received the name Bedell upon his baptism at St. Andrew's Episcopal Church in Philadelphia, USA, on 15 June 1856, at the age of 22. His wife was baptized at Canton in 1861 by the Revd Dr A.P. Happer. Bedell Lee Yune retired as first interpreter in the Magistracy in 1886 after twenty-six years of service. He died in 1889 at Canton. He was the first of the Chinese interpreters to give life-time service to the Government.

One other former interpreter to the Allied Commission appointed to the Magistracy at the same time as Bedell Lee Yune was Chan Achoy. He was regarded as having less ability than Bedell and left his position in 1865.

Tam Tin-tak (譚天德) became a student interpreter in August 1864. He was soon transferred to the Harbour Master's Office. He had been a student at St. Paul's College and was baptized with the name Thomas. In May 1866, he was married to Mary Cheung Mui (張梅).[15] She was a student at the Diocesan Female Training School. In October of the same year, Tam Tin-tak was arrested and charged with the theft of two bills of exchange, which resulted in his dismissal as interpreter.

As far as the records indicate, none of the various members of the Fan family, Bedell Lee Yune, Chan Achoy, or Thomas Tam Tin-tak rose to prominent élite status. With the appointment of Chan Ayin (陳亞賢), alias Chan Oi-ting (藹亭), as fourth interpreter in 1864, this pattern was broken. Like his St. Paul's College classmate, Ng Achoy, alias Wu Ting-fang, he served in the Ch'ing Government's Legation in America. Later, he was Director of the Chinese Engineering and Mining Company and the Shanghai-Nanking Railway Administration. While in the service of the Hong Kong government he received steady promotions and when he left in 1871 he was receiving a salary of £175 per annum.[16]

Lee Lum-kwai was appointed third interpreter in October 1866. He left about 1868 and shortly afterwards became a clerk for John Joseph Francis, a solicitor. In August 1870, Mr Francis charged him with embezzlement. The newspaper account states that Lee Lum-kwai was from Hoifoong (Hai-feng, Hui-chow District, Kwangtung) and had the Ch'ing rank of blue button. He was found not guilty and entered a suit against his former employer for false imprisonment. In 1874, however, he was in more serious difficulties being charged with threatening to institute a false charge of murder before Chinese authorities against a wealthy Hong Kong merchant, Yeung Amow (楊亞茂), alias Yeung Sing-kwong. The alleged murder was said to have taken place in Swatow, where the Yeung family had been agents for the tea trade of Jardine, Matheson and Company. Lee Lum-kwai threatened to use his connections with Chinese authorities at Swatow against Amow and his brother, Apat, to bring about their arrest and conviction unless he was paid $5,000. Lum-kwai was convicted and sentenced to penal servitude for life. However, after ten years' imprisonment, he was released under the condition of banishment from the colony. He had put his abilities to good use while in prison by undertaking much of the translation and interpretation work of the gaol. He also rendered valuable help in the gaol hospital. Upon his release, he returned to China where he is said to have received an important appointment from the Chinese Government.[17]

In December 1866, Ng Ashing was appointed supernumerary Chinese interpreter to the Police Magistracy. He had entered government service two years previously as interpreter on the convict hulk *The Royal Saxon* off Stonecutter's Island. After serving as supernumerary for six years he was promoted to interpreter but left government service soon afterwards. He then became a solicitor's clerk in the office of H.L. Dennys.

At times, the offices of clerk and interpreter were combined. The first to hold this position was Choong Aon (鍾亞安), appointed in 1857. He had been a student at St. Paul's College. He was dismissed from government service in 1861. After his dismissal, he entered the Chinese maritime customs service and he was still in that service in 1880.

In 1871, Chan Yau-lok, alias Chan Sz-wa, alias Chan Iu-ting, was appointed clerk and interpreter. He remained only about a year before becoming a solicitor's clerk in the office that was to be known as Sharp, Johnson and Stokes. He died in Hong Kong in 1906. For probate purposes, his estate was estimated at only $4,000, perhaps indicating that he was not among the financial élite. This estimate, however, may not have represented his true wealth.

Ho Atim (何亞泰), alias Ho Shan-tim (神泰), the second son of the Revd Ho Fuk-tong, brother of Sir Ho Kai[18] and brother-in-law of the Honorable Wu Ting-fang, was appointed third Chinese interpreter in 1873. He left the service in 1875, became a real estate broker, and was a large speculator in the 1881 land boom in Hong Kong. The collapse sent him into bankruptcy. At the time that he was speculating so heavily in land, he was also a leading promoter of a Hong Kong syndicate bidding for the Macau Government Wai Sing lottery monopoly.[19] After his bankruptcy, he moved to Canton but later returned to Hong Kong, dying there in 1907 or 1908. Although he had been an important figure in Hong Kong financial circles in the 1880s, by his later years his importance had declined.

Upon the resignation of Ho Atim from the third interpreter's position, Li Hong-mi was appointed in 1874. He had had two years' previous service in the Government. In 1877, he was made third clerk in the Magistracy and in 1881 was promoted at a salary of $1,800 per annum to be assistant interpreter and translator of the Supreme Court. The newspaper notice of the appointment remarks that 'he was the only one in government service who could accurately translate some of the inland dialects'.[20]

It is interesting to note that, upon the promotion of Li Hong-mi from second interpreter to third clerk, his replacement was a member of the Hong Kong Muslim community, Abdoola Fuckeera. Fuckeera left the service of the government in 1879 and became a clerk in the firm of Wing Kee.[21] At the same time, a Chinese, George Ng Fook-shang, was the Hindustani interpreter in the Magistracy.

The ranks of interpreter in the Magistracy underwent numerous changes in the 1870s. In 1875, Ng Achoy, who had been first interpreter since 1866, resigned to go to England to study for the Bar. Bedell Lee Yune was promoted from second to first interpreter, a position he held until his retirement in 1887. Li Hong-mi was moved from third to second interpreter, leaving the position of third interpreter vacant. The following year, Li Hong-mi was promoted to the position of third clerk and replaced by Abdoola Fuckeera, who only remained a year, so that in 1878 the posts of both second and third interpreter were vacant. Li Acheung was appointed second interpreter in April 1878, and Hung Kam-shing was appointed third interpreter in September 1879; thus, a full complement was provided for the interpretation staff after a three-year shortage.

Li Acheung was the son of Li Tsin-kau (李正高), alias Li Sik-sam (錫三), the evangelist of the Basel Missionary Society's Hakka congregation at Sai Ying Pun. Li Acheung had been a student at Queen's College and received a prize for best scholar in 1871. After leaving school, he became a charge-room interpreter for the Police; in 1875, he was made a clerk in the Magistracy, and in 1878 was appointed second interpreter, a position he kept until 1882 when he was appointed Chinese interpreter to the kingdom of Hawaii. In Honolulu, he became one of the leaders of the Hawaiian Chinese community.

Hung Kam-shing, appointed third interpreter in 1879, had been, like Li Acheung, a pupil at Queen's College. He had enrolled in 1873 at the age of 14 and had completed his studies before receiving his appointment in the Government. He replaced Li Acheung as second interpreter when Acheung left for Hawaii. On the retirement of Bedell Lee Yune in 1887, he became first interpreter. In 1892, he resigned and was replaced by Hung Kam-ning, presumably his brother. Both Kam-shing and Kam-ning were Eurasians and the family later used the surname Anderson. Records suggest that the sons of Hung Kam-shing were Charles Graham Overbeck Anderson, alias Hung Kwok-chi, born in 1890, died in 1935, student at Cambridge University and practitioner of law in Shanghai; G.C. Anderson; Joseph Overbeck Anderson, alias Hung Kwok-leung, born in 1880, died in 1904, who studied law at Lincoln's

Inn, London; and Hung Kwok-wah. All were students at Queen's College, Hong Kong.

Hung Kam-ning was appointed second interpreter in 1887. He had been a student at Queen's College, where he received the Steward Scholarship in 1884. While still a student, he had been appointed a provisional clerk in the Marine Survey Office in 1881, and in 1883 became fifth clerk in the Harbour Master's Office. From there, he entered the Magistracy as interpreter. He was placed on the government pension list in 1896 upon the abolition of the office he then held. After his retirement from government service, he was usually known as Henry Graham Anderson. His children were Hugh G. Anderson, born in 1887, died in 1922; Ernest G. Anderson, born in 1888, died in 1920; Charles (Carl) Graham Anderson, born in 1889, died in 1949 (Carl Anderson was the father of Mrs Joyce Symons, a member of the Legislative Council); James G. Anderson of Shanghai; Dr Henry M. Anderson, one-time member of the Royal Army Medical Corps; John G. Anderson; Catherine Anderson, wife of Ho Sai-wing, the son of Ho Fook and adopted son of Sir Robert Ho-tung; Mabel Anderson, a sister in the Canossian Religious Order in Hong Kong; Irene Teresa Anderson, born in 1895, died in 1959, a government nurse; Agnes Anderson, born in 1899, died in 1946, unmarried; and Edith Anderson, born in 1900, died in 1959, unmarried, one of the first physiotherapists to be trained in Hong Kong.

English-speaking Chinese as Compradores

It was natural that Chinese with a formal English education should increasingly dominate the compradore system in Hong Kong. The better his English, the more competent the compradore was to perform an important function of his position: middleman between Chinese employees and business men, and his foreign employer. In the days before formal English-language education was offered in the missionary and government schools, the compradores depended upon China coast pidgin English as the bridge of communication. Pidgin, as we saw, seriously limited the areas of communication and could be a source of misunderstanding. On the English side, a person often had to guess the exact meaning of the garbled language; on the Chinese side, knowledge of pidgin did not enable a person to understand the subtleties of English.

The compradore system, as it developed in nineteenth-century

China, grew out of the 'Co-hong' system instituted by the Chinese Government at Canton to control foreign trade. An official group of Chinese linguists was licensed to bridge the language gap. They were to be the medium of communication between the foreigners and government officials. In addition, each foreign firm or *hong* had a compradore secured by a Chinese *hong* merchant; all servants and household affairs were under his supervision. He was also in charge of the treasury and its contents.[22]

After the abolition of the Co-hong monopoly in 1842, the compradore assumed functions which had previously been performed by the linguists. 'Linguists', as an official category, disappeared, though in some sense official translators and interpreters may be considered as continuing the linguist tradition.

On 19 June 1871, the *China Mail* published an editorial on the compradore system in which it set forth a compradore's duties, responsibilities, and privileges under seven points, which are summarized here:

(a) He was guaranteed to his employers by the chop of respectable and wealthy sureties, generally in an amount which, though large, was very frequently of little practical protection against defalcation, by reason of the very large sums of money and the value of the goods placed under his care.

(b) In default of banking facilities, the compradore had entire charge of all monies, bullion, and cash, and in addition was not unknown to have acted somewhat like a banker in finding monies, and paying cheques and orders on him, in excess of his employer's balance, i.e. in honouring overdrawn accounts.

(c) He engaged the servants, coolies, and so on, and was held responsible for any losses incurred by their misconduct.

(d) He was the go-between in his master's commercial dealings with native merchants. All transactions were conducted through him or his agents and he was accountable for the honest fulfilment of all contracts entered into by his master with them, whether in the sale of goods or purchases of merchandise. All commercial dealings went through his hands.

(e) He was paid only a nominal wage, but in consideration of his service he was permitted to charge native buyers or sellers a commission on every transaction which passed between them and his employer.

(f) He also usually traded on his own account. This was not con-

sidered to affect his services as compradore or his relationship to his master. Whatever trading the compradore engaged
in was outside and distinct from his services as compradore.

(g) Large operations were frequently entered into between employer and compradore on joint accounts, but these were
also distinct and apart from compradore duty, and were
friendly agreements for mutual profit.

From this description of duties and privileges it can be seen that
the compradore was a central figure in the organization of business
between Chinese and foreigners. His position provided him with
the opportunity to trade on his own and in private partnership with
his employer. He was enabled to acquire capital, which he used to
promote commercial, financial, and industrial enterprises mod-
elled on Western patterns. The compradore financed Chinese-
owned steamship companies, banks, and insurance companies,
which in the latter half of the nineteenth century increasingly made
inroads on the foreign domination of these business fields. In the
Kwangtung area, Hong Kong compradore capital was a significant element in the promotion of railroads, telegraph, and public
utilities.

In Hong Kong, the development of the compradore system was
strengthened in the 1850s with the influx of foreign firms seeking
refuge from the disturbed conditions in Canton caused by the outbreak of the second Sino-British war in 1856. It was in the 1860s
that the foreign firms began to recruit a larger number of their
compradores from students of the English-language schools. In the
first half of the century, most of the compradores used pidgin English. In the larger foreign firms, the compradoreship became a
family position, sons and nephews succeeding fathers and uncles as
they retired or died. The second generation had usually been educated in English in anticipation of their future responsibilities, and
in turn, they sent their sons to English-language schools.

English-speaking Chinese in the Legal and Medical Professions

As early as 1845, the author of an article in the *Chinese Repository*
suggested the propriety of Chinese practising in the courts of Hong
Kong: 'As friends of the Chinese, we should like to see this Court
[the Supreme Court] provided with its learned Chinese advo-
cates'.[23] However, it was not until 1856 that a Chinese expressed

a desire to practise in the Hong Kong courts. At that time, Yung Wing had returned to China after graduation from Yale University in the United States. After acting as personal secretary to Dr Peter Parker, the American Commissioner at Canton, he moved to Hong Kong. He arrived at a time when the Supreme Court was in desperate need of a qualified interpreter. Yung Wing offered himself and was eagerly accepted. But his future as an interpreter in the Hong Kong courts did not meet the expectations of either himself or his patrons. He was urged to prepare himself to qualify for acceptance for practice as a solicitor. In consequence, he entered the office of Ambrose Parsons as an articled clerk for a three-year apprenticeship, after which he hoped to apply for permission to practise. In this move he had the support of Thomas Chisholm Anstey, the Attorney-General. Anstey prepared and introduced into the Legislative Council an ordinance, No. 13 of 1856, 'for the admission of candidates to the rolls of practitioners in the Supreme Court, and for the taxation of costs'.[24] Section seven clarified the position of Chinese applicants: 'No person bona fide domiciled within the Colony and who complied with the provisions of the ordinance, was disqualified from obtaining such admission as aforesaid merely by reason of alienage, or that he is by birth a Chinaman.'

While the ordinance was under consideration, members of the legal profession, who according to the editorial in the 19 June 1856 issue of the China Mail 'imagined their craft to be endangered, and their gains jeopardized, by the introduction of the new element amongst them' held a meeting, drew up a memorial, and sent a deputation to the Governor to protest against its enactment. In spite of this opposition, the ordinance was adopted by the Legislative Council on 21 June 1856. When the Supreme Court re-opened on 1 July, Yung Wing tendered his resignation as interpreter, acting upon the advice of Attorney-General Anstey, who said that it was not compatible with the terms of the new ordinance for him to act as court interpreter and at the same time be an articled clerk in a solicitor's office.

In anticipation of qualifying under the terms of the ordinance, Yung Wing drew up a memorial requesting that he be granted letters of naturalization as a British subject. The memorial bore the recommendation of the Bishop of Victoria and other prominent members of the community. Before submitting it, he sent the memorial to Chief Justice Hulme asking the favour of his recommendation and signature to the document. But here Yung Wing met with a rebuff, for according to the account of the incident published in the *China Mail* on 19 June 1856, 'with marked and inexplicable discourtesy, the humble petition was returned, not only without signature, but in an open envelope, and unaddressed.'

However, a subsequent explanation was given in a letter from the Chief Justice's clerk, W.F. Bevan, published in the *China Mail* of 26 June 1856, stating that the Judge had wished to interview Yung Wing and had sent his messenger to invite him, but the messenger, instead of issuing the invitation, had returned the memorial to Yung Wing, who then left.

The controversy aroused by Yung Wing's intention to qualify for the legal profession was accompanied by articles in the press, which, according to the *China Mail* of 19 June 1856 'by inuendos and under cover of reflections upon the Chinese as a body to villify [*sic*] Awing, whose reputation hitherto has been stainless ... and whose good qualities have won for him the esteem of all foreigners with whom he has come in contact.'

The editor of the *China Mail*, Andrew Shortrede, was sympathetic to Yung Wing and his ambitions. Shortrede had been one of the principal supporters of the three students of the Morrison Education Society School whom Samuel R. Brown, the principal of the school, had taken to America to be educated in 1847. Yung Wing had been one of these students.

These attacks were an important element in Yung Wing's decision to move to Shanghai in August 1856, where he became an interpreter in the Chinese maritime customs service, although he did not find this position satisfactory either. He could not accept the system of graft practised in the service and resigned after four months to enter the business world.

It was not until 1877 that a Chinese was admitted to practise in Hong Kong. He came fully qualified, having been accepted as a member of Lincoln's Inn in London. Norton-Kyshe published a 'Roll of Barristers admitted to practice before the Supreme Court of Hongkong'.[25] Out of forty-six admitted between 1844 and 1898, three were Chinese: 18 May 1877, Ng Choy, of Lincoln's Inn; 29 March 1882, Ho Kai (何啟), alias Shan-kai (神啟), of Lincoln's Inn, Bachelor of Medicine of Aberdeen University and a member of the Royal College of Surgeons; and 22 October 1888, Wei Pui, of the Middle Temple.

The 'Roll of Proctors, Attorneys, and Solicitors admitted to practice before the Supreme Court of Hongkong'[26] contains sixty-seven names, of which three were Chinese: 23 August 1887, Ho Wyson, a solicitor of the Supreme Court of Judicature in England (admitted on 8 July 1887); 3 July 1897, Tso Seen-wan (曹善允), a solicitor of the Supreme Court of Judicature in England (admitted on 1 October 1896); and 26 July 1897, Wei Wah-on (韋華安), a solicitor of the Supreme Court of Judicature in England (admitted on 12 January 1897).

Wei Pui and Wei Wah-on were sons of Wei Akwong, compradore of the Mercantile Bank of India, London and China. Ho Kai and Ho Wyson were sons of the Revd Ho Fuk-tong.[27] Ng Choy had married their sister. Another brother, Ho Yow (何祐), alias Ho Shan-yow (神祐), became an articled clerk to his brother, Ho Wyson, when the latter began practising in Hong Kong in 1887. In 1897, Ho Yow accompanied his brother-in-law, Ng Choy, to the United States. The latter had been appointed Chinese Minister in Washington. Ho Yow was appointed Chinese Consul-General in San Francisco. Ho Wyson died in Hong Kong on 25 June 1898. He was not a forceful personality and Norton-Kyshe remarks 'it is feared, that Mr. Ho Wyson, who was much respected, did not take advantage of the opportunities which offered themselves to him'.[28]

Tso Seen-wan, who was born in 1868 and who died in 1953, belonged to a wealthy Macau family.[29] He received a Chinese education at Shanghai and went to Cheltenham College in England in 1886. He left the college in 1890 to join a solicitor's firm as an articled clerk, passing his final law examination in 1896. He practised in Hong Kong, where his firm become known as T'so and Hodgson.

Of the above six Chinese legal professional élite, three became members of the Legislative Council, Ng Choy (1880–2), Ho Kai (1890–1914) and T'so Seen-wan (1929–37). Two others, Wei Pui and Wei Wah-on, were brothers of another member of the Council, Sir Boshan Wei-yuk (1896–1914).

The first Chinese to receive a medical degree from a Western university was Wong Fun (黃寬).[30] He had received his English-language education at the Morrison Education Society School. In 1847, accompanied by two of his classmates, he went to America for further study. After several years at the Monson Academy in Massachusetts, he went to Edinburgh University, Scotland, under the patronage of the editor of the *China Mail*, Andrew Shortrede. He graduated with high honours in 1857. Before his return to China, he was appointed a missionary of the London Missionary Society, which intended to send him to work at Canton. However, the second Sino-British war prevented his departure from Hong Kong. While waiting for the settlement of the conflict, he opened a dispensary in Hong Kong for a short period, but in October 1858 he was able to open a dispensary in Canton. Both were under the auspices of the London Missionary Society.

In 1860, the relationship between Wong Fun and the Society became strained and he resigned to take up the post of administrator of the Civil Hospital in Hong Kong, but he did not remain long in Hong Kong, leaving soon afterwards to become medical adviser to Viceroy Li Hung-chang. Again, his service in this position was short, and he then entered private practice at Canton, at the same time assisting Dr Kerr in the Canton Medical Missionary Society Hospital and serving as medical officer in the Chinese maritime customs service. He died a wealthy man in 1878.

During the long history of the Canton Medical Missionary Society Hospital, a number of Chinese were trained in Western medicine but none seems to have practised in Hong Kong. The second Chinese to receive a Western medical degree was Ho Kai, alias Ho Shan-kai, the fourth son of the Revd Ho Fuk-tong. He was born in Hong Kong in 1859 and died in 1917. Educated at Queen's College, he was sent to Britain for advanced study. There he earned degrees in both law and medicine.

Dr Ho Kai was a key figure in the development of a medical Chinese élite in Hong Kong. He was the liberal donor of the Alice Memorial Hospital, named in memory of his deceased wife and operated in close association with the London Missionary Society. After many delays, the hospital was opened in February 1887 and, in the same year, in October, a College of Medicine for Chinese was opened in the hospital. Dr Ho Kai was one of the originators of the scheme. The Hong Kong Government relied heavily upon Dr Ho Kai's advice in respect of issues affecting the Chinese community. He was appointed to most of the important advisory boards and was a member of the Legislative Council from 1890 to 1914.

The graduates of the College of Medicine for Chinese were too young to rise to élite status in the nineteenth century, but by the early part of the twentieth century many of them were recognized leaders in Hong Kong and in one important instance, in China. The most famous of the graduates was Sun Yat-sen, the father of Republican China. There was a strong Christian influence in the college and hospital and a number of Dr Sun's classmates were baptized.

Under the patronage of Li Hung-chang, a medical school was opened at Tientsin in 1881. Two of its graduates came to practise in Hong Kong. Chun King-ue was staff surgeon at Alice Memorial Hospital from 1890 to 1895. He died in 1908. The other graduate of the Viceroy's hospital medical school was Dr Wan Tun-mo (尹端模), alias Wan Man-kai (文楷). He was the son of Wan Wei-tsing (尹維清), an ordained minister of the London Missionary Society. After his graduation at Tientsin, Dr Wan returned to Canton, where he was associated with the hospital of Dr Kerr. In 1897, he came to Hong Kong as staff surgeon of Nethersole Hospital, and after the death of U I-kai (胡爾楷) in 1898, Dr Wan replaced him as staff surgeon at Alice Memorial Hospital. He married the daughter of Au Fung-chi, and several of his brothers-in-law were graduates of the College of Medicine for Chinese and practised with him in Hong Kong.

U I-kai graduated from the College of Medicine for Chinese in 1895. He died during the plague of 1898. Among his children were Dr Arthur Wai-tak Woo and Miss Katie Woo, late headmistress of St. Paul's Girls' School.[31]

English-speaking Chinese as Advisers to the Government

Hong Kong English-speaking Chinese were used as advisers to government officials in both Hong Kong and China. In China, their knowledge of Western practices in business, commerce, and industry qualified them to advise those officials who were interested in promoting the military, commercial, and industrial modernization of China. Such officials recruited Hong Kong Chinese as members of their personal staff. These appointments were not part of the official system based on success in government examinations. However, the patron of these Hong Kong Chinese often recommended them to an official position as advisers or they were rewarded with an official honorary rank. Examples were Ho Shan-che, adviser to the Viceroy of Fukien, Wu Ting-fang, adviser to Li Hung-chang, and Yung Wing, adviser to Tseng Kuo-fan.

While officials in China chose English-speaking advisers on the basis of their intimate acquaintance with Western practices, the Hong Kong official sought the advice of English-speaking Chinese for their knowledge of Chinese ways and thought. The Government also relied heavily for advice on those Chinese-speaking Europeans in their employ who had intimate knowledge of Chinese ways and thought: such men as John Robert Morrison, Charles Gutzlaff, E. J. Eitel, and J. Dyer Ball, all with missionary connections; and Daniel Richard Caldwell whose wife was Chinese. The Government, however, realized more and more the value of Chinese as advisers. For example, when the Governor, Sir John Pope Hennessy, was at one time concerned about the practice of flogging prisoners, he sought the opinion of Wei Akwong, compradore of the Chartered Mercantile Bank.

The most significant step in securing Chinese opinion in government decisions was the appointment of Chinese to the Legislative Council. The first such appointment was made in 1880, when Pope Hennessy recommended Ng Choy, alias Wu Ting-fang. He served until 1882. In 1884, Wong Shing was the second Chinese member of the Council. He resigned in 1890, to be succeeded by Dr Ho Kai, a brother-in-law of Wu Ting-fang. He served until 1914. Wei Yuk, the son-in-law of Wong Shing was appointed in 1896. He also left the Council in 1914. All had received English-language education, both locally and abroad, and were in some measure connected with the missionary presence in China.

The Government also appointed English-speaking Chinese to certain boards and committees which dealt with specific aspects of Chinese life in Hong Kong. In the nineteenth century the most important of these was the District Watch Committee.[32]

At times, the Government turned to its Justices of the Peace for advice. All appointees were English-speaking. The first Chinese to be appointed Justices were Ng Choy, Ho Kai, Wei Yuk, and Wong Shing. The following were also appointed before 1900: in 1883, Chan Quan-ee, Choa Chee-bee, Luk Sau-theen, Wong See-tye, and Woo Lin-yuen; in 1886, Kaw Hong-take; in 1891, Ho Tung and Lau Wai-chun; in 1892, Chan Afook, Ho Fook, and Tseung Sz-kai; in 1893, Chan U-fai; and in 1899, Fung Wa-chun, Leung Pui-chi, Leung Shiu-kong, and Wei Long-shan.

The following biographical notes on these individuals are taken from various materials I have gathered on Hong Kong people, not all of which have as yet been collated.

(a) Chan Quan-ee (陳關意), alias Chan Shut-cho, alias Chan Man-shing, lived for some years in Burma, where he learned English. From there he came to Hong Kong and in 1857 was clerk in the office of George Cooper-Turner, solicitor. Upon the removal of the American firm of Augustine Heard and Company from Canton to Hong Kong at the time of the second Sino-British war, he became compradore. Through the years, he invested in property and became a large real estate owner. He was one of the first among the Chinese to live in the 'Mid-levels' area of Hong Kong Island, developing Lower Mosque Terrace, now known as Ying Fai Terrace. He died in 1901 or 1902. According to my records, his sons were Chan Yau, born in 1861, died in 1938; Chan Pat; Chan Wei, died in 1911; and a daughter, Chan Man-ng, alias Chan Kam-ying, alias Alice Martha Chan.

(b) Choa Chee-bee (蔡紫微), alias Choi Tse-mei, alias Tsoi Tsz-mi, was a member of a Fukien family which had been settled in Malacca for several generations. Choa Chee-bee came to Hong Kong in the early 1870s, where he was compradore for the newly-organized Wahee, Smith and Company Sugar Refinery. Later, the partners in the Company went bankrupt and the business was taken over by Jardine, Matheson and Company; Choa Chee-bee continued as compradore under their management. He died in 1901, apparently without children. His nephew, Choa Leep-chee (蔡立志), born in 1859, died in 1909, came to join his uncle at the refinery. He later became compradore. Both uncle and nephew had received an English-language education in the Straits Settlements. Choa Leep-chee was survived by ten children. There are many of his descendants still in Hong Kong, including Dr George Choa and Dr Gerald Choa, the Director of Medical Services in 1973.

(c) In 1881, Luk Sau-theen (陸壽四), alias Luk Sow-tin, was an assistant in the Yew Cheong Hong of Bonham Strand.

(d) Wong See-tye (黃祉帶), alias Wong Yiu-chun (曉川), alias Wong Siu-kwong (詔光), was the eldest son of Wong Yook (黃玉), who died in Hong Kong in 1877. The father owned real estate in Hong Kong that he had bought in 1866 from Kwok Acheong, the compradore of the P. & O. Steamship Company. Wong Yook also appears to have been a compradore for the company. His son, Wong Shu-tong (黃樹堂),

alias Wong Ka-yau (家猷), alias Wong Wing-kwan (榮坤), alias Wong Achai, certainly was compradore, as well as his grandson, Wong Ping-sun (黃屏蓀), alias Wong Shau-ying (壽應). The latter died in Hong Kong in 1942. Another son of Wong Yook, Wong Yam-ting, alias Wong Wa-hee, had interests in the sugar business. He was a principal in Wahee, Smith and Company Sugar Refinery and the Oriental Sugar Refinery. In neither company was he successful and he went into bankruptcy in 1878. Wong See-tye was compradore of Belilios and Company in Hong Kong. In 1880, he was a member of the Tung Wah Hospital Committee. He died at Canton in January 1889. The value of the property he left in Hong Kong was estimated at $118,000. It was administered by Wong Ping-lam (黃炳林), alias Wong U-kai (雨溪), compradore of Belilios and Company, and Wong Tat-kwan.

(e) Woo Lin-yuen (胡連元), alias Woo Tsit-san (捷山), came to Hong Kong about 1867. He was a member of the Fukien community in Hong Kong. In 1887, when the Fukien merchants entertained a member of the Royal family of Siam, the only English-speaking hosts at the dinner were Hong Bing-kew, secretary to the Viceroy of Kwangtung, and Woo Lin-yuen, who was secretary of the Man On Insurance Company. In 1887, Woo was appointed Hong Kong agent for the China Railway Company of Tientsin. In 1883 and 1884, he was a member of the Committee of the Po Leung Kuk, originally established as a refuge for kidnapped girls and women,[33] but he does not appear to have served on the Tung Wah Hospital Committee, which was another important Chinese élite organization.[34] Woo was appointed to the Sanitary Board but resigned in 1892, presumably because of ill health, for he died in Canton in June 1893. His Hong Kong estate, valued at $1,000, was administered by a wealthy merchant, Li Sing, and by Lai Siu-tang.

(f) Kaw Hong-take was a member of the Singapore firm that received the Hong Kong opium monopoly in 1881. He last appears on the roll of Justices of the Peace in 1904, and probably returned to Singapore.

(g) The career of Sir Robert Ho-tung is so well known that it is not necessary to give full biographical details here.[35] Born in Hong Kong, he was educated at Queen's College. Upon graduation, he accepted a post in the Chinese maritime customs

service in October 1878, but resigned in June 1880. He returned to Hong Kong and entered the employ of Jardine,
Matheson and Company, becoming in time their head compradore.

(h) Lau or Lai Wai-chun (劉渭川), alias Lau Sai (西), alias Lau
Kwok-cheung (國祥), was a native of Tsin Shan, Heung Shan
District, Kwangtung. His family had business connections in
Vancouver, Canada, and as a young man he was sent there to
gain overseas business experience. While there he learned
English. He later come to Hong Kong, where he was naturalized in 1891. He was twice elected to the Tung Wah Hospital
Committee, in 1884 and 1893. In 1892, when the compradore
of the Hongkong and Shanghai Banking Corporation embez-
zled a large sum of the Bank's money, Lau Wai-chun took
over his position. Formerly, he had been a member of the
Tung Shang Wo firm engaged in the California and Australian trade. In the same year that he became compradore for
the Bank, he was appointed by the Government as Justice of
the Peace, member of the Sanitary Board, and member of
the District Watch Committee. Lau Wai-chun became involved in the complicated affairs of the Wong Fung firm,
which was established in 1895 to take over the management
of the Wai Sing lottery monopoly in Kwangtung Province.
Associated with him were the two brothers, Wei Yuk and
Wei Long-shan. The latter was the assistant compradore of
the Hongkong and Shanghai Banking Corporation. However,
when the Viceroy of Kwangtung shut down the lottery in
1905, the Wong Fung firm, as well as several other businesses
connected with it, became insolvent, causing Lau Wai-chun
to go into bankruptcy in 1906. He is said to have had liabilities of over two million dollars, although one source puts his
liabilities at the more conservative figure of $503,657. His
assets were only $66,554, consisting of his furniture and a
share of property on Lyndhurst Terrace. Lau's bankruptcy
ended his connection with the Bank, although a relative, Lau
Pun-chin (劉泮樵), alias Lau Ting-cheung (廷章), succeeded
him as compradore.[36]

(i) Chan Afook was appointed clerk in the Registrar-General's
Department in 1867. In 1870, he was transferred to the Survey Department as fourth clerk. In 1881, he was made acting
second clerk in the Police Magistracy. He left government

service in 1882 and entered the office of Danby and Leigh, civil engineers, architects, and surveyors. Later, he went into business on his own and also became a director of Watkins Ltd.

(j) Ho Fook, a brother of Sir Robert Ho-tung, left Queen's College in 1881 and joined a Haiphong Chinese *hong* as shipping clerk. He soon returned to Hong Kong and was appointed Chinese clerk and interpreter in the Registrar-General's Department. In 1885, he entered the office of Dennys and Mossop, solicitors, as interpreter. He then became assistant compradore at Jardine, Matheson and Company and eventually succeeded his brother as head compradore.

(k) Tseung Sz-kai or Tsz-kai (薛士楷), alias Tseung Ying-fong (應芳), was a native of Amoy who, when young, went to Jamaica; he later spent some years in Puerto Rico. In about 1872, he returned to Hong Kong. In time, he became compradore to the Japanese firm of Osaka Shosen Kaisha; in 1887, he was Vice-Chairman of the Po Leung Kuk Committee; and in 1891, he was appointed to the District Watch Committee. He either left Hong Kong or died about the year 1910.

(l) Chan U-fai was appointed pupil teacher at Queen's College in 1873 and in 1874 was promoted to assistant master. He later left and engaged in business. He is not listed as a Justice of the Peace after 1897.

(m) Fung Wa-chun (馮葉川), alias Fung Tat-cheung (穗祥), alias Fung Shui, was appointed a pupil teacher at Queen's College in 1874 and promoted to assistant master in 1876. He left his teaching position in 1881 and became an assistant in the Yan Wo opium firm. In 1892, when he was elected to the Tung Wah Hospital Committee, he was compradore of the National Bank, but by 1901 he was compradore of Shewan, Tomes and Company. In 1898, he was appointed to the District Watch Committee; in 1899, to the Sanitary Board; and in 1906, he held the lease for quarries in Fa Yuen District, Kwangtung. His name does not appear on the list of Justices of the Peace after 1912.

(n) Leung Pui-chi (梁培芝), alias Leung Long-cheung (龍章), alias Leung Chung (忠), was a native of Heung Shan District, Kwangtung. He was naturalized in 1899. He had at that time been in the colony for thirty-seven years. In 1889, he was elected to the Tung Wah Hospital Committee. He had business interests in the Shui Fung Bank. His name last appears on the lists of Justices of the Peace in 1917.

(o) Leung Shiu-kong was, in his younger years, a clerk in the Mercantile Bank. In 1898, he was compradore to A.H. Rennie, and in 1900, Chinese agent of the Canadian Pacific Railway. After 1904, his name is not listed as a Justice of the Peace.

(p) Wei Long-shan, alias Wei Song, was a son of Wei Akwong and brother of Wei Yuk. In 1882, he was an assistant compradore in Shanghai. He later returned to Hong Kong, where he invested in real estate and became involved in the management of the Wai Sing lottery monopoly of Kwangtung Province. With the lottery's collapse in 1905, he went into bankruptcy. He took up residence in Macau, where he died in 1929.

Conclusion

In this examination of the progress of Chinese to élite status in nineteenth-century Hong Kong, the focus has been mainly on the development of English-education institutions, and the education and careers of particular individuals. One purpose of the examination was to refine some of the raw material, to systematize some of the data, before any positive sociological statements about the emergence of Chinese élites in the nineteenth-century period could be made. However, I would like in this final section to make some general observations on the basis of my material and from what I know about the backgrounds of some élite individuals.

English-language education clearly fulfilled a need in the colonial situation of Hong Kong. The colony was ruled and dominated by a minority foreign population. Both the Government and the foreign firm needed individuals with dual-language ability to bridge the gap between the non-Chinese-speaking foreign community and the non-English-speaking Chinese community, and there were not many who had this facility. A very small group of foreigners had studied Chinese. A somewhat larger group of Chinese young men had received an English-language education. Dual-language ability opened up a new type of employment: as interpreter or compradore. Both positions had roots in the Canton Co-hong system. The positions of linguist and compradore, established as they were to facilitate and control relations with foreigners, did not command much 'face' among traditional Chinese, but an education outside the traditional Chinese system meant, at least at a formal level, a break with the prevailing cultural system. And, in Hong Kong, the old values relating to status did not have the same importance. In China, the community would have looked to the literati-gentry class for leadership (although even there English-educated individuals were beginning to assume important roles). In Hong Kong, such a class scarcely existed (although some members of the élite reinforced their status by purchasing degrees and titles). Leadership was assumed by those who accumulated wealth. Because the demand for dual-language speakers exceeded supply, it was not difficult for a Chinese speaking standard English to secure a position which at the same time gave him opportunities to accumulate wealth (perhaps not always by legitimate means). Many members of the élite had humble beginnings but English-language ability in a dual-language community enabled them to rise from poverty to wealth; from obscurity to prominence. The dual-language-speaking group formed the pool from which the Government recruited its top advisers on affairs relating to the Chinese community at large.

Élite persons did emerge among those who did not understand English, particularly those operating in strictly Chinese social and business organizations. But wherever such organizations moved beyond a strictly Chinese context, those members with facility in English were placed in influential positions. This is evident if we look at such institutions as the Tung Wah Hospital:[37] established to provide medical services for the traditionally-minded Chinese, it came to assume responsibility for various quasi-political activities within the Chinese community. And inasmuch as the hospital was accountable to the Hong Kong Government, members of the organization able to speak English were at an advantage. Practically all the Chinese on the councils and committees established by the Government were at one time members of the Tung Wah Board of Directors.

As a man of wealth and position, the English-educated member of the élite had the qualifications necessary for becoming a 'founding ancestor' of an élite 'dynasty' or descent group. The fortunes of the family in a new geographical setting centred on him. The family was basic to Chinese life and its importance was reflected in certain aspects of the structure of Chinese élite groups in Hong Kong. The present Chinese élite, indeed, is still largely dominated by families whose ancestors grew to élite status in the nineteenth or early twentieth century. Practically all these ancestors were individuals discussed in this chapter.

The Chinese family system operated on a principle of first responsibility to members of the immediate family, and then, in varying degrees, to other members of the wider descent group. This often resulted, in Hong Kong, in the introduction of brothers, cousins, sons, and nephews to positions over which an individual could exercise some influence on employment policies. Certainly, we find that in some government offices and departments, employees were kinsmen. A compradore might staff the lower positions under his control with remoter kinsmen, but reserve the better places for those nearest in relationship. In some cases also the position of compradore was held in the same family for some three or four generations.

The position of the family in élite circles also appears to have been strengthened and extended by intermarriage with other élite families. Although intermarriage among élite families follows a general pattern, in the Hong Kong Chinese case, the situation was influenced by degrees of Westernization and Christianization. A person might have a foreign-acquired aversion to foot-binding, preferring to have a wife who had not been subjected to this practice; and she, in all likelihood, would be a member of a Westernized and élite family. Christian families wished to find Christian marriage-partners for their sons or daughters and again they tended to be in the Westernized and élite family groups. And given these marriage 'qualifications', partners also tended to come from the same dialect group and place of origin.

Special attention needs to be paid to the role of Eurasians in the nineteenth-century élite of Hong Kong, particularly towards the turn of the century when they began to come into prominence. Two groups of Eurasians appear to have existed according to whether they used a Chinese or a non-Chinese surname. During the period of concern, the Eurasian was almost universally the child of a non-Chinese father and a Chinese mother. Eurasians with English surnames do not as a group enter into this study with the exception of a few persons who began their careers with Chinese names and later changed to a non-Chinese surname.

Eurasians bearing English surnames usually appear to have been children of foreigners with a low social status: tavern-keepers, lower-grade Chinese maritime staff, and government servants of lesser rank such as police, prison staff, sanitary inspectors, and so on. Some members of this group had neither the financial means nor the desire to return to their countries of origin. Hence, they frequently married or cohabited with a Chinese woman, established a family, and remained in Hong Kong until they died. Their children then bore their father's surname.

Eurasians bearing Chinese surnames were usually children of a father who remained in the colony for a limited time. A number were merchants and business men of good social position and wealth, but who, after amassing a competence, returned to their home country. They had not married the Chinese women by whom they had children in Hong Kong. These women were called, locally, 'protected women' and formed a special class. They tended to be particularly independent and were usually girls from the so-called 'Tanka' floating population.[38] Their patrons often arranged to provide for their financial security. This was usually in the form of an annuity, a property in trust, or an outright gift of real estate. These provisions assisted the Eurasian offspring to begin their careers with some financial advantage. In the absence of her patron, the mother returned to the Chinese community. Here, the children were reared in a Chinese-speaking household and bore a Chinese surname. The mother, however, appears to have realized the importance of English for the future career of her son and sent him to an English-language school. When Eurasian boys sought employment, the firm with which the father had been connected often employed them and provided them with special advantages. This assisted them to rise more rapidly to élite status.

English-educated Chinese were also significant as a bridging element between Chinese and Western culture and social institutions in the adjustment period following European imperialism. Having been trained outside the traditional Chinese educational system with its emphasis on the conservation of the values of the past, the English-language student was open to innovations in social behaviour, business methods, and the uses of capital. He functioned to open up various avenues in commerce, finance, and industry for the Chinese.

In China, such students served as middlemen for progressive Chinese government officers in their efforts to modernize China during the closing years of the Ch'ing dynasty. They not only filled the positions of interpreter and translator, but also provided the much needed knowledge of Western law, customs, attitudes, and modes of behaviour. Moreover, they provided specialized technical and professional knowledge for the development of a modern army and navy and for the introduction of railways, telegraph services, steamships, Western medicine, and journalism.

I have been looking at general trends. In fact, conditions affecting English-language-educated Chinese in the 1850s were different from those found at the end of the century. In the first period, a Chinese élite group was only just beginning to emerge in Hong Kong. By the turn of the century élite groups were well established. The elements composing the élite and the origins from which members of this élite sprang became more diverse. This increasing complexity and diversity have continued to the present day.

8 The Hong Kong Church and Nineteenth-century Colonial Attitudes

THE Church has held to certain basic beliefs since its foundation, but these have been subject to historical development and adaptation within different cultural settings. In the process, church thought and practice have interacted with the context in which they have existed.

China provided a new context for an old faith, with a different language, different thought forms, customs, economic and political structures, and social institutions. The propagation of the Christian faith accompanied an aggresive foreign trade. Both were resisted by China, which maintained it needed nothing from the West.

The missionary to China came from a tradition where civilization was equated with Christianity. Non-Christian peoples were 'heathen' and hence barbarian. The Chinese, on their part, identified their own nation and culture with civilization and those outside the Middle Kingdom as barbarians.

The Chinese literati-gentry élite were not about to abandon their traditional views, and Christianity made few converts among them. The common man generally accepted the traditional view, even though his participation in the higher Chinese culture was limited. He was more ready, however, to submit to the inferior position the missionary expected him to accept as a person of an 'inferior' and 'heathen' nation. The missionary was slow to acknowledge the Chinese as equals in culture and character.[1] The result was a tendency towards denationalization of the convert. This process was reinforced when the Church established itself in a colony.

In Hong Kong, missionary efforts had the support of a familiar legal system, they were tolerated, and they had an established (as in the case of the Anglicans)[2] or a semi-established status (other groups *vis-à-vis* traditional Chinese religions).

This chapter will examine aspects of the adaptation of the Protestant Church in a colony with a predominantly Chinese population and will focus particularly on the ways in which the Church has dealt with cultural distance and superior-inferior relationships.

Distance and Dependence

Thirteen days after the British flag was planted on Possession Point, a party of eight Protestant missionaries came to Hong Kong from Macau on an exploratory trip. They found a temporary village rising on the beach where the town of Victoria was to be. It was made up of a cluster of huts and matsheds hastily thrown together. The missionary party also visited some of the agricultural and fishing villages. They estimated the entire population of the island to be less than 2,500, practically all of them very poor. The island's significance as a Chinese settlement did not impress them, but they envisaged a glorious future for it as a British possession. 'There is no question but that in the course of time, the island of Hong Kong will, if retained by the British, rise in importance and influence until it becomes the first insular emporium in these Eastern waters.'

As to its missionary prospects, they felt that Hong Kong might form, 'in the providence of God, a place on which to establish, under the auspices of the flag that now waves on its summits, the true principles of commerce, justice and the Christian religion, which protected, these may flourish untrammeled until the nation (China) be enlightened and saved'.[3]

The missionaries, after reflection, were divided in their views as to the advantages of a British colony as a field for their work. They felt that, with the political and military power of Britain behind them, they would have protection and security, whereas there were uncertainties on Chinese soil. However, it was soon evident that Hong Kong was not China and the Chinese settlers did not represent the best of Chinese society.

In 1847, a missionary contrasted the difference between Hong Kong and Canton as it affected missionary work. 'Hong Kong is English soil, with a Chinese population of various dialects, and mostly unsettled in residence, going and coming constantly. Here (at Canton) is a Chinese society in all its primitive state. This is Chinese soil, and the people do not feel themselves to be bondsmen or servants. We come to them as men in their own houses and homes.' Unfortunately, he did not have a high opinion of Chinese character. 'The Canton people are covetous, avaricious, selfish, extortioners.'[4] The Revd George Smith, after a visit to various cities of China, noted that in the northern cities the foreigners everywhere met intelligent and friendly people representing the best of China; not so in Hong Kong, where the Chinese were mostly of the lowest order.[5]

Missionaries and clergy did not make the impact hoped for. At the time the missionaries were opposing the introduction of legalized gambling houses for Chinese, Mr Turner, of the London Missionary Society, described the sad state of affairs:

Anyone at all acquainted with the Chinese and their feelings toward Christianity knows that the conduct of the British government in the opium trade and the war consequent thereon, has been an immense obstacle in the way of the missionary. This is a bye-gone conclusion to which it would be useless and unwise now to refer to publicly. But another scandal is threatened in some respects more shameful than the opium trade. This is the licensing of gambling houses by the British government in the only spot of land where the Chinese have any opportunity of observing what the British government is. The Chinese Christians agree with me that this measure will make our Government a laughing stock to the Chinese, and will be a great disaster for the mission work. You know, I dare say, from similar experience in India, how the natives refuse to be disabused of the notion that the missionaries are government agents. It follows that we and our work are made to bear directly the odium of any wrong acts on the part of the government.... Nothing but utter ignorance of the Chinese could have impelled him [the Governor] to such a step.[6]

In spite of petitions and protests from the missionaries, the gambling houses were licensed. To the missionary, this was but another example for the Chinese that 'barbarian' governments were immoral. In his yearly report to the mission board in London, Turner wrote: 'Three great vices of China, opium smoking, fornication, and gambling, are carried on [in Hong Kong] under license and regulation of Government'. The Chinese expected the Government to uphold morality, and Turner admitted that their Government usually maintained 'a consistant [sic] profession of adherence to virtue, and in its laws and edicts aims at the suppression of vicious practices. For a Christian government in the sight of these people to even appear to patronise vice is a terrible stumbling block to the way of the Gospel.'[7]

In the process of adapting to a Chinese and a colonial situation, the Protestant Church encountered problems of distance and position: distance in terms of a gap in attitudes and cultures, position in terms of inferior-superior relationships. A letter written in 1840 by a Chinese convert will be used as a framework to discuss these problems. The points raised in the letter will be illustrated by other examples from the early period of Protestant mission work in Hong Kong.

The letter was written by Chu Tak-leung.[8] He had been baptized in England in 1838. He had been taken there from Indonesia by the Revd Walter Henry Medhurst, of the London Missionary Society, to assist in the translation of the Scriptures. By 1840, he had returned to China to visit his family. He was then attached to the mission at Macau as a language teacher to William C. Milne, the son of the pioneer Protestant missionary at Malacca.

Upon his return to China, Chu was regarded by the missionaries as an employee and of inferior status. Even such a valuable and well-qualified pastor as the Revd Ho Fuk-tong was not accepted as an equal. It is true that Dr James Legge treated him as a trusted friend and colleague, but during Legge's absence from Hong Kong another missionary refused to hand over money sent for the care of some girls whom Dr Legge had left under the supervision of the Revd Ho Fuk-tong. The missionary justified himself to his board with the following explanation.

We object to the proposal [to hand over the money] as calculated to lower us in the eyes of Tsun-shin [Ho Fuk-tong was also known as Ho Tsun-shin] and the other natives around us. What is it, but saying, we can trust Tsun-shin with the disposal of this money, but not the missionaries. Mrs. Cleland may engage in the work of instructing these children, but cannot be entrusted with the funds for their support. Could any Christian lady brook to apply to a native, however estimable and trustworthy Tsun-shin certainly is, for the monthly allotment for the support of these children—thus exalting one we have been sent to teach and be an example to, above the missionaries themselves in point of trustworthiness ... Nothing should be done to lower us in the eyes of the Chinese, otherwise how shall they regard us as examples in all things.[9]

From any point of view, this expression of missionary superiority and condescension towards Chinese hardly provided the example on which to produce a church built on trust and mutual respect.

Another example of these same attitudes is shown in the case of Dr Wong Fun. He was commissioned by the London Missionary Society in England in 1856 with the same status and salary as their other agents. Wong Fun had been educated at the Morrison Education Society School at Hong Kong. He and several schoolmates were taken by their headmaster, the Revd S.R. Brown, in 1847 to the United States for further study. After several years in the United States, Wong Fun proceeded to Edinburgh to study medicine. He received his degree there in 1856.

The news of the commissioning of Dr Wong Fun produced different opinions regarding its wisdom among his future colleagues in Hong Kong. Many of the reservations about the appointment seemed to arise from an awareness of Dr Hobson's reluctance to work as an equal with a Chinese. Wong Fun's status as a commissioned missionary was viewed as a wedge to undermine missionary authority among the Chinese. All this leads one to believe that if Wong Fun were to succeed as a missionary, it would not be because of the friendly reception by his Western co-workers.

If it was thought there would be prejudice against a Chinese missionary which could only be counterbalanced by the presence of a foreigner, no account was being taken of the great ill-will the Chinese held against the foreigner. Wong Fun himself was not deceived in this matter. After his return to Hong Kong he wrote, 'There are always many obstacles to missionary labors, but at present there is, and there will be for many years to come, a strong prejudice against Englishmen for what they (the Chinese) think, the high-handed way in which they carry everything. Which prejudice works very strongly against the missionary'.[10]

But let us return to Chu Tak-leung. After his return to Macau, where he was employed as a language teacher, he was charged with smoking opium. Later, some opium-smoking equipment was found hidden in his room. He was sent away and all connections with him were severed. He replied, however, with a long letter justifying his acts and asking to be forgiven and reinstated. He accused the missionaries of being a party to the corruption of China through the opium trade:

Where does this opium come first, if not from your Christian country? Why [are] men of Christian land so kind, to send this opium to China and kill so many people. Christ came to save them, but not condemn. Now you came to be missionary. I think your Society spend money in vain. Why? Because one save, and one kill. If you say, 'they are they, you are you', but think where comes your Society's money. Are collected from them.[11] It is you and they are just one. How can make difference. I think it is better for you to go back to your country, tell your own people, and to ask your Queen give orders, from this time any merchants shall not trade with opium to China.

The missionaries were accompanied by the taint of the record of their 'Christian' nation. They were open to the charge that the opium policy of their country contradicted the missionary claim to be seeking salvation of souls, the betterment of life, the improvement of moral standards, and the introduction of a 'civilizing' influence.

The first missionary comment on the opium trade appears to have been in 1837, when the Revd E.C. Bridgman, editor of the *Chinese Repository*, published an article entitled 'The Traffic in Opium'.[12] He wrote to his mission board in America, 'The subject of opium is at length broached. What will be the issue of it is not possible for man to conjecture with much confidence. I will do what I can to make known the whole truth concerning it.'[13]

In 1842, during the course of the war between China and England, the missionaries drew up a statement. They polarized the two contestants as two mighty empires, 'one of them as it were a mass of inert mind, indurated by the "old customs" of ages; and the other a nation, whose mind seems to be destined, by its activity and energy, to leaven the whole world'. The meeting of these two great nations, even though it was on the field of battle, 'will be productive of advancing the final triumphs of Christian civilization, the war with China must be regarded as "the leading star" in the political horizon'.[14]

The possibilities the war opened up, if it resulted in the humiliation of China, pushed into the background the objectionable features, from the missionary view, of its origins.

As its succeeding acts one after another developed, the observer is carried along with them, and the originating causes ... lose somewhat of their obnoxious character, from seeing how grand and unexpected are the results likely to flow from them. The conduct of the foreigners in bringing opium, against their wishes ... cannot on any ground be defended ... But we rather desire to regard the occurrance [sic] of the last four years as a new exhibition of God's power and goodness in causing the wrath and avarice of man to work out his ends.[15]

The war against the Chinese was a just retribution for their pretensions against the sovereignty of God. The British bullet was seen as the thunderbolt of God against an impious nation which was an affront to those eager to defend the honour of their God.[16]

This kind of reaction by Protestant missionaries in China reflected attitudes and theological views current at the time. It indicated the great gap they would have to overcome before they could correctly understand the setting in which they expected to work. On the practical side, they saw no end to the opium traffic, in spite of its evils. 'The love of money will continue to lead men to raise it and bring it here, as long as the lust of appetite drives thousands to take it and die.' Unfortunately, this prediction was true. Only the pressure of world opinion finally induced the British Government to suppress the trade in Hong Kong. This was well into the present century.

The opium trade and British policy were a great hindrance to missionary work. The Revd Ho Fuk-tong, in a letter to Dr Legge, tells how in Hong Kong one of the mission's Chinese colporteurs 'has often been abused by many. They say, "The English came here to distribute these books, which teach men to do good. How is it that they come likewise seeking to fight with us, and to usurp our land? There is no good doctrine in that" '.[17]

In Hong Kong, antagonism was muted. In China, it was more open. Dr Benjamin Hobson observed in 1851, 'I had myself no conception of the difficulties of the Mission work till I resided here (at Canton) some time, and been taught by bitter experience how deceitful, proud, and self-satisfied the Chinese are. In their native village and towns you see them in their natural element. In Hong Kong and other places where a higher and foreign power reigns, the Chinese prove accommodating and even servile.'[18]

Some missionaries did not feel free to express their true feelings about the opium question publicly, though they were willing to share them with their board. To the directors at home, a missionary wrote in 1847, 'I do not wish anything I have said concerning the opium trade or the merchants here made public, for if it should reach their ears, it would bring down their wrath upon me.' He cited the fate of Dr Macgowan at Ningpo, 'Two years ago a strong protest was published in the Baptist papers. The captains of vessels going up the coast and the merchants engaged in the coasting trade were so vexed that they would not forward any letters or parcels to him.'[19]

Not all missionaries were so averse to letting their true opinions be known. Dr Julius Hirschberg resigned in 1849 as Director of the Medical Missionary Society Hospital in Hong Kong because of his opposition to the opium trade. He gave his reasons to the board of the London Missionary Society:

From the beginning and more particularly now my conscience reproves me for being united with a Society [the Medical Missionary Society] most of the Members of which are Opium Dealers.... I know that there is hardly any Society which does not receive contributions from ungodly men, and I know also the reasonings which are brought forward in favour of this, but what, if my conscience reproves me and tells me daily that I ought to avoid giving any countenance to evil, and as a Christian I ought to show the world that I disapprove of the traffic.[20]

As the years passed, the missionaries became increasingly outspoken in their criticism of the opium trade and other social evils. The missionary seldom adopted a Chinese mode of life, particularly those who remained in Hong Kong or the treaty ports of China. This unwillingness to live as their converts reinforced the distance between them.

Chu Tak-leung, in his apologia, criticized the first Protestant missionary to China for adopting a life-style that was too comfortable:

Dr. Morrison first be missionary to China, after a few years he put away his own duty, turning to be interpreter to opium merchants.[21] He think to be missionary could not get much money but to be interpreter may get much money, may live well with fine house, may keep many servants, may put on fine cloth, may eat fine food. Allow me a question to you, are truly Christians who love money in this way.

Unlike Morrison, the German-born missionary Charles Gutzlaff made a conscious effort to identify with the Chinese during the early years of his mission to the Chinese. Later, he followed a more usual missionary style of living. On his first journey up the coast of China in 1831, he wore Chinese dress and lived with the Chinese. He speaks of having become 'a naturalised subject of the celestial empire, by adoption into the clan of family of Kwo, from the Tung-on district of Fukien ... [and] wore occassionally [sic] the Chinese dress. Now I had to conform entirely to the customs of the Chinese'. A traveller who met him at this time said, 'that those who know him to be a foreigner believe that his grandfather must have been Chinese, and thus the jealousy which exists in regard to the barbarians generally, is in a measure removed from him.'[22]

When in 1846 four young men arrived from Europe to assist Gutzlaff in his Chinese Christian Union, he placed them in rooms in the Chinese section of Hong Kong. One died within the year, and some believed his death was the result of unsanitary conditions in the district. While his assistants were acclimatizing themselves to Chinese life in Hong Kong, Gutzlaff himself was living with his wife in a large European-style house in Gough Street. He was at the time a government employee, receiving a large salary as Chinese Secretary. As head of a government office, he was able to staff the office with his Chinese converts.

The missionary found family responsibilities an obstacle to a fuller identification with a Chinese way of life.

At the same time that Gutzlaff was putting his bachelor recruits into a Chinese environment, the Revd Samuel W. Bonney, also a single man, was living in the upper room of a tea warehouse in Canton outside the foreign settlement. He had adopted Chinese dress, but without the queue (Gutzlaff had sometimes worn a false queue) and ate in the Chinese style. Some parts of this new way of things he considered temporary. He informed his home board that 'after my neighbours see that I am not a foreign devil but a foreign friend, I will dispense with those parts of the dress inconvenient, especially with soled shoes. I will also put spoons on my table to show how much neater it is to take food with than to shovel it down with chopsticks'.[23] Perhaps after becoming expert in the use of chopsticks he would have found their use more acceptable, but at least he was making an effort to fit into the Chinese scene.

He further noted how Chinese dress broke down distance between peoples. 'When foreigners approach a house in a foreign dress, the dogs bark, the children run away and cry out "*fan qui*", the door is quickly shut and barred, and like demonstrations of non-intercourse are exhibited. But when he goes in the dress of the people, the dogs are quiet, the children laughing, the master of the house or shop is pleased and offers tea or a tobacco pipe.'[24] Bonney's American friends at Canton did not receive his innovations in the same spirit as the Chinese appeared to. He was accused of adopting a 'heathen costume' as opposed to 'Christian' dress. One told him, 'I hope that you enjoy your heathenish costume, and that the natives pity rather than resent your weakness.'

In the view of most foreigners in China at that period, any concession to Chinese customs was an admission of inferiority and weakness. Such attitudes pervaded missionary circles and contributed to their separation from the people they had come to serve. The Chinese felt that missionaries did not have a proper understanding of Chinese culture and customs. Chu Tak-leung's principal accuser was a youth aged 25. To him Chu wrote, 'You are too young, have not much knowledge, cannot be missionary, and you come to China a short time, not understand of my custom.'

In spite of the distance between missionary and convert, they were bound by a tie. It was one of dependence. The convert had received something from the missionary, and it was thought by the missionary that he had nothing to give in return but gratitude and loyal obedience. In the opening stages of missionary activity, a convert was usually an employee or a student of the mission, or, perhaps, he was taken into the pay of the mission after his conversion, for in this period there was a demand for pressmen, teachers, translators, preachers, catechists, medical aides, and other assistants.

The convert also looked to the missionary as the agent who had brought him into a state of grace through baptism. He was the source of spiritual instruction. He directed church affairs. Chu's last point in his letter was that the missionaries in Macau had no right to cut him off without the permission of the Revd W.H. Medhurst, who had baptized him. This showed a special sense of 'belonging' to an individual missionary.

This dependent relationship between the Chinese Christian and the foreign missionary continued to characterize the Church in China for many years. Among some Christian groups in Hong Kong, vestiges of it can still be found.

From its establishment, the Protestant Church in Hong Kong has been somewhat different in its development from the Church in China. The Church in China today is both fully independent and Chinese. The Hong Kong Church sooner or later will be a part of that Church. As a Church in a colony, however, its experience has been different. Both the positive and negative aspects of this experience should enable it to make its own contribution to the Church of China.

9 The Hong Kong Situation as it Influenced the Protestant Church

How has the colonial status of Hong Kong affected the Chinese Christian Church? Have the attitudes and experiences of Hong Kong Christians been significantly different from Christians in China? The differences will be examined using four aspects arising from the colonial situation of Hong Kong: (a) Hong Kong as a place of refuge for those who wished to remove themselves from conditions in China; (b) the marginal character of the Chinese community in Hong Kong; (c) the relative absence of a challenge to the Chinese Christian to come to terms with his faith in relation to national identity; (d) the close identification of the Church with the objectives of a colonial government. In conclusion, some questions are raised about the future.

Hong Kong as a Place of Refuge

Hong Kong is an urban centre on the edge of China beyond the jurisdiction of the Chinese Government. This has resulted in its becoming a haven for Chinese wishing to escape from Chinese law or from disturbed social, political, or economic conditions. This has affected the quantity and the quality of the Chinese population of Hong Kong. In both these aspects, the history of Hong Kong has reflected the prevailing conditions within China.

In the years immediately following the British occupation, many of the least desirable elements of the population of the Canton delta came to Hong Kong. The first Chinese landowners were those who had supplied the British forces with provisions or had otherwise co-operated with the enemy of China in the first Opium War. An extract from George Smith's description of the Chinese population of Hong Kong published in his account of a visit to Hong Kong describes this situation:

The lowest dregs of native society flock to the British Settlement, in the hope of gain or plunder ... The principal part of the Chinese population in the town consists of servants, coolies, stone-cutters, and masons engaged in temporary works.... The colony has been for some time also the resort of pirates and thieves, so protected by secret compact as to defy the ordinary regulations of police for detection or prevention. In short, there are but faint prospects at present of any other than either a migratory or a predatory race being attracted to Hong Kong, who, when their hopes of gain or pilfering vanish, without hesitation or difficulty remove elsewhere.[1]

Like many overseas Chinese communities in their earliest periods, the population of Hong Kong was predominantly male. There were few families and little sense of belonging. Missionaries did not consider this type of inhabitant promising material with which to establish and build a strong Chinese Church. In spite of this, the Church in Hong Kong prospered. It produced a group of young men educated in the English language who by the 1860s were rising to positions of importance in the political, educational, and commercial life of China. They were sought out by those progressive Chinese officials interested in strengthening China. These officials engaged them to serve on their staffs as advisers on Western techniques and ways of thought. These young men proposed a pioneer project for the foreign education of Chinese, the Chinese Educational Mission, and they introduced new methods and procedures into Chinese commerce and industry.

From the standpoint of an independent Chinese Church, perhaps the first self-supporting, self-governing, and self-propagating congregation was the To Tsai Church. It was established in 1843; a Chinese pastor was ordained in 1846; a congregation with deacons and elders was formed in 1849; a constitution was adopted in 1876; and the To Tsai Church became fully independent in 1888. Today, the congregation bears the name Hop Yat.

How do we reconcile the unpromising prospects of early Hong Kong for missionary success and its production of leaders in the modernization of China and the establishment of an independent Church? The answer may be found in the colonial status of Hong Kong, which attracted and produced what may be termed 'marginal Chinese'. The marginal character of Hong Kong Chinese and their effect upon the Church will be examined in the next section of this chapter.

The post-war period witnessed a different type of person flocking into Hong Kong to escape conditions on the mainland. It was not the adventurer seeking quick gain or the criminal. The composition of the post-war refugee population was varied, but a significant number were middle-class and educated. A large number, however, were destitute and the rapid increase in population created serious problems in terms of education, employment, and housing. There was a basic need for clothing and food. This need aroused the compassion of foreign Christian communities, which responded by sending personnel and money to Hong Kong. Those churches which had a well-developed local leadership became the channel through which relief was administered, though financed by foreign contributions and organized with foreign administrators co-operating with the local church. Other groups which did not have an established local base found that the opportunities provided by a relief programme assisted them in establishing new religious communities. Sometimes, these new groups were recruited from refugees who had come from areas where churches of a particular denomination had been established on the mainland. The result within both the established churches and the more recently organized churches was a rapid increase in membership, so that the growth rate of the Hong Kong churches in the 1950s and into the 1960s was among the highest in the world.[2]

Apart from the obvious danger of attracting 'rice Christians' inherent in the programmes of relief conducted by churches and church agencies, the church offered security to people who were uprooted and faced with the necessity of restructuring their lives. It provided values to those whose traditional values had been rendered ineffective by changing political, social, and economic structures.

In the early years of Hong Kong's history as a colony and in more recent years the situation of Hong Kong as an easily accessible place of refuge has been a factor in the development of the Hong Kong Church.

Hong Kong as a Marginal Community

The low status of Hong Kong's original population in relation to the traditional structure of Chinese society has been noted. Some, serving the interests of foreign aggressors, had been traitors to their country; some, unsuccessful in achieving economic security in their home community, sought to make a quick fortune in the new economic structure of Hong Kong; others were of the criminal class. The first converts of the Protestant Church in its mission to the Chinese were often individuals of similar status. They belonged to a group of misfits who had been unable to establish or maintain their proper place in Chinese society: opium-smokers, unemployed and unsuccessful literary aspirants, and servants of the proscribed 'barbarians'. Some had been converted in overseas Chinese communities such as Singapore, Malacca, or Bangkok and were thus from the group of emigrants who defied Chinese law by living outside the Middle Kingdom. When the missionaries came to Hong Kong, they brought some of their converts with them as assistants and servants. These became the nucleus upon which the Hong Kong Church was built.

The Chinese convert found in Hong Kong an environment in which he could establish his identity in a way he could not have done were he in China proper. In Hong Kong, he was not under the same pressure to adjust to the demands of the traditional Chinese social structure. Once the convert had given up the observance of traditional Chinese rites associated with worship of ancestors, burial, marriage, and festivals, he did not fit into the social organization of his clan or village. He had become an outsider not participating in the rites which supported social cohesiveness and established personal identity. In a large urban centre like Hong Kong, however, he could participate in a new social organism, the Church. The supportive function of the Church is mentioned by the Revd A.B. Hutchinson in his annual letter of 1875 to the Church Missionary Society. He explains why his congregation, St. Stephen's, did not grow as fast as the other two Protestant Chinese congregations in Hong Kong, those of the Basel Missionary Society and the London Missionary Society. 'A large community amongst which are several wealthy members has a great attraction for the young convert, cut off from old friends and associations and needing to realize whatever support there may be for him in human brotherhood—thus many are led to cast in their lot with the older and larger body in preference to joining our church.'[3]

Unlike most of the other Chinese residents of Hong Kong in the early period, the Christian usually established a family and bought property. Thus, he became a founding ancestor. Following the traditional practice regarding founding ancestors, the Wong family of Fu Mun, Tung Koon District, Kwangtung, whose members have contributed both to the Hong Kong Church and to the diplomatic, judicial, and educational life of China, published a genealogy in 1954 which begins with the first Christian convert of the family. Property was left in trust by a descendant to finance semi-annual visits to the grave of his ancestor, the Revd Ho Fuk-tong, the first Chinese pastor to be ordained in Hong Kong. The creation of a genealogical branch or '*fong*' in a clan and the use of income from property in trust for visits to an ancestor's grave indicate the rise of a strong family unit.

One of the positive aspects of marginality was that it opened up new creative possibilities. One was released from the demand for strict conformity to a traditional social order. The marginal person was released to carve out a new way of life. In theory, the individual had great flexibility. On the one hand, if he valued the traditional structures from which he had been excluded, he could try to re-establish them in his new environment. On the other hand, he could try to move into the new patterns introduced by an alien culture. However, he was unlikely to find either alternative totally successful.

His experience in a marginal situation often made him an agent of change. When he returned to China, either from Hong Kong or overseas, he was different. His values had been affected by the need to adapt to a different cultural situation. He rebuilt his village house so that it would have more windows; he often promoted and financed schools and clinics for his village. In Hong Kong, as an instrument of social change, he promoted the introduction of Western-style medicine, journalism, and education for the Chinese. He also acquired a new concept of the role of women. The Revd Ho Fuk-tong was persuaded by a missionary to change his will and provide legacies for his married daughters. Chinese Christians, in their obituary notices and gravestone inscriptions, included the names of daughters and granddaughters long before non-Christian Chinese began doing so. Christian families no longer bound the feet of their daughters. They sent them to schools established by missionaries. Mature women were trained for a career as Bible women. The unmarried female missionary provided an image to some of the Chinese girls of the possibility of remaining single and pursuing an independent career. In the earliest period, this career was in teaching, nursing, or medicine. As early as 1879, graduates of the True Light Seminary were being trained as doctors at the Medical Missionary Hospital in Canton. Later, a separate medical school was organized for women. In Hong Kong, however, medical training was too closely linked with a male-dominated Government to accept female students. The missionary movement, in providing education, different images, and new roles for women, prepared the way for the emancipation of women in modern China. This was preceded, however, by the impact of the missionary educational programme for boys.

The introduction of Western education in the first half of the nineteenth century produced profound changes in the development of China in the last years of the Ch'ing dynasty. This education attracted those who were in a marginal situation. The earliest schools providing English-language education for Chinese were opened at Malacca, Singapore, and Macau. Some of these were later transferred to Hong Kong. Students were recruited among those too poor to pay for training in the traditional manner or among those whose parents realized the advantage of English as a means to advancement in areas where the foreigner had intruded. In these schools the student acquired the qualifications to serve as a bridge between two cultures. Dr Margaret M. Coughlin suggests, in her unpublished doctoral thesis, 'Strangers in the House: J. Lewis Shuck and Issachar Roberts, First American Baptist Missionaries to China', for the University of Virginia in 1972, that the Christian convert fulfilled a function similar to that of the compradore on the China coast and that an important contribution to the understanding of the modernization of China would be made by a study of this role of the Chinese Christian similar to that of Yen-p'ing Hao on the compradore in nineteenth-century China.[4]

In the early period of the China mission, the convert was often the Chinese of marginal status. In turn, once becoming a Christian, his new situation reinforced his marginality for he came under the influence of foreign ideas and institutions. Hong Kong provided a setting for the marginality to produce a new type of Chinese élite which contributed both to the development of Hong Kong as a colony and to the modernization of China and the changing of its traditional structures.

Christianity in a Colonial Setting and National Identity

The Chinese Church in Hong Kong tended to develop a colonial mentality. There was not a strong Confucian literary tradition in Hong Kong in the nineteenth century. The Hong Kong resident was seldom exposed to the representative of the classical Chinese tradition. In the latter part of the nineteenth century, some of the wealthy merchants purchased degrees, which entitled them to wear mandarin robes and display the usual symbols of literary achievement, but they were only playing a game. For the average resident of Hong Kong, his identity as a Chinese was not challenged in the way it would have been if he had been living in China.

Those among the Chinese population who intended to make Hong Kong their permanent residence—and the Christians were a disproportionate part of this group—realized that it was in their best interests to accept and take advantage of the colonial institutions and structures. This meant Westernization: use of the English language, a Western-style education, and accepting honours and titles in recognition of their contribution towards the implementation of the policies of the colonial Government.

In Hong Kong, the Government tended to regard Chinese who were Christians as a step above the rest of the Chinese population. This reinforced their marginality and made it easier for them to become Anglo-Chinese. An example of the special treatment of converts is reflected in the *Hong Kong Register*'s account of the public administration of a sentence of sixty strokes laid upon Julian Ahone, otherwise known as Wei On. He had been baptized in America and on his return to China became a member of the Baptist Church in Hong Kong. In the issue of 26 October 1843, the paper reported:

The culprit was paraded down the Queen's Road from prison to the place of punishment. He was dressed exactly as a European, white hat, jacket and trousers, but his tail being cut off, we suppose at the time of his conversion, he walked surrounded by police but not in bonds ... The usual 'man of rattan' did not officiate, but a European who did not strike him the blow half so severe as the usual rattaner would have done.

In this case two missionaries had appeared in court on his behalf. There are other instances of missionaries appearing to plead for a convert who had become involved in legal proceedings. Such intervention had its effects upon the judgments of the courts. Even after death, Chinese Christians were granted special privileges. Until the granting by the Government of a site for a Chinese Protestant Cemetery in 1858, the Chinese Christian was buried in the Colonial Cemetery, and even after the Chinese Protestants had their own place of burial, some of the more wealthy members of the Chinese Church were permitted to be buried in the Colonial Cemetery. These examples show how Hong Kong provided a setting in which the Christian could find a new identity *vis-à-vis* his identity in terms of Chinese nationalism, and it continued to do so in other subtle ways.

Within China, the Christian was under open attack with the rise of the Chinese nationalist movement in the 1920s. This movement produced anti-Western and anti-religious criticism of foreign influence upon China. The Hong Kong Christian experienced these attacks only in a secondary way, if at all. By this time, most of the Christians in Hong Kong, particularly the decision-makers in the Church, had accepted the Government's conception of their role in the British Empire.

The policy of the Government regarding the Chinese population is set forth in a speech that Governor John Pope Hennessy gave at the Prize Day of Central School (now Queen's College) in 1880.

It is my wish—it has been the ambition of nearly every man who preceded me in the Government of this Colony, and it has been the policy of all Secretaries of the State, who have written to my predecessors and myself—that Hongkong should be made an Anglo-Chinese Colony, where Her Majesty should have thousands upon thousands of Chinese subjects, with a thorough knowledge of the English language—amenable to English law and appreciating the British Constitution, loyal to their Queen, and a strength to this distant part of Her Majesty's Empire. Our education scheme will accomplish a practical result if it assists in achieving this. An Anglo-Chinese Colony, such as I have over and over again expressed my wish to see here, must spring from the children in the Colony.

That the influential section of the Chinese population had accepted their role as defined by the Governor is evident in his further remarks:

Last year there came a deputation of Chinese merchants and shop-keepers. Some of them said, 'We have children and grandchildren born in this Colony, and we ourselves desire to become naturalized. We desire to see the property we hold transmitted to our children as from British subjects to British subjects.'... They also told me they desired to keep their children here, with all their future interests wrapped up in Hong-kong as their permanent home, their real country and last resting place.[5]

In a 1925 report of the baptism of a student of St. Stephen's Girls' College, Hong Kong, both denationalization and a commitment to serve China are reflected. Her teacher stated:

She asked for the baptismal name Victoria ... She has discovered that the great English queen determined, while still a girl, to do her utmost to lead her people in the right direction, and to be worthy of her great responsibility as a Christian queen. It is this example which has fired the Chinese girl, as she sets out upon the Christian life, to be a Christian leader—to serve her people and to help them forward and upward toward God and toward a new and better China. Where has she learned this ideal? From one of the English missionaries who had looked across the sea to 'a great nation in great need' and determined to go and help to meet the need.[6]

The question arises whether the image of the British queen she had acquired in Hong Kong would have been an impediment to the realization of her hope 'to serve her people and to help them ... toward a new and better China'.

As a result of the anti-religious movement of 1922 in China, there was an organized movement for the 'Recovery of the Rights of Education'. The movement sought to bring all education under government regulations. It required registration of schools and, in 1925, the Private School Regulations of the Ministry of Education required half of the board of directors and the head of the school to be Chinese. This posed a problem for those Christian institutions which had not yet developed Chinese leadership or handed over management to local control. The Church in Hong Kong did not have to face this problem as there had been a long and close association between the Government and the Church. As early as 1845, the Revd Charles Gutzlaff, at the time part-time missionary and Chinese Secretary to the Governor in his capacity as Superintendent of Trade in China, recommended that the Hong Kong Government should grant a subsidy to the Chinese schools on Hong Kong Island. A committee of three was named with the Colonial Chaplain as chairman to administer and supervise the grant. Later, when a Bishop was appointed for Hong Kong, he replaced the Colonial Chaplain as chairman. The committee, dominated as it was by religious interests, favoured the appointment of Christian teachers. Some of the incumbent teachers were baptized and in other cases Christian converts replaced what were considered unsatisfactory non-Christian teachers. Within a few years all the subsidized schools had Christian teachers. From 1856 to 1860, the Revd William Lobscheid, a missionary of the Chinese Evangelization Society, was Inspector of Schools. Another former missionary, the Revd E.J. Eitel, was Inspector of Education from 1879 to 1897. Sir John Bowring, a Unitarian, was an advocate of secular education, but this policy could not be implemented until the retirement of Bishop Smith in 1864. A great deal of the burden of educating Chinese in Hong Kong was assumed by the Church. Its contribution was recognized and brought into direct government relationship by the grant-in-aid scheme in 1873. Until the present day, the Church has been an ally of the Government in its educational policies and programmes.

It is to be expected that the Government would wish its educational system to prepare students to fit into and support the given structures of Hong Kong as a colony. The result is a blunting of national consciousness. How relevant for Hong Kong today are the remarks of Bertrand Russell made in *The Problem of China*, published in 1922. 'Education in mission schools ... tends to become denationalized, and have a slavish attitude toward foreign civilization ... and of course their whole influence, unavoidably if involuntarily, militates against national self-respect in those whom they teach.'

The Church's Identification with the Objectives of the Government

The relationship between the Church in a colony and denationalization, particularly as it relates to education, has been discussed. This section will further develop the role of the Church and its members in their relation to a colonial government.

The nineteenth-century British Christian, considering his country's ever-expanding colonial empire, was impressed with the obligation this entailed for missionary endeavour. The Revd George Smith, the first Bishop of Hong Kong, expressed this in a report of a visit to China in the 1840s. Speaking of Hong Kong, he stated:

While contemplating this rapidly formed colony, the circumstances under which it has been gained, and its probable influence on the future destinies of a race amounting to one third of the estimated population of our planet, many novel considerations obtrude themselves on the mind of a British Christian. Believing that his country has been honoured by God as the chosen instrument of diffusing the pure light of Protestant Christianity through the world, and that the permanency of her laws, institutions, and empire is closely connected with the diffusion of evangelical truth, a British Missionary feels jealous for the faithfulness of his country to her high vocation, and 'rejoices with trembling' at the extension of her colonial empire.[7]

But in fact, when Smith viewed more closely the actual conditions in Hong Kong, he concluded that the British administration and the presence of a foreign population were hindrances to the missionary cause. He cites particularly:

the frequent spectacle of European irreligion, and the invidious regulations of police ... It is with unfeigned regret and reluctance that the author states, that scenes frequently occur in the public streets, and in the interior of houses, which are calculated to place the countrymen of the Missionaries in an unfavourable aspect before the native mind ... The Chinese also are treated as a degraded race of people. They are not permitted to go out into the public streets after a certain hour in the evening, without a lantern and a written note from their European employer, to secure them from the danger of apprehension and imprisonment till the morning.[8]

There was a serious gap between the ideology which viewed the empire of a Christian nation as a divinely given opportunity for evangelization and the sober reality of actual conditions created by the imposition and exercise of a colonial administration.

The Revd George Smith was describing Hong Kong a few years after the British occupation. With the passing of years, attitudes and conditions changed. The missionary continued to be grateful for certain advantages the colonial status of Hong Kong provided for the missionary enterprise. In time, however, a new relationship was established between the Government and the Chinese population. In this change, the Chinese Christian played a significant role.

The Church provided an English-educated élite through which the Government could relate to the general Chinese population. Sometimes with government approval and sometimes without it, the Chinese community developed institutions to manage its internal affairs and its relations with the Ch'ing Government of China. This was done through quasi-governmental structures such as the Man-Mo Temple Committee, the Kai Fong organization, and the management committees of the Tung Wah Hospital and the Po Leung Kuk. A dual administrative structure appeared to be emerging, the official one controlling the European population and its contacts with the Chinese and unofficial organizations through which the Chinese managed their own affairs. To counteract this, the Government created official structures for Chinese representation and advice. English-speaking Chinese were admitted to the roll of jurors. The first juror was Wong Shing in 1858. He was a deacon of the Chinese congregation of the London Missionary Society. Chinese were appointed to the Legislative Council. The first was Ng Choy, otherwise known as Wu Ting-fang, in 1880. He had been baptized as a student at St. Paul's College. The second appointment of a Chinese was Wong Shing in 1884. The third was Ho Kai in 1890. Sir Ho Kai was the son of the Revd Ho Fuk-tong. The Government also named Chinese as Justices of the Peace. It reconstituted the District Watch Committee (Kai Fong), and appointed Chinese to the Sanitary Board (the predecessor of the Urban Council). In all of these there were a more than proportionate number of Christians or of those who had come under the influence of the missionary endeavour and were sympathetic to it. These structures, through which the Government could better relate to the Chinese community, have been continued to the present day.

The Government realized the important role that the English-speaking product of mission education could play in its effort to bridge the gap between an expatriate-dominated administration and the local resident. The Chinese Christian accepted this role and became a part of the colonial establishment. Perhaps following the pattern set forth by Max Weber in *The Protestant Ethic and the Spirit of Capitalism* and R.H. Tawney in *Religion and the Rise of Capitalism*, a portion of the Christian community had become wealthy, thus further qualifying them for élite leadership. Their wealth and their prominence in the community made them important figures in the Church. They served on church councils and were on the boards of church institutions. When members of the Church have both an economic and status stake in the established order, this tends to blunt the prophetic role of the Church and may be an impediment to the Church acting as an agent for social change.

Thinking of the future of Hong Kong as it is envisaged in the Sino-British Joint Declaration, I would pose the following questions. Will the Church have the motivation to participate in the social changes of the future? Has its prophetic and creative role been seriously blunted by its close association with the policy of a colonial government? How much are the decisions of the churches determined by the interests of the decision-makers in the status quo? Is the Church overconcerned with the value of individual liberty, especially if the exercise of this liberty benefits the privileged section of the community to the detriment of a whole-hearted endorsement of efforts to change the conditions of the deprived section of the community? Traditionally, Western Christianity has thought of its responsibility to the poor and exploited in terms of charity and benevolence. Both within the Christian faith and within the ideology of the People's Republic of China there is the possibility of a different relationship.

10 The Early Hong Kong Church and Traditional Chinese Ideas

THE place of the family in the development of the Hong Kong Protestant Church must be seen in relation to the traditional Chinese family structure. In what ways did Christian faith and the standards required of converts by missionaries conflict with the traditional structure of Chinese family life? Could the integrating factors of the old system be preserved within a different ideology? Have the adjustments and adaptations that have been made been consistent with the theological implications of Christian faith to family life?

It is obvious that prevailing social patterns constitute a significant element in the adaptation of the Church to a new situation when it is establishing itself in an area and culture where it has not previously existed. Certain structures and their ideological base may promote or retard church growth and determine the quality of Christian life established. When the Church established itself in China, it had to come to terms with a central unifying value of Chinese society, the concept of filial piety as expressed in the worship of ancestors within the context of the basic social organization of Chinese society, the clan. Certain implications of the Christian's new faith produced changes in practices and values related to filial piety, the clan, and family patterns.

Filial piety is so important because fatherhood and the production of sons are essential for the continuity of the family and as a link between past and present. It is associated with respect for age, and thus looks backward to the preceding generations, the ancestors. It emphasizes the duty to produce descendants and thus looks to the future. The ancestors and descendants must be bound in an unbreakable biological chain. The genealogical expression of this chain is the clan, and the basic structure of traditional Chinese society is the large family within a clan organization.

One of the most interesting aspects of the relationship between Chinese social organization and Chinese ideology is the concrete character of the ideological base. The clan is a visible entity, it is rooted in history, and certain objects represent this history, such as ancestral tablets, a clan temple, ancestral graves, and a clan genealogy. The value system is permanently recorded in clan rules.[1] These tangible entities embody transcendent values. The individual, whatever his hierarchical rank, finds his identity both as a recipient of the blessings of the ancestor and as a contributor to the biological continuity of the family in the future, and with the destiny of heaven on his side, he will enhance the family prestige and honour.

The system provided the individual with a sense of identity and a system of values. He was a part of the greater whole that had a concrete historical identity. He was surrounded by a ready-made set of values which provided meaning and purpose, as well as a given structural form to life.

There were always in China, however, those who for one reason or another did not participate fully in the system. They constituted a restless substratum beneath the stability of the given order. The early Christian convert was often a member of this substratum. In the first decades of the Chinese Protestant Mission, its work was located not in China proper, but among the overseas Chinese population in Singapore, Penang, Malacca, Bangkok, and Batavia. The very fact of their overseas residence removed these Chinese from the structures we have been examining. They had committed the unfilial act of 'deserting the graves of their ancestors'. Their marginal sociological, psychological, and geographical situation made them amenable to a transfer to another value system and to adjustment to a different social organization, that provided by the Christian Church. Once they had made the change, they were removed from those structures which provided identity and value to a Chinese.

In an earlier period, the Jesuits had attempted to hold Christian commitment and the place of ancestors together. It was a bold, well-intentioned attempt at indigenous adaptation and was realistic in its awareness of the importance of the ancestral cult for the Chinese. But the question is whether the transcendent aspect of the ancestral cult could have been transferred to the transcendent ideological symbols of Christian faith, particularly those of God and the communion of saints.

The nineteenth-century Protestant missionary usually demanded a clear break by the convert. He was not to participate in the 'heathenish-idolatrous' ceremonies associated with marriage, burial, or 'sweeping the graves'. This meant that the convert could not be a contributing member of the supportive rituals of village life. The rituals reinforced the given social and ideological structure of the village and clan. This exclusion from customary community ritual forced the convert to become involved in new structures. It was here that some of the tensions and problems lay for the missionary, the convert, and the new Christian community.

The supportive character of a missionary and/or a Chinese congregation could soften the trauma of a break with an inherited sociological structure which embodied meaning and identity. Adaptation of certain traditional Chinese methods of reinforcing a strong family sense in terms of relation to ancestors could be employed by Christians. There are examples of such adaptation among well-established Hong Kong Christian families. The Wong family, originating from Fu Mun in the Tung Koon District of Kwangtung, published a genealogy that begins with the first Christian convert as the founding ancestor, though mention is made of the line of descent from an earlier ancestor probably taken over from their traditional clan genealogy.

Another feature of Chinese family life that shaped its structure was concubinage. The practice was closely related to the necessity of maintaining family biological continuity. Its ostensible purpose was to provide male descendants when the first wife did not do so. It was also a status symbol fitting into the cycle of the more virtuous, the more prosperous, the more wealthy, the more sons and descendants. Concubinage ensured that a wealthy family would not lack descendants. Of course, behind the customs was also a pandering to the male sexual appetite. The monogamous tradition of the Church conflicted with this Chinese practice.

The custom was particularly prevalent among the well-to-do. This conflict between Chinese and Christian attitudes towards plural marriage may be an element in the failure of the Church to attract the wealthy. This relation between wealth and the custom of concubinage as it affected the Hong Kong Christian Church is illustrated by an aspect of the first work of the Anglican Church among the Chinese.

Initially, the Anglican Church in Hong Kong directed its missionary thrust towards education, most notably St. Paul's College. Here were educated and converted a number of boys of humble origin. Their English-language ability enabled them to rise to positions of importance and acquire wealth at a relatively young age. In a number of cases, when they began to be prosperous, they took on additional wives. They were excluded from the Church, or their Christian connections grew increasingly tenuous. Examples are Wu Ting-fang, twice Chinese Ambassador to the United States, Chan Oi-ting, first Chinese Consul-General at Havana, and Sun Yat-sen.

The record book of the London Missionary Society congregation in Hong Kong contains a number of entries of disciplinary action because of concubinage. A deacon was admonished because he consented to his daughter being taken as a secondary wife of one of the nominal Christian old boys of St. Paul's College. At times, a married convert would be accepted in Hong Kong, and only later would it be revealed that he had another wife in his village. There were instances in which men with several wives were received into the church. In one case, the member made special financial provision for his secondary wife, on the understanding that she would not be a part of the household, nor would he have further conjugal relations with her. My impression is that the policy of some of the churches eased regarding concubinage in the early decades of this century, though I have not precisely documented this assumption.

Another model for the traditional Chinese family was a large family house. Its existence depended on financial ability as well as a will to maintain harmonious relations. The Government of Hong Kong was always hopeful that the responsible elements of the Chinese community would establish family houses as some of the Chinese community had done in Malacca. The congested conditions of the Chinese sections of Hong Kong were not conducive to the type of large family house which could contain a number of apartments for nuclear family units of uncles, brothers, and cousins.

Most of the better-off Chinese in Hong Kong maintained their family house in their home village, having a smaller establishment in Hong Kong with a secondary wife. The Christians who were able to become financially secure occupied larger premises near the European section of the city. A deacon of the London Missionary Society congregation, a man of some property, left each of his sons a piece of Hong Kong real estate in his will, but stipulated that each should contribute to the expenses of their common family house in which they and their families were expected to live with their widowed mother.

In some cases, the household of the Christian family was opened to more distant relatives from the country. An interesting example of a large household was that of Mrs Ko, as she is designated in Chinese church records, or Mrs Caldwell, as she was known by the English community. She was the Chinese wife of Daniel Richard Caldwell. He began his career in Hong Kong as a translator and rose to the position of Registrar-General or 'Protector of the Chinese'. He was a colourful and controversial figure. This was in part due to his close connection with certain members of the Chinese community. About 1845, he went through a traditional Chinese marriage ceremony with his wife, Chan Ayow. In 1850, she was converted and became a member of the London Missionary Society congregation. In March 1851, a Christian marriage service was performed in St. John's Cathedral. The children born before the Christian ceremony were baptized shortly afterwards. The Caldwell children were members of the Anglican Church and grew up as part of the English community. As they grew older, Mrs Caldwell received into her household an assorted collection of Chinese, most of whom, if not all, were baptized and became members of her church, the London mission congregation. The unmarried were subsequently matched off, presumably by Mrs Caldwell. The church register lists some twenty-four persons connected with the Caldwell household, including a table boy, a number of girl servants, a relative, several blind people and 'the tall woman'.

Of special interest is an orphan she raised who, at his baptism in 1872, was table boy. He was married to one of the servant girls. He became the progenitor of a large family, many of whose members are still prominent in the life of the Hong Kong Church. After the death of his first wife, the former table boy married the daughter of a wealthy and socially prominent doctor, also a member of the London mission congregation. This second marriage illustrates the opportunities for social mobility provided by the Christian community.

For several years, Mrs Caldwell employed a young man from Fatshan, Kwangtung, to act as a private chaplain for the household. She remained a faithful member of the Chinese Church and was a generous contributor to the building of To Tsai Church, which occupied the site of the old Caldwell residence on Hollywood Road. A picture and plaque in her memory are located in a prominent place in the present Hop Yat Church, the successor of the To Tsai congregation.

In the period in which she lived, Mrs Caldwell would not have
fitted well into a European congregation, particularly as her husband was a civil servant. His marriage to a Chinese was not looked
on with favour by many of his colleagues, especially those who
believed and circulated a slanderous rumour regarding the social
background of his wife. This rumour was not substantiated by an
official inquiry regarding possible connections of Mr Caldwell with
criminal elements in the Chinese community.

Living in an urban centre, the Hong Kong Christian family was
often quite mobile. The standard pattern for the ordinary rural
Chinese was to function as one link in a centuries-old tradition of
cultivating the family fields. Disturbed political and economic conditions or an excess of population in a particular village upset this
pattern and encouraged removal to urban centres or emigration
overseas. We have already noted that the first Protestant work
among the Chinese took place in overseas communities. Hong
Kong itself was a nearby urban centre to the Kwangtung delta and
overseas in the political sense of not being under Chinese jurisdiction. This resulted in the movement of Hong Kong Christians between the urban centres of Hong Kong and Canton, or a return to
their home village, or possibly emigration, especially to the places
most frequently mentioned in the church records, namely Annam,
Singapore, Australia, California, Hawaii, British Guiana, and
North Borneo.

As certain of the Christian families, or those with Christian
backgrounds or connections, became more prominent and
assumed leadership in the political and economic life of China,
there was a tendency for the well-established Hong Kong-based
families to disperse. They moved back to China, but in times of
political change, Hong Kong or America became places of refuge.

Another aspect of this dispersal and mobility is the strong connection between the Hong Kong Christian community and overseas communities, particularly those in Australia and the United
States. Various factors in overseas residence were conducive to
acceptance of the Christian faith. Among these were the interest
that was shown by the host community 'to the heathen in our
midst' and the opportunity presented to 'a Christian land' to reach
non-Christians with the gospel; the desire of the immigrant to
learn English and the Chinese Sunday School movement, which
provided 'the bait of English while fishing for souls', an expression
used at times by promoters of the movement; the supportive

strength of a close community of Chinese converts for an immigrant experiencing personal loneliness and cultural isolation; and a natural desire to conform to the expectation of the larger community. These and other factors, not to mention the working of the Holy Spirit, contributed to the susceptibility of the immigrant to conversion. Once converted, taught the Christian moral values, and introduced to non-Chinese patterns of behaviour and thought, he sometimes found, on his return to his home village in China, that it was difficult to adjust to what had been natural before his emigration. Thus, he often found Hong Kong a more acceptable place of residence. It was Chinese enough for him to feel as though he had returned home, but also a place where he was not expected to conform to all the old patterns, with some of which he found himself out of sympathy.

Notable among these returned overseas Chinese converts were the several members of the Kwok, Ma, To, and Choy families of the Sincere, Wing On, and Sun companies. They returned not only with the Christian faith, but with new merchandising principles and business methods which were both popular and financially rewarding.

I have mentioned that those who left the ancestral village were regarded as 'deserting the graves of the ancestors'. Hence, they were regarded as unfilial. Certain graves of the clan, such as the original founding ancestor and other distinguished or wealthy members, particularly heads of separate branches (*fong*) of the clan, were regularly visited. Funeral customs and graves were a village concern. Overseas Chinese usually tried to arrange to ship back to the home villages bodies of their compatriots who died. The Christian who had been cut off from the clan structure was still desirous of a proper burial. It soon became apparent that provisions should be made for a burial place in Hong Kong. Sites for the burial of Christians might still be bought near home villages if the family had sufficient funds and could find someone who would sell to them, or perhaps they still retained property suitable for burial near the home village, but as increasingly Hong Kong Christians considered Hong Kong their permanent home and ties with the home village diminished, the Christian found it more convenient and appropriate to be buried in Hong Kong.

At first, Chinese Christians were buried in the Colonial Cemetery at Happy Valley, but in 1858, representatives of the London Missionary Society, the Church Missionary Society, and the Basel

Evangelical Missionary Society were granted a site in what is now Western District by the Government. With the expansion of the town in this direction, it became necessary to move to another location, and the original plot was exchanged for the present one at Pok Fu Lam Road.

It is an interesting feature in the development of church life in Hong Kong that the cemetery has been an important factor bringing the Church together in a common concern. It has helped to finance certain joint projects of the Chinese churches. The Chinese Christian Churches Union, which manages the Hong Kong and Kowloon cemeteries, is a significant feature of Protestant church life, uniting in a common purpose groups that otherwise might have no integral relation to one another. In like manner, in traditional China, the maintenance of graves of certain important members of a clan served to unite its members in a common interest, who otherwise, in time, might have little in common other than the tradition of a common biological origin.

In the case of some wealthy or prominent individuals, one will find at the Pok Fu Lam Cemetery a large impressive stone marking the grave, and on the same lot in subsidiary position the graves of sons, daughters-in-law, grandchildren, and sometimes daughters and sons-in-law. Such an arrangement reinforces consciousness of family solidarity.

My examination of Chinese wills written in Hong Kong indicates that it was traditional to regard prosperity as the favour of the ancestors and to exhort the testator's survivors to maintain harmony and to practise economy and diligence to ensure the future good fortune of the family. In the case of two Christian wills, those of a father and a son, these values relating to the family are transferred to God. A deacon of the London Missionary Society congregation, writing his will in 1869, stated, 'I have to thank God the Father for enabling me to possess certain houses and land at Hong Kong'. His son, dying as a young man in 1873, entrusted his property, his wife, and two small children to the care of his elder brother. In doing so, he stated that 'being of the same parents (life breath), I need not make too many orders, but I pray ten thousand times that God, the Heavenly Father, will bless our whole family, this is ordered what my heart sincerely wishes'. In the son's will, there is reflected much of the awareness of traditional Chinese family unity, but with the introduction of an appeal to God for continued blessing rather than the traditional virtues of economy and diligence as the means to ensure continued family prosperity.

These examples illustrate a significant transfer of values from family biological continuity to a transcendent reality not as immediately tied to the material and tangible.

The most significant factor affecting Christian family life was the break with the traditional ancestral cult. The cult was the ritual expression of identity as a part of a large family or clan. The clan was the basic social organization of Confucian China, and biological continuity was essential for the clan. Values, life-meaning, and personal identity were resident within the biologically- and historically-based family-clan structure. This tended to tie transcendent values to a concrete continuum.

In Christianity, family continuity does not bear transcendent values. These values are transferred from the biological family to the communion of saints. This communion is spiritually based in that it is centred on man as a child of God, rather than as a child of an immediate or ancestral father. The basic value is not found in a continuing biological line, but in a relationship to a spiritual reality, God the Father. Fatherhood is spiritual. Filial piety for a Chinese Christian is lifted to a different realm. In both Christian and non-Christian attitudes, the piety has transcendent dimensions. In Confucian piety, this dimension is focused on concrete historical personages. In Christian piety, it is focused on a God who is both in and outside history.

The Christian belief in the community of saints provides a theological base for the equality of sexes which theoretically should liberate women from their historically subordinate position. The Chinese sensed that the attitudes maintained by the foreigner regarding the relationship between the sexes would, if introduced among the Chinese, break down old-established practices and change traditional structures. Medhurst, a missionary of the London Missionary Society in Batavia in the 1830s, summarized an anti-Christian tract in which the author charged that the missionary was deficient in four out of the five cardinal virtues, saying that 'It was monstrous in barbarians to attempt to improve the inhabitants of the celestial empire, when they are so miserably deficient themselves ... allowing men and women to mix in society, and walk arm in arm through the streets, they shewed that they had not the least sense of propriety.'[2]

The same fear, but with an added sexual element, was expressed in the anti-Christian feelings during the 'genii powder' hysteria of the early 1870s, which originated in Nam Hoi, Kwangtung, and spread northwards. One of the placards posted at Fatshan, Kwangtung, embodied some of the fears felt concerning breaches of propriety in the relation between the sexes:

Barbarians erected churches and chapels to incite women and girls to become converts and to have lewd intercourse with them. Women and girls originally knew the rules of propriety, and when they saw that the barbarians were detestable from their features and their differences of race, how was it possible that they should become converts and associate with them? They used money to bribe people to go in disguise of Tao priests, or to get old procuresses, to mix themselves among villagers, to falsely proclaim an epidemic at hand and distribute 'San Sin Fan' (Genii Powder).[3]

The powder, when mixed with rice flour to make dumplings, caused those who ate the dumplings to become ill; in women their stomachs swelled and in men it was their feet. Then the missionaries appeared offering a cure, but with the primary intent thus to gain converts, 'only to cause women and girls, when once converts, to let barbarians have free sexual intercourse with them.'[4] These quotations indicate that the Chinese critics of the missionary movement were aware of the changes that would be produced in the relationship between the sexes, and particularly in the role of women.

In traditional China, a woman was supposed to assume a submissive role, as a daughter, wife, daughter-in-law, and even as widowed mother. Normally, her status increased with age. Within these limits, there were many levels in the family hierarchy. At the bottom was perhaps the purchased female servant (or slave). A concubine was considered subordinate to the first wife.

A young woman lost her original identity upon marriage. She was expected to be a full part of her husband's family. Often her lot was not easy. Her husband might be dominated by his mother. The mother might be jealous of the daughter-in-law, and remembering the difficulty she had as a young bride under the surveillance of her own mother-in-law, might now find satisfaction in making the life of her daughter-in-law as difficult as possible. If, in time, the husband took a secondary wife or wives, the female portion of the household could become a hotbed of jealousy and strife. The situation was aggravated in that there were few or no external outlets to serve as an escape valve for the frustrations and restrictions experienced.

Against this background the increasing liberation experienced by girls in Christian families should be considered. If born into a Christian family, they would not have to undergo the binding of their feet and the resulting limitation on their physical mobility. If they were of a family of financial means, their big feet would in itself put them into a special group.

The Chinese female was not expected to attend public meetings. The church, of course, encouraged the attendance of women at public worship, or rather, one might say, the missionaries urged it, for it is not certain that husbands and fathers were always eager for the women of the family to attend worship. They may still have been influenced by the traditional attitude that it was not proper for a woman to go out into a public place, even if it was a church gathering. This separation of the sexes extended, of course, to the seating arrangement in the church. When the London Missionary Society congregation instituted the practice of a monthly 'tea-meeting', women did not attend, though an annual tea-meeting was held for them.

Attendance of women at a church service could be a nuisance. There is a delightful account given by the first female agent of the London Missionary Society to work in Hong Kong of services in the Chinese congregation on Sunday afternoons at Union Church. The report was written in 1891 and relates other aspects of her work among women.

In the Spring of 1877, I was appointed to work among women and girls in Hongkong, with instructions to do what seemed best for the improvement of the Female members of the Church and evangelization of surrounding masses. At the first meeting with the deacons, I sensed the sense of the meeting, that old women, wives and mothers of the church members, were to be accepted as they were, and left undisturbed in their ways.

Many of the men were married to heathen women, and even among the deacons there were several whose homes were ruled and influenced by idolatrous mothers. All told [there were] about fifty-five women [in the] church membership, but of these about half were very lax in observance of religious duties. Excuses were: some too old and feeble, others too young to traverse streets, all had household cares, and many declared it was too expensive to have their heads dressed and chairs engaged to take them to the service in a manner suitable to their position. Few could read, and of the rest, a large number fell back on the Chinese notion of the stupidity of the feminine mind, and asserted that consequently they could not understand Sermon, Scripture lesson, or Psalmody, and it was a waste of time, and wear and tear of garments to go to church regularly. When they did go, they made it a social function; babies were brought, and old women to nurse them, little children and girls to play with them, other children because they could not be left at home, and even the family dogs to please the little folks. Baskets and bundles, of course, accompanied them, and a kind of subdued picnic went on all over the women's side of the beautiful Union Church. Children and dogs played about the aisles, babies were handed from one to the other, and carried in and out screaming, while the mothers compared notes of admiration and whispered with their gossips, and the bigger girls looked about them and giggled at their friends in neighbouring pews. The missionary voice rose higher and higher above the occasional tumult, and the men on their side, sat stolidly indifferent to the behaviour of their female relatives. Babies and noise were accepted as necessary evils, the women could not come and leave them at home. Anything like control or compulsory reverence in the House of God was beyond the power of man. Any interference with the views of the 'Sisters' or their privileges would cause them 'to lose face'.

The singing was dreadful. An acquaintance who lived on the same Street, told me he was obliged to change his lodging, because our vocalization utterly destroyed the rest and calm of the Sabbath Day. Everyone who could read the characters felt it was his and her duty to shout them aloud, as if like the priests of Baal, they thought God was sleeping and 'must be awaked'.

Now in 1891 ... Bible women work from house to house, reading Scripture in the colloquial, explaining them and exhorting ... Two evenings a week there are special meetings for women. One on Sunday mornings in Wantsai Chapel has gradually become a mixed assembly of men, women and girls. At the Chinese Chapel Sunday afternoon service, the women's side is fairly well filled with an orderly, attentive, interested congregation. Children of all ages are still brought, but the art of keeping them in order has been learned. Many of the young women and all the elder girls can read their Bibles. The habits and attitudes of respect learned in schools have proved useful in revolutionizing the attitude of the youthful members of the audience.[5]

Miss Rowe's report documents changes effected in behaviour, attitudes, and education of women within a Christian congregation. They increasingly acquired a different understanding of their position and capabilities.

An interesting example of the influence of missionary attitudes on inheritance patterns as they affected females in the family is provided by the example of the family of the Revd Ho Fuk-tong.

In his will, he left the management of his considerable estate to his widow. The Revd John Chalmers states that he had some difficulty in finally convincing the widow that she ought to break with traditional Chinese custom and leave an outright bequest to her daughters as well as her sons. It is probably the share of one of the daughters, Ho Mui-ling, which enabled her husband, Ng Choy, better known as Wu Ting-fang, to study for the bar in England. Further evidence of a more inclusive view of female members of the family is the early appearance of the names of daughters and granddaughters on the gravestones of Christians. It was common practice among all Chinese to record names of sons and grandsons, but not daughters.

The Church was a pioneer in the education of females. In the early period, the missionary wife would sometimes care for orphans or unwanted girls, and at a proper age form them into a small class. Otherwise, it was difficult to induce parents to send their girls to school as they could be more useful at home caring for the younger children or performing household tasks. When one of the first agents of the Church Missionary Society opened a girls' school in Hong Kong, he offered the inducement of a subsidy, though the experiment was soon abandoned.

The first school for girls supported by the Government was organized at Stanley and was taught by a convert of the Anglican Church. It was so successful that the leaders of the Chinese community in Hong Kong requested that the teacher be transferred and placed in charge of a similar school to be opened there.

An interesting project was organized by the wife of the first Bishop of Victoria, Mrs Smith. She enlisted the aid of interested women in the education of Chinese girls of the better class. They formed a committee and appealed to the Society for the Promotion of Female Education in the East to send teachers out from England. The new school was called the Diocesan Female Training Institute, and the girls were given instruction in English. This, however, was found to be a mistake, as it made the young girls too attractive to that section of the male European community who were looking for local household companions with whom they could communicate in English. After several of the students had entered into such irregular positions, the language of instruction was largely confined to Chinese.

One of the purposes of the Diocesan Female Training Institute was to train teachers and provide suitably educated marriage partners for the young male converts of St. Paul's College. This purpose was fulfilled by a number of pupils of the Institute.

In response to the appeal from Hong Kong to the Society for the Promotion of Female Education in the East, several unmarried women came from England. Among the first, arriving in 1860 and 1861, were the Misses Baxter, Magrath, and Eaton. They opened and conducted schools, male and female, boarding and day, for Europeans, Chinese, and children of mixed race. The energetic and devoted service of Miss Sophia Harriet Baxter attracted particular notice and has had a lasting influence, particularly in the schools which have been under the patronage of the Anglican Church.

These women were the forerunners of the unmarried female worker, though Gutzlaff had persuaded some unmarried women to come to Hong Kong in about 1850 for the purpose of missionary work among the Chinese. It was charged that he had misled them in portraying the prospects in much too optimistic a vein. The ladies were disillusioned and their missionary service was brief. Following the example of the Society for the Promotion of Female Education in the East, the mission boards increasingly sent out single female workers. They devoted themselves largely to education or house visiting, though some female doctors were also sent. Their presence was important, as they provided a model for a positive female vocation other than that of wife and mother. They inspired some of the girls who came under their influence to resist the pressure to marry, but instead to remain single and pursue a career in education, medicine, or church work. The churches also opened up positions as a means for young widows to achieve financial independence.

In some fashion the nineteenth-century improvement in the status of women in the Christian community in China laid the foundation for demands for women's suffrage, appointment to government office, and the broadening of job opportunities made in the early 1920s at the time of the establishment of the Canton-based southern constitutionist Government. The leaders in the effort for women's rights were largely young returned overseas students. Many had received their earlier education in the Christian schools in southern China, and were thus already conditioned to think in terms of greater freedom for themselves as girls and women. Their hopes were reinforced by their overseas experience as students.

There is a theological foundation for the liberation of women and equality between the sexes. In God's sight there is no distinction of ethnic origin, social status, or sex; though this implication of equality has seldom been realized fully in the Church at large, the concept of equality did support movements towards improving the role and status of women in the Chinese Christian community. In the community created by clan solidarity, there is a well-defined hierarchy on the basis of age, generation, sex, and social status. If the equality of the saints includes equality of male and female in their fellowship with God and each other, it should logically provide an impetus to the liberation of women from a subordinate position within earthly society.

Epilogue

THIS volume has discussed various aspects of the Protestant Church in Hong Kong in the nineteenth century. The developments since then and a look at the future can only be briefly suggested.

Before the Second World War, Pentecostal and Holiness groups had long been established in Hong Kong. Missionaries were sent out by other fundamentalist and faith groups, mostly American. There were also several congregations unrelated to any missionary body.

After the establishment of the People's Republic of China, some of the main-line denominations that had not previously had congregations in Hong Kong, such as the Lutherans and the American Methodists, organized congregations. The great influx of refugees in the 1950s directed world-wide attention to the needs of these people. During this period, the sectarian-fundamentalist presence was strengthened. The longer-established main-line denominations were independent of foreign control but were dependent on foreign funds for educational and relief work and the financing of major building projects. The land boom of the late 1970s freed main-line groups from a need for foreign funds to support their large programmes. The Church as a whole has reached maturity, though in some groups there is still a relatively strong missionary presence.

The fact that Hong Kong was a British colony resulted in its own particular characteristics which distinguished it from cities in China, though there was always a reciprocal influence between them. What is true of the colony is also true of the Churches.

The relationship between the Churches in Hong Kong and on the mainland was altered after the establishment of the People's Republic, and during the cultural revolution of the 1960s the contact between the two was virtually broken. In recent years, contacts have been re-established. There has been increasing interchange, though neither the Church in China nor the ecumenical Churches in Hong Kong wish to return to pre-liberation patterns.

The Protestant Church in China operates within the context of the national policies of the People's Republic. It is still exploring the best methods to participate in China's reconstruction and to assume its proper role in a new social order.

There have been some misgivings about the possible position of the Hong Kong Church in the period after 1997, but many of these doubts have been assuaged by the terms of the Joint Declaration of 1984, which ensures the Church its freedom of operation. The details will have to be worked out within the context of a developing situation.

The histories of the Church in China and of the Church in Hong Kong have been different. This difference has influenced attitudes and policies. In the future, there should be a sharing of the uniqueness of each group, a searching for the most effective way for the Church to contribute to the national life of China and to assume a positive role in the life of its own particular community, yet also to participate in a universal community of faith.

Appendix

A Register of Baptized Protestant Chinese (1813–43)

My interest in obtaining more information on the Chinese converts and their careers led me to search archives of several missionary societies that worked among the Chinese. In the letters and reports sent back by missionaries I found numerous references to the Chinese converts. Many times, these references had been omitted by authors who used these archival sources for their published missionary histories.

The spelling of the names is copied from the original sources. At this period, there was no settled form for Romanizing Chinese names. Most of my material has been from English and German language sources.

The material is largely from the following sources: Archives of the American Board of Commissioners for Foreign Missions, Houghton Library, Harvard University (Cambridge); Archives of the Presbyterian Board of Foreign Missions (New York); Archives of the London Missionary Society (London); Archives of the American Baptist Church (Valley Forge, Pennsylvania); *Calwer Missionsblatt*; and Gaihan's *Chinesische Berichte* (Cassell, 1850).

1813 Batavia (Java), a convert of 'Chinese extraction' baptized by W. Robinson, an English Baptist missionary.

1814 Macau, Tsae A-ko (Choi A-ko) baptized on 16 July by Morrison. Born 1776, died 1819. He worked for Morrison as a pressman.

1816 Malacca, Leung A-fa baptized on 3 November by Milne. He was a block-cutter for the mission press. Born 1787, died 1855. Ordained as an evangelist-preacher by Morrison in 1827.

1821 Malacca, Johanna, daughter of a Chinese father and a Siamese mother, and formerly mistress of a European, baptized by Milne.

1821 Kwangtung Province, Ko-ming District, Loh-tsun village, Lai, wife of Leung A-fa, baptized by A-fa. She died in 1849.

1822 Macau, Tsae A-heen, elder brother of T'sae A-ko, requested baptism by Morrison. However, there is no record of his actual baptism.

1823 Canton, Leung Tsun-tak, son of Leung A-fa, baptized on 20 November by Morrison. Born 1820, died about 1862. In 1859, he was received into a church at Shanghai by the Revd Elijah C. Bridgman.

1824 New York, Lieaou A-see, alias William Botelho, a Chinese student of the Foreign Missions School of the American Board of Commissioners for Foreign Missions at Cornwall, Connecticut.

1828 Kwangtung Province, Ko-ming District, Kwu Tin-ching, a school-teacher and relative of Leung A-fa, baptized in January by A-fa. There is no further information regarding him.

1828 Tavoy, Burma, Kee Zea-chung baptized on 3 August by an American Baptist missionary.

1829 Kwangtung Province, Ko-ming District, Loh-tsun village, Leung A-chin, infant daughter of Leung A-fa, baptized by A-fa.

1829 Malacca, Choo Hea, a cripple, baptized by Kidd. He was still a member of the Malacca church when it was disbanded in 1843.

1830 Macau, Keuh A-gong, alias Wat Ngong, employee of the London Missionary Society press, baptized in February by Morrison. Born 1785, died 1867. For many years, a preacher for the LMS in Hong Kong.

1830 Bangkok, Bun Tai, baptized by Gutzlaff. Rebaptized by an Ameri-
-1 can Baptist missionary, the Revd John Taylor Jones on 8 December 1833. He separated from the Siam Baptist Mission in 1836. Returned to the church for a short time in 1843–4.

1832 Canton, Choo Tsing, a literary graduate, teacher at the Anglo-Chinese College at Malacca, baptized by Morrison on 16 December. When the British Government was established at Hong Kong, he became a government employee, but was dismissed in October 1843. He was seen by the Revd George Smith in Canton in 1844. He was an opium-smoker.

1833 Bangkok, Peng (Pong), aged 50, baptized on 8 December. Died March 1836. Sang Seah, aged 40, baptized on 8 December. Both were baptized by Jones.

1834 Malacca, a Chinese girl, aged 17, baptized in June.

1834 Surabaya (Java), the missionary Jacob Tomlin mentions meeting Fek-suy, a baptized Christian, in August.

1834 The small Chinese Christian Church at Canton was scattered by the persecution of the Chinese authorities. Most of the members had been baptized by Leung A-fa between 1831 and 1834. A list of the members was published in a circular letter from E.C. Bridgman and J.R. Morrison dated Canton, 15 January 1835.

    1. Leang Afa, aged 48, an evangelist.

    2. Keuh Agan, aged 50, an assistant.

    3. Le, aged 31, wife of A-fa.

    4. Leang Atih, aged 15, son of A-fa.

    5. Leang Achin, aged 11, daughter of A-fa.

    6. Le Asin, aged 31, bricklayer. (He is said to have been afraid to associate with foreigners after the 1834 persecution.)

    7. Chow Asan, aged 25, pencil-maker. (Renounced his faith and became an informant on his fellow Christians in 1834.)

    8. Woo Achang, aged 31, assistant printer. (Fled to Singapore and became head printer for the American Board mission.)

9. Leang Ataou, aged 28, pencil-maker.

10. Leang Asun, aged 24, pencil-maker. (There is a record of A-fa baptizing his relative, a literary graduate, aged 62, and his sons, aged 21 and 17, in February 1831.)

11. Ashun, ... , ...

12. Afuh, ... , an assistant to A-fa.

13. Lew Che-chang, aged 38, a literary graduate.

14. Choo Tsing, ... , a literary graduate.

(There is also a record of A-fa's baptism of Lam, an innkeeper at Canton in 1831. His name was not included in this 1835 list of baptized persons at Canton.)

1835 Bangkok, baptized by American Baptist Mission, 20 and 30 December: Chek Han (How? Ho?), aged 40, died June 1843; Chek Ete, aged 60, a tradesman; and Pay-chun, aged 70, a gardener, died 19 May 1844.

1836 Malacca, fifteen Chinese baptized; of these, four were students of the Anglo-Chinese College and the remaining were three married couples and five children.

1836 Macau, on 28 December, the Revd E.C. Bridgman married Lewis Hamilton, an American shipwright, to Mary, a baptized Chinese. Their adopted daughter was baptized in 1837. Lewis Hamilton, born 1799, died 1845, was buried in the Old Protestant Cemetery at Macau.

1837 Singapore, Ke Seng, former student of the Anglo-Chinese College, Malacca, baptized on 1 January by an American Board missionary. He was a teacher in the American Board school at Singapore.

1837 Macau, Ah Loo, a Chiu Chow house servant of the Shucks', was baptized by Shuck in January. In April 1838, he went with Dean to Bangkok. He was excluded from the church (for immorality?) in June 1838.

1837 Malacca, between November 1836 and April 1837, Evans reports baptizing twenty, including four families of four men, four women and five children, and six young men aged from 18 to 24. (Among these may have been the above-mentioned individuals baptized in Malacca in 1836.)

On 31 December, Evans baptized eighteen persons, and on 21 May, ten persons; of the latter group there were three young men, two families totalling six persons, and an old man aged 65, formerly a schoolteacher. On 14 August, the mission at Malacca reported a 'devoted flock of between 40 and 50'.

Among the persons baptized at Malacca in 1837 were probably: Ho A-sun, alias Ho Ye-tong, a printer for the London Missionary Society press. He accompanied Legge to Hong Kong in 1843, and was a useful and faithful member of the LMS congregation. He died in 1869. Wong A-muk, alias Wong Kwong-ching, a printer, from

Malacca went to Singapore, whence he came to Hong Kong in 1846. He was a deacon in the LMS congregation in Hong Kong. Born in 1810, he died in Hong Kong in 1884.

1838 Bangkok, the following were baptized by the American Baptist mission: Kiok Cheng, Chek Hwa, and Chek Kok. The mission reported six Chinese members in the church.

1838 Singapore, A-tei, a young man who came with Leung A-fa from China was baptized by the American Board mission. In 1840, he returned to China.

Lee (Seen-shang) was baptized by Johnson of the American Board. He was employed as a teacher by the Board.

1838 Hackney, England, Choo Tih-lang, Medhurst's language teacher. Excluded from church at Macau for opium-smoking in 1840. Later, a clerk for a commerical firm in Hong Kong.

1838 Malacca, on 2 April, twenty-nine Chinese men and women partook of Holy Communion.

September 1838 to April 1839, nineteen Chinese were baptized at Malacca. Among them was Ho Fuk-tong, alias Ho Tsun-shin, a student of the Anglo-Chinese College. He accompanied Legge to Hong Kong in 1843. He was ordained in 1846. Until his death he served as pastor of the London Missionary Society congregation in Hong Kong. Born 1818, died 1871.

1839 Singapore, A-bi, student of the American Board school, baptized by their missionary. Died of leprosy about 1856.

Tang Kwan, language teacher of the Revd Robert Orr, baptized by the American Presbyterian mission in November.

1839 Baltimore, USA, Wei Ang, alias Julian, baptized in Baptist Church. Returned to China in 1842 and joined Shuck's congregation at Hong Kong. Was excluded from congregation in 1843. Apparently was mentally unbalanced.

1839 Bangkok, three Chinese baptized by American Baptist mission in October. One of them, Chek Yet, came to Hong Kong with Dean in 1843, and was killed in April, when he intervened as a peacemaker in a quarrel. Dean also brought with him to Hong Kong, Hong Hek, who had been baptized in Bangkok before 1842. He was a charter member of Dean's Hong Kong Chiu Chow congregation. Nine Chinese are reported as members of the Baptist Bangkok mission.

1839 Macau, in a letter dated 10 November, Gutzlaff mentions the following as coming into the Christian Church: Chang Ye, Schin-se, Gno, a Hokien, and Setschong (Schitschang), a youth. (He became a member of the Chinese Christian Union, and in 1847 was preaching in Ho-nan.)

1839 Eton (Eason) Apping, USA, returned to Singapore in 1840. Accom-
-40 panied American Presbyterian missionaries to Amoy. He left their employ in 1845.

1840 Canton, Leung A-fa baptized four in April. He reports that there are 'altogether now twelve baptized persons' at Canton.

1840 Bangkok, American Baptist mission baptized four on May 13 and two on 11 October. Dean reports 16 Chinese in Bangkok mission.

1840 Macau, Gutzlaff reports following baptized persons: two youths; Hin, a doctor; a young man; a teacher, who is also a tradesman; a scholar; an aged man of 70 years. One of these must have been Siao Tao Ching, from Kwei-shan District, who became an active member of Gutzlaff's Chinese Union.

1840 Singapore, Teum Chi, a native of Chiu Chow, baptized by McBryde, American Presbyterian mission, on 15 November. He is described as 'a poor laborer'.

1841 Surabaya, Java, Yang Pang-ke, a 'country-born Chinese' baptized by Medhurst in September.

1841 Malacca, a Chinese man baptized in October.

1841 Canton, Kwan, aged 35 years, sister-in-law of Leung A-fa, a widow, baptized by A-fa in October.

1841 Singapore, Tsang Lai-sun, former pupil of the American Board
  -2 school baptized by McBryde of the American Presbyterian mission. In 1843, he was taken to America by Mr Morrison, a Presbyterian, and was educated at Hamilton College, New York. Upon his return to China, he became assistant of the American Board mission at Canton from 1848 to 1853. Then he went to Shanghai as mercantile assistant. He was one of the Commissioners of the Chinese Educational Mission to the United States in 1873. He was a member of the staff of Li Hung-chang. He married Ruth Ati in 1850 (see below).

1842 Batavia, Java, Medhurst baptized two girls from Miss Aldersey's school, Ruth Ati, who married Tsang Lai-sun in 1850 (she was born in 1825, died in 1917 at Shanghai) and Christiana Kit, who married Kew Teen-sang in December 1847 (he had been brought up in a mission school at Batavia and was baptized in Shanghai on 13 November 1845). The two girls accompanied Miss Aldersey when she moved her school to Ningpo. They were assistant teachers in the school.

1842 Macau, some time before Gutzlaff's departure for Chusan in June, he had baptized Liapo; Jong, a teacher; Nia; Kwu, a teacher; Sa (Siau?), a dentist, and his assistant. Among the members of the Chinese Union at its organization in June 1844 were Yung, a teacher, Kwo, a teacher, and Leap, catechist. On 25 July 1844, Roberts reports one of his assistants at Canton as A-fa, dentist. This may be the same as Le A-sam whom Roberts reports as deceased in 1845. The teacher Jong (Yang) may be the Yeang Chi-yuen, a member of Dean's Chiu Chow congregation in Hong Kong, but excluded in 1847 for opium-smoking. Two of Hamberg's assistants in 1848 were reported as being baptized in the year 1842. They were Tai, aged 27, from San-on District, and Siao Tao-ming, aged 48 years, from Kwei-shan District.

1842 Bangkok, baptisms by American Baptist mission: Chek Team, in January; Chir Sun, on 16 April by Goddard; and Chek Chin, on 7 August. The number of baptized Chinese in Siam was reported by the Baptist mission as eighteen, of which four moved to China and one died, leaving thirteen Chinese in the Bangkok mission.

1842 Hong Kong, Chun baptized by Roberts at Chek Chu (Stanley) on 12 June. He was Roberts' first convert, a member of Shuck's Baptist congregation formed on 1 April 1843. He accompanied Roberts to Canton in 1844, and died in 1845.

1843 Malacca, Legge reported in May that there were six members in the church: Keuh A-gong, Ho Tsun-shin, and Ho A-sun (these three accompanied him to Hong Kong), a man and his family moved to Singapore to work at the London Missionary Society press (this was probably Wong A-muk), one remained with the son of the Revd John Evans, and another remained in Malacca (one of these must have been Choo Hea, baptized in 1829).

1843 Singapore, five church members are reported: a language teacher named Tan Le-chun, a Christian from Malacca, and three who had been baptized by the American Board missionaries.

1843 Hong Kong, Chow and Wong were baptized by Roberts on 2 July. They were received as members of Shuck's Hong Kong Baptist congregation. Wong was excluded on September 1843. Chow accompanied Roberts to Canton as an assistant in 1844. Tang Tui, a coolie contractor for the Government, and Koe Bak were baptized by Dean on 27 April. Both were charter members of the Chiu Chow Baptist congregation at Hong Kong organized by Dean on 28 May 1843. Both became active members of the congregation.

Notes

Notes to Chapter 1

1. *Chinese Repository*, Vol. X, 1841, p. 583.
2. *Chinese Repository*, Vol. XIII, 1844, pp. 634–8 for Brown's analysis of the Chinese language and quotations cited in the text.
3. *Chinese Repository*, Vol. XI, 1842, p. 549.
4. *Chinese Repository*, Vol. XIII, 1844, p. 636.
5. *Chinese Repository*, Vol. X, 1841, p. 572.
6. *Chinese Repository*, Vol. XI, 1842, p. 550.
7. *Chinese Repository*, Vol. XIII, 1844, p. 632.
8. *Chinese Repository*, Vol. XIII, 1844, p. 633.
9. *Chinese Repository*, Vol. XIII, 1844, p. 633.
10. *Chinese Repository*, Vol. XIV, 1845, p. 476.
11. Gunther Barth, *Bitter Strength, A History of the Chinese in the United States, 1850–1870* (Cambridge, Harvard University Press, 1964), p. 147.
12. Mrs Gutzlaff, the former Miss Wanstall, had conducted a girls' school at Malacca as an agent of the Society for the Promotion of Female Education in the East. After marrying the Revd Charles Gutzlaff and moving to Macau, she opened a similar school there. She also accepted a few young boys into the school but soon gave up having a mixed school. The school was begun in 1836 and was discontinued when the Opium War broke out. Mrs Gutzlaff, accompanied by several blind girls she had in her care, then went to Manila.
13. Yung Wing, *My Life in China and America* (New York, Henry Holt and Company, 1909), pp. 2–3.
14. Yung Wing (1909), pp. 9–10.
15. *Eighth Annual Report of the Morrison Education Society for the Year ending September 30, 1846* (Hong Kong, China Mail Office, 1846), p. 33.
16. *Eighth Annual Report* (1846). p. 36.
17. *Chinese Repository*, Vol. XIII, 1844, p. 640.
18. *Chinese Repository*, Vol. XII, 1843, p. 628.
19. *Chinese Repository*, Vol. XII, 1843, p. 628.
20. *New York Observer*, 9 January 1841, 25 June 1842; W.E. Griffis, *A Maker of the New Orient, Samuel Robbins Brown* (New York, Fleming H. Revel and Co., 1902), pp. 77, 79–80; *Chinese Repository*, Vol. XI, 1842, pp. 339–40, Vol. XII, 1843, pp. 362–8, Vol. XIII, 1844, pp. 383–5; *Fourth Annual Report of the Morrison Education Society read September 28th 1842* (Macau, S. Wells Williams, 1842), pp. 27–31; and *Eighth Annual Report* (1846), pp. 33–6.
21. This is probably a misreading for Ats'euk. The apparently complete record of the students does not mention the name Auseule.
22. *New York Observer*, 9 January 1841, p. 6.
23. *New York Observer*, 25 June 1842, p. 101.
24. *Fourth Annual Report* (1842), p. 27. The identification of the authors of the essays printed in this report is deduced from a comparison of the information given in the report concerning their age and time at the school with the published lists of students.
25. Griffis (1902), p. 77.
26. Griffis (1902), p. 80.
27. *Chinese Repository*, Vol. XIV, 1845, pp. 506–9.

28. *Chinese Repository*, Vol. XIV, 1845, p. 509. The essay proceeds to spell out the corrupt practices of the mandarins under six points:
(a) They forcibly take money from the people;
(b) Opium-smugglers can buy their way out of punishment;
(c) They extort gifts from the rich under the pretence of borrowing;
(d) The customs officers and tax collectors extort excessive levies;
(e) They employ underlings but do not pay them, though they charge their services to the public expenses;
(f) A prisoner is tortured into a confession before any attempt is made to ascertain if he is innocent or guilty. If guilty, the judge will accept a ransom for his release.

29. *Chinese Repository*, Vol. XI, 1842, p. 340.
30. *Chinese Repository*, Vol. XI, 1842, p. 340.
31. *Chinese Repository*, Vol. XI, 1842, p. 340.
32. *Eighth Annual Report* (1846), p. 34.
33. *Chinese Repository*, Vol. XII, 1843, p. 364.
34. *Chinese Repository*, Vol. XIII, 1844, p. 384.
35. *Fourth Annual Report* (1842), p. 28.
36. Lo Hsiang-lin, *Hong Kong and Western Culture* (Honolulu, East-West Center Press, 1963), pp. 57-8.
37. *Chinese Repository*, Vol. XIII, 1844, pp. 383-4.
38. *Chinese Repository*, Vol. XIV, 1845, pp. 516-19.
39. *Chinese Repository*, Vol. XIV, 1845, pp. 515-16.
40. *Eighth Annual Report* (1846), pp. 34-6.
41. *Chinese Repository*, Vol. XIV, 1845, p. 512.
42. *Chinese Repository*, Vol. XIV, 1845, pp. 304-5.

Notes to Chapter 2

1. 徐潤, 徐愚齊自敍年譜 (Hsü Jun, *Chronological Autobiography of Hsü Jun*) (1927), pp. 57-8; 劉廣京, 唐廷樞之買辦時代 (Liu Kuang-ching, 'T'ang T'ing-shu, His Compradore Years') in 清華學報 (*Tsing Hua Journal of Chinese Studies*), New Series 2, Vol. 2, 1961, pp. 143-83; 沈鎮桂, 唐廷樞傳 (*Biography of T'ang T'ing-shu*), in 匏隱廬文稿 (*Literary Notes of P'ao-yin-lu*); Albert Feuerwerker, *China's Early Industrialization* (Cambridge, Harvard University Press, 1958), pp. 110-11; Yen-p'ing Hao, *The Comprador in Nineteenth Century China* (Cambridge, Harvard University Press, 1970), see index; Chan Hok-lam, 'Four Chinese Students of the Hong Kong Morrison Memorial School', in F.S. Drake (ed.), *Historical, Archaeological and Linguistic Studies* (Hong Kong University Press, 1967), pp. 285-6; Ellsworth Carlson, *The Kaiping Mines (1877-1912)*, in Harvard University Chinese Economic and Political Science Studies, Special Series (Cambridge, 1957); and Kwang-ching Liu, 'A Chinese Entrepreneur', in Maggie Keswick (ed.), *The Thistle and the Jade* (London, Octopus Books, 1982).

Difficulties arise in research because of the complex Chinese system of naming. A Chinese may have several names and one of his names may be used in one document and another in another document. Alternatively, several aliases, as they are usually termed, may be given. Where aliases have been found, I have included them for further identification. In Chinese names, the surname comes first. This is most typically followed by a 'generation' name, which identifies the individual in terms of his descent group. Then comes the personal name. More rarely, there is no middle name, the generation being identified by the use of a particular radical attached to the phonetics of the characters for all personal names of individuals of one generation of the descent group. An individual may further have several names which identify him as an actor in particular roles. Thus, he may have a name given by his parents, another added when he enters school, another when he marries; perhaps another when he joins an association or society; and another Western name if he is baptized a Christian. Chinese also have nicknames used by friends and close associates and it is quite common to replace the generation name by the appellation 'a' for informal use.

A confusion has arisen over the identity of Tong A-chick. Chan Hok-lam, in his article on the students of the Morrison School, identifies him as Tong King-sing. I myself had done so until Mr H. Mark Lai, President of the Chinese Historical Society of America, kindly drew my attention to the chop, Tong K. Achick, affixed to his translation into Chinese of a California law for the collection of the foreign miners' tax. The chop reads Tong Cheuk Mow Chee (唐植茂枝) (Bancroft Library, Berkeley, F862.3/C148x). When A-chick was admitted to the Morrison School in 1839 he was 11 years of age (hence born in 1828); his brother Akü was admitted in 1841, aged 10 (hence born in 1831). The sixty-first birthday celebration for Tong Mow-chee was held on 19 December 1888 (hence born in 1827); a similar celebration for Tong King-sing was reported on 3 June 1892 (hence born in 1831). *Daily Press*, 25 December 1888; *North China Herald and Supreme Court Consular Gazette*, 3 June 1892, p. 741.

2. *Chinese Repository*, Vol. XIV, 1845, pp. 504-19. This is one of the six essays written by pupils of the senior class. Unfortunately, the names of the writers are not given, so we are unable to relate the sentiments and interests of an essay to a particular member of the class. The titles of the other essays were 'Chinese Government', 'Labour', 'An imaginary voyage' (including a tour of the United States; this is interesting in view of the fact that all but one member of the class later travelled to America), 'Scriptures' (at least four of the class later professed Christianity), and 'Notions of the Chinese in regard to a future state'.

3. An incident in the later career of Tong King-sing illustrates this principle. While in the employ of Jardine, Matheson and Company in 1866, some question was raised regarding his honesty. He refutes this aspersion on his character by referring to his youthful education: 'Having received a thorough Anglo-Chinese education, I consider squeezing an Employer is a sinful and mean act' (Liu Kuang-ching, 1961, p. 165). When the foreign community at Tientsin organized a sixty-first birthday celebration for Tong King-sing, they did so to express 'their deep appreciation of the splendid straight-forwardness and rectitude of principle he had displayed in all his dealings with them' (*North China Herald and Supreme Court Consular Gazette*, 3 June 1892, p. 741).

4. As the name suggests, Tong-ka was the village of the 'Tong family'. The family had been resident in the Heung Shan District for generations and this was their family seat. In the Republican period there was an ambitious project to make the village a major port of China.

5. An uncle of Tong King-sing was a compradore to Charles G. Holdforth, Sheriff of Hong Kong from 1845 to 1849. Holdforth left Hong Kong for San Francisco and this may have influenced the uncle to follow him.

6. *Archives of the Presbyterian Board of Foreign Missions*, Microfilm Reel 192, Vol. 6, No. 83, Macau, 26 January 1847, Vol. 2, No. 63, Macau, 24 February 1846, and Vol. 2, No. 66, Macau, 28 March 1846.

7. 'Seventh Annual Report of the Morrison Education Society', *Chinese Repository*, Vol. XIV, 1845, pp. 473-4. The father quoted is not identified by name, but a detailed analysis of the student rolls of the school has led me to identify him as the father of Tong A-chick. With reference to the father, there is a baffling item in the Hong Kong Probate Calendar for 1897 in the *Government Gazette*. On 1 June 1897, an administration on the estate of one Tong A. Tow, who died on 28 November 1845 in Heung Shan District, was granted to Tong Chick, the only son. The estimated value of the estate was given as $5,000. This may be the father of the three

boys. Tong King-sing died in 1892, the youngest brother may also have been dead by 1897, thus leaving Tong Mow-chee (Tong Chick or Tong A-chick) his only surviving son. Tong Mow-chee died at Shanghai on 6 July 1897.

8. The first five students were Aling, aged 16, from Macau, who was dismissed on 12 October 1840 for bad conduct; Atseuk, aged 14, from Shan Cheung, was driven from the school by his father on 19 August 1840, but returned on 1 June 1842; Ayun and Awai, both aged 11, from Shan Cheung, were removed by their father on 19 August 1840; and A-chick, aged 10, from Tong-ka. More students were admitted later. On 11 November 1839, Ahop, aged 12, was admitted from Tsin Shan, but after a few months' trial he was dismissed for stupidity. In March 1840, five more students were enrolled. Of these, the youngest, Alun, aged 10, could not adjust because of homesickness and was dismissed for going home repeatedly without permission. Tanyau, from Nam-ping, was also dismissed in June for bad conduct. Lee Akan, aged 14, from Ngau-hung-lai, Chau Awan (Chow Wan), aged 13, from Macau, and Wong Atu, aged 11, from Tung-nong, remained as permanent members of the first class. On 1 November 1840, Yung Wing, aged 13, from Nam-ping, was enrolled, and on 1 January 1841, Wong Ashing, aged 15, from Macau, became the last member to join the class. See student roll, *Chinese Repository*, Vol. XII, 1844, p. 263.

9. For the missionary orientation of the school, see Carl T. Smith, 'A Study of the Missionary Educational Philosophy of Samuel R. Brown from the Perspective of Inter-faith Encounter', *Ching Feng*, Vol. XII, No. 2, 1969, pp. 2–22.

10. *New York Observer*, 9 January 1841.

11. *New York Observer*, 25 June 1842.

12. A notice of the death of T'in Sau appeared in the *Hongkong Register* on 6 December 1853: 'Death of Hwang T'een Siu (commonly known as "Teen-sow") for some time in the service of the *T'aoutae* here, known as one of his linguists. Whether born in China or one of the Chinese settlements at "The Straits" does not appear. For some years he was in one of the Mission Schools at Singapore or Malacca, and came from thence to Hongkong and subsequently Shanghai. His arrival here was very soon after opening of the foreign settlement in 1842. For a time in service of foreigners, then went into service of native merchants. He professed himself a Christian and was often seen in worshipping assemblies on the Lord's day. During naval operations on the river below Chin-kiang he was sent back and forth between the fleet and the *T'aoutae*. His sympathies were with the rebels. Probably the reason his master *T'aoutae* Wu dismissed him. He applied to foreign houses for employment, but was not successful, so he joined forces with the *T'aoutae*'s foes in the city. He had not been a week in the city when he became obnoxious to his new master. He was charged with being a spy, and was "cut to pieces". The reasons for his breaking friendship with his new master, and undertaking to act as a spy, do not appear; but that he did so, his best friends admit. The circumstances of his death are too terrible to be related. At their recital Samqua (*Tao-tai* Wu) is said to have cried like a baby.'

13. See Carl T. Smith, 'Commissioner Lin and His Translators', *Chung Chi Bulletin*, No. 42, 1967, pp. 29–36.

14. *Chinese Repository*, Vol. XIII, 1844, p. 625. Several years after the first boys were sent, Governor Davis requested more students. This time, Mr Brown took a firmer stand and was willing to have a show-down on the issue. The Presbyterian missionary, Andrew P. Happer, reported the matter in a letter to his mission board: 'Within a week Mr. Brown writes he has had correspondence with the Governor terminated rather crabbily on the part of the Governor in relation to boys for the public service. The Governor asking for some as if he felt he had a perfect right to call for any anytime he might wish them. Mr. Brown wrote to him that the boys are engaged to stay for a certain number of years and that he had no authority from the Trustees to let any leave the school until their term of study was com-

pleted, when they were at liberty to enter upon any service that they chose. The Governor thought that this was a new interpretation of the matter and that through giving a lot free of rent and Sir Henry Pottinger having given some $1,300 from the public fund and the civilians and military of Hong Kong contributions for its support, gave them the right to expect Interpreters from it. He closed the correspondence by saying to Mr. Brown that he was at liberty to call from Shanghai two boys that have been in the consulate there for more than a year, and Mr. Brown thinks that Governor Davis himself may order them home. All the Trustees support Mr. Brown but the Governor can set influences at work which will sooner or later result in removing Mr. Brown. Mr. Brown inquired if our Board would be willing to receive him—that he was that tired of laboring for the world that had no Christian sympathy or prayers for the great object he had in view.' *Archives of the Presbyterian Board of Foreign Missions*, Vol. 2, No. 41, Macau, 4 August 1845.

15. *Chinese Repository*, Vol. XIV, 1845, p. 475.

16. *Eighth Annual Report of the Morrison Education Society for the Year ending 30 September, 1846* (Hong Kong, China Mail Office, 1846), pp. 33–6.

17. Hong Kong Land Registry Office, Memorials 943, 1098 and 1179.

18. Legge Collection, Archives of the London Missionary Society.

19. Colonial Office Records, Series 129–23, No. 15, 25 January 1848.

20. *China Mail*, 18 December 1850.

21. *Friend of China*, 17 September 1851; *Parliamentary Papers*, Vol. XLVIII, 1860, p. 174.

22. *Hongkong Register*, 16 September 1851, 7 October 1851; *China Mail*, 23 October 1851.

23. Colonial Office Records, Series 129–45, No. 24, 11 May 1854.

24. For a summary of the case, see G.B. Endacott, *A Biographical Sketch-book of Early Hong Kong* (Singapore, Eastern University Press, 1962), pp. 97–9.

25. *Queen* v. *Tarrant*, 7 August 1858, *Parliamentary Papers*, Vol. XLVIII, 1860.

26. Colonial Office Records, Series 131–1, 1855–6.

27. *China Mail*, 3 April 1856.

28. Mentioned in Liu Kuang-ching, 1961.

29. Bonney writes that 'one of the overseers of the company had been a teacher of our deceased brother J.G. Bridgman, and another of the emigrants was formerly my pupil in Morrison School and has been baptized'. *Archives of the American Board of Commissioners for Foreign Missions*, 16.3.8, Vol. 2, No. 232, 21 January 1852.

30. The St. John's Cathedral Baptismal Register, entry Nos. 15, 16, and 17 for 29 June 1851 are blank, but written in pencil is the notation, 'Chinese—students in St. Paul's College'. This fits with the statement made in the Bishop's report for 1851: 'Three pupils were baptized during the last summer: Ching-tik, sent back to Ningpo, his native place, dangerously ill, and apparently dying, where he has, however, unexpectedly recovered, and continues under the kind care of his former friends and instructors, the missionaries of the Church Mission Society. Achick is at present unsettled, on account of an uncle wishing to take him to California, and Kum-shoo, a boy of fifteen, considerably advanced in Chinese reading and possessing a fine intellect and disposition', *Letter to the Archbishop of Canterbury containing the Annual Report of St. Paul's College and Mission at Hong Kong, George Smith, D.D., Bishop of Hong Kong* (Hong Kong, 1852). Tong A-chick later stated that he had received the baptismal name 'Laying cheu'. The Revd Albert Williams of San Francisco reports this, stating that A-chick had said that this meant 'belief of the Scriptures'. It is likely, however, that if the Chinese words had been heard and transcribed correctly, the name was 來認主, meaning, 'confess the Lord'. *The Presbyterian*, Vol. XXII, No. 31, 1852, p. 82.

31. *Annual Report of the Bishop of Victoria to the Archbishop of Canterbury*, 7 April 1854, Archives of the Society for the Propagation of the Gospel, London.

32. *The Presbyterian*, Vol. XXII, No. 31, 1852, p. 82.

33. 'Journal of William Speer', *Home and Foreign Record of the Presbyterian Church in the United States of America*, Vol. IV, 1853, p. 214.

34. There is little evidence that, in his later career, Tong King-sing was an active Christian. However, a newspaper correspondent, reporting from Tientsin in 1886, comments that Li Hung-chang 'prefers to promote the interests of his countrymen who have embraced the Christian religion and pushes them on to rank and high position'. As examples, he mentions Tong King-sing and his brothers. *Daily Press*, 9 March 1886.

35. Letters regarding the Chinese mission in California 1852–65, from Speer to Lowrie, No. 6, newspaper clipping of contribution list, Presbyterian Historical Society, Microfilm Records of Presbyterian Church, USA, Board of Foreign Missions, Microfilm 2, C. 441, Reel 1, No. 5, 15 September 1853, San Francisco. Along with Tong A-chick, there were two other individuals who contributed $100, Chun Ching and Lee Kan and Co. Lee Kan is probably a former classmate of Tong A-chick's at the Morrison Education Society School in Hong Kong, who died some years later in San Francisco. Three of the five district associations contributed. The Sz Yap Company gave the largest contribution, $200, and the Yeong Wo Company and the Ning Yeung Company each gave $100.

36. I have followed the account of this issue as given in Gunther Barth, *Bitter Strength, A History of the Chinese in the United States 1850–1870* (Cambridge, Harvard University Press, 1964), chap. VI.

37. Reprints from a pamphlet, 'An Analysis of the Chinese Question', *Friend of China*, 2 June 1853.

38. Quoted in *Barth* (1964), p. 147, from a newspaper notice in the *Herald*, 7 June 1852.

39. This and subsequent quotations are from an account of the Chinese case published in *Friend of China* on 2 June 1853. Gunther Barth (1964), p. 146, doubts whether the two letters were actually written by Chinese. He says, 'it was not according to Chinese procedure'. This is true, but he overlooks the experience Tong A-chick had gained in such matters during his service as interpreter in the British Consulate. Nor was Tong A-chick a stranger to the effectiveness of a 'letter to the Editor', a popular method employed by readers of the China coast newspapers to air their grievances or special concerns.

40. Theodore H. Hittell, *History of California* (San Francisco, N.J. Stone and Company, 1897), Vol. IV, p. 110.

41. Letter from the Revd W. Speer dated 30 November 1852, *Home and Foreign Record of the Presbyterian Church in the United States of America*, Vol. IV, 1853, p. 51.

42. *Annual Report of the Bishop of Victoria to the Archbishop of Canterbury* (1854).

43. *Daily Press*, 25 December 1888.

44. *Daily Press*, 17 July 1869; *Government Gazette*, 2 January 1870.

45. Hong Kong Land Registry, Memorials 11687 and 13264.

46. Feuerwerker (1958), pp. 113 and 129.

47. *O Macaense*, 9 July 1883.

48. *North China Herald and Supreme Court Consular Gazette*, 3 June 1892, p. 741.

Notes to Chapter 3

1. Arthur Waley, *The Opium War Through Chinese Eyes* (New York, Macmillan and Company, 1958), pp. 65–6.

2. Letter from T.T. Leang to Mrs Morrison dated Macau, 4 November 1841, *Evangelical Magazine*, Vol. XX, 1842, p. 295.

3. *Archives of the American Board of Commissioners for Foreign Missions* (Houghton Library, Harvard University), 16.3.3, Vol. I, No. 119, 1840 (hereafter *AABCFM*).

4. *Chinese Repository*, Vol. VIII, 1840, pp. 635–6.

5. Waley (1958), pp. 95–6.

6. Bridgman's journal, 1 May 1830, *AABCFM*, 16.3.8, Vol. I, No. 26.

7. London, Kegan Paul, Trench and Company, 1885, pp. 260–5.

8. *Chinese Repository*, Vol. XVIII, 1849, p. 407; *Fourth Annual Report of the Anglo-Chinese College* (1826), *Fifth Annual Report* (1827), *Report of the Eleventh Year* (1829).

9. William C. Hunter, *Bits of Old China* (London, Kegan Paul, Trench and Company, 1885), pp. 261–2, quoting from the *Canton Register* of 3 October 1829.

10. *Chinese Repository*, Vol. VIII, 1839, pp. 167–8.

11. *Missionary Herald*, Vol. XVII, 1821, p. 2.

12. *T'ien Hsia Monthly*, Vol. XI, 1940, pp. 128–39. La Fargue states (p. 137) that Lieaou Ah-see, another of the students at Cornwall, was mentioned by 'Robert Morrison and David Abeel ... as serving as an interpreter in the yamen of Commissioner Lin'. Unfortunately, La Fargue has not documented this statement. It is questionable inasmuch as Robert Morrison died in 1834 and the Lin Commission took place in 1839–40. Perhaps Dr Morrison's son, John Robert Morrison, is meant. Abeel mentions seeing Ah-see at Canton but does not suggest any connection with Commissioner Lin. It would appear that La Fargue assigns rather arbitrarily to Ah-see the role of Lin's translator out of the five Chinese boys who studied at Cornwall. He was probably using as his source the notice in the *Chinese Repository* which does not definitely name the translators. G.W. Overdijking, in his study of Lin, *Lin T'se-hsü, een Biographische Schets* (Leiden, E.J. Brill, 1938, *Sinica Leidensia*, Vol. IV), picks up this identification of Ah-see as an interpreter indirectly from La Fargue through the mention of Ah-see in George H. Danton's *The Culture Contacts of the United States and China, the Earliest Sino-American Culture Conflicts 1784–1844* (New York, Columbia University Press, 1831).

13. *AABCFM*, 16.3.8, Vol. I, No. 220, 18 May 1834.

14. *AABCFM*, 16.3.11, Vol. I, p. 25.

15. *Archives of the London Missionary Society* (London), South China, Box 2, Folder 2, Jacket C.

16. Bridgman's journal, 23 October 1830, *AABCFM*, 16.3.8, Vol. I, No. 30.

17. *AABCFM*, 16.3.8, Vol. I, No. 61.

18. Letter dated Macau, 5 December 1840, *Archives of the London Missionary Society*, South China, Box 4, Folder 1, Jacket C.

19. A letter from Bridgman dated 29 November 1840, *AABCFM*, 16.3.3, Vol. IA, No. 65.

20. Letter from Bridgman dated 11 July 1841, *AABCFM*, 16.3.3, Vol. IA, No. 71.

21. Letter from Bridgman dated 1 March 1841, *AABCFM*, 16.3.3, Vol. IA, No. 67 and note appended to the printed semi-annual letter of the missionaries at Macau dated 1 January 1841, *AABCFM*, 16.3.3, Vol. IA, No. 73.

22. Letter from Bridgman dated Victoria, 14 February 1844, *AABCFM*, 16.3.3, Vol. IA, No. 84.

23. Letter from Bridgman to Prudential Committee dated Hong Kong, 20 September 1844, *AABCFM*, 16.3.3, Vol. I, No. 56. Hong Kong Land Registry Office, Memorials 33, 34, 36 and 37.

24. Letter from Bridgman dated Hong Kong, 26 May 1845, *AABCFM*, 16.3.3, Vol. I, No. 57.

25. Letter from Bridgman dated Canton, 25 December 1845, *AABCFM*, 16.3.3, Vol. I, No. 63.

26. George H. McNeur, *China's First Preacher, Liang A-fa, 1789–1855* (Shanghai, Kwan Hsueh Publishing House, 1934), p. 93.

27. Letter from Bridgman dated Canton, 18 March 1847, *AABCFM*, 16.8.3, Vol. III, No. 72.

28. Letter from Bridgman dated Shanghai, 25 August 1848, *AABCFM*, 16.8.3, Vol. III, No. 93.

29. *AABCFM*, 16.8.3, Vol. III, No. 206.

30. *Daily Press*, 14 May 1878.

31. *Chinese Repository*, Vol. VI, 1837, p. 231.

32. *Archives of the London Missionary Society*, London, South China, Box 3, special red folder.

33. For an account of the life of Liang Tsen Teh, see Carl T. Smith, 'Commissioner Lin's Translators', *Chung Chi Bulletin*, No. 42, 1967, pp. 29–36.

34. Minutes of Singapore mission dated 28 November 1837, *AABCFM*, 16.2.6, Vol. 1, No. 129.

35. Roll of American Board mission school, Singapore, 1 February 1840, *AABCFM*, 16.3.1, Vol. 2, No. 180.

36. *AABCFM*, 16.3.1, Vol. 2, No. 151.

37. *AABCFM*, 16.3.1, Vol. 2, No. 151.

38. Morrison Education Society reports for the years 1861–2, 1862–3, and 1863–4.

39. Semi-annual report by Bridgman dated Hong Kong, 20 July 1843, *AABCFM*, 16.3.8, Vol. 1A, No. 23.

40. Hong Kong Government Land Registry Records, Memorials 36–7.

41. Letter from Hirschberg dated 25 September 1852, *Archives of the London Missionary Society*, South China, Box 5, Folder 3, Jacket A. 'The Chinese have contributed $250 to the erection of the new hospital. One Tam Ah-choy, a rich building contractor, had been several times a looker in at the hospital. Another Loo Ah-qui, who owns a number of houses in the Lower Bazaar and who obtained a button for some services to his country, received me most friendly and in a very good English said to Lee Kip Tye, a Chinese broker, who went with me to collect the money "Do not trouble that gentleman to come here again, I shall send you the money ($15) to your house tomorrow mornings" and then turning to me said "A very good cause, Sir. A very good cause" and then took my hands and shook them most heartly according to English fashion. Another Ah-Yang, late teacher of Rev. Dean, sent me $2 during his illness and after his death received from Dean: "Enclosed is $5 as a small bequest for your hospital from my late Chinese teacher, who died this morning." Lee Kip Tye has taken great interest from the start and procured by his untiring zeal the greatest number of subscribers and at his own expense has undertaken to erect a stone in the hospital with the names of all subscriptions engraved, as an evalasting memorial of the first assistance given by the Chinese to Europeans for a good cause.'

42. *China Mail*, 23 September 1852.

43. Hong Kong Government Land Registry Records, Memorials 684, 685, and 737. Ho A-seck, who also bore the names Ho In-kee and Ho Fei-in, first appears in Hong Kong records in March 1849 when he purchased Inland Lot No. 239 C in Tai Ping Shan (Memorial 468). At the time, he was compradore of the opium-importing firm of Lyall, Still and Company. The firm closed in 1867. Ho A-seck engaged in his own business ventures under the firm name of Kin Nam. He was a dealer in opium and in 1871 he held the gambling house monopoly in Hong Kong. In an action brought against him in 1871, he testified that he operated with a capital of $200,000. He was one of the leaders of the Chinese community, a member of the

Joss House Committee in 1872, a member of the Committee to Establish Tung Wah Hospital in 1870, and Vice-President of the Tung Wah Committee in 1872. He died in Pang Po (probably Ping Po (平步)), San Tuk District, on 29 April 1877. His wife, Ho Leong, obtained letters of administration, but as she was blind, she gave power of attorney to Wei Akwong.

44. Hong Kong Government Land Registry Records, Memorial 2629.

45. Cheung Achew (鄭亞朝) was a neighbour of Wei Akwong. He bought Inland Lot No. 189 from William Scott on 17 August 1855 (Memorial 876) and a month later purchased the adjoining lot No. 193 (Memorial 891). He died at his home village of Kai Choong in Heung Shan District on 7 December 1865. Probate of his estate was granted to Wong Shing, a neighbour. His widow, Cheung Chew-shi, died at Hong Kong on 16 December 1880. Probate of her estate was granted to her son, Cheung Tsun, of Macau. An adjoining lot to those of Cheung Achew, Inland Lot No. 197 (Memorial 917), was bought by Cheung Mung (鄭明), a compradore, in August 1855. He died in 1858, and his property in Hong Kong fell to his administratrix, Cheung Chew-shi. Lum Ayow is listed as a lorcha owner in the *Hong Kong Government Gazette* of 26 January 1856, 'Return of Vessels Owned by Chinese Residents Holders of Land in the Colony'. 1854, No. 15, October, *Good Chance*, 149 tons, owner Lam Yow, Captain Lam Yuen, securities Amoon and Ty-sing.

46. Article from *China Review* reprinted in the *China Mail*, 23 October 1875.

47. Hong Kong Government Land Registry Records, Memorials 2447, 2977, 2978, 4312, 5237, and 5093.

48. Letter from Wong Shing to James Legge dated 20 February 1869, Hong Kong, Legge Collection, *Archives of the London Missionary Society*.

49. Arnold Wright (ed.), *Twentieth Century Impressions of Hong Kong, Shanghai and other Treaty Ports of China* (London, Lloyd's Greater Britain Publishing Company, 1908), p. 109.

50. Wei family genealogy, 1908 (韋氏族譜, 光緒戊申). Made available to me through the courtesy of Dr David Faure.

51. Probate File 1151 of 1878 (4/368), Public Record Office of Hong Kong.

52. This is my interpretation of his remarks and may not be a completely accurate assessment.

53. See Tin-yuke Char, 'In Search of the Chinese Name for "Lai Sun"', *Journal of the Hong Kong Branch of the Royal Asiatic Society*, Vol. 16, 1976, pp. 107–111. The character for his surname appears to have been (佾). In his signature he used the romanization 'Chan'.

54. 'Brother Tsung Lai Shun in Massachusetts', *Journal of the Hong Kong Branch of the Royal Asiatic Society*, Vol. 21, 1981, pp. 179–84. Reprinted from *Chater-Cosmo Transactions*, Vol. 2, 1980.

55. *Spirit of Missions* (Journal of the American Episcopal Church), Vol. 22, 1857, p. 350.

56. Vol. 58, p. 258.

57. *South China Morning Post*, 23 January 1917.

Notes to Chapter 4

1. In an appendix to Dr Margaret M. Coughlin's unpublished doctoral thesis, 'Strangers in the House: J. Lewis Shuck and Issachar Roberts, First American Baptist Missionaries to China', University of Virginia, 1972, there is a letter from Roberts to Shuck dated 27 March 1847 giving details of Hsiu-ch'uan's spiritual development.

2. *Southern Baptist Missionary Journal*, Vol. 2, No. 10, 1848.

3. For an English-language account, see Jen Yu-wen, *The Taiping Revolutionary Movement* (New Haven, Yale University Press, 1973).

4. When my sources have not given names in Chinese characters, I have used the Romanization of the original manuscript, except for Hung Hsiu-ch'uan, Hung Jenkan and Feng Yun-shan. There are particular difficulties in determining the proper surname for individuals who appear in the sources as Fung. This was the accepted Hakka form of the surname Hung (洪), but it was also the Cantonese spelling of the surname Fung (馮).

5. Letter from Hamberg dated May 1854, *Die Evangelischen Heidenboten*, October 1854.

6. *Die Evangelischen Heidenboten*, June 1868, p. 73.

7. Li Tsin-kau, otherwise known as Lee Sik-sam, died on 8 April 1885, aged 62. On the letters of administration issued to his widow, Ho Lai-yau, the value of his estate was estimated at $400. His assets consisted principally of a small house beside the Basel Missionary Society's church and mission house in Sai Ying Pun, which he had purchased in 1878 for $480. He sold a portion of the lot in 1878 for $370.

Li Tsin-kau's wife was baptized in Hong Kong in 1861 and died there on 21 September 1888, leaving four surviving children. The family property after her death was conveyed by Li A-cheung, an interpreter, Li Shin-en, a missionary, and Li En-kyau, unmarried, to their brother, Li A-po, a trader.

The eldest son of Tsin-kau, A-lim, had died in 1864 'in trouble with the police'. A-po, the second son, was betrothed in 1865 to Kong Oi-fuk from Lilong. She was a student in the Basel Missionary Society girls' boarding-school in Hong Kong, and he was a student at their boys' school at Lilong.

The third son, A-cheung, studied at Hong Kong Central School (Queen's College) and in 1871 was given the prize for best scholar. After leaving school, he entered government service, beginning as a charge-room interpreter for the police, but in 1875 was transferred to the Magistracy as a clerk. Three years later he was promoted to second interpreter in the Magistracy. In 1882, he was offered the position of interpreter to the Kingdom of Hawaii. Like his brother, he had married one of the students at the girls' boarding-school in Hong Kong, Tshin Then-tet. She accompanied him to Hawaii.

In 1883, the Revd Frank Damon, who was in charge of Chinese Christian work in Hawaii, visited Hong Kong. In a report of his visit published in *The Friend* (New Series, Vol. 33, No. 2, 1883, p. 9) he expresses his pleasure at meeting 'the venerable and interesting father of our government interpreter in Honolulu, Mr Lee Cheong. A brother and sister are engaged in teaching here, while another brother is missionary to his countrymen'.

The fourth son, Li Shen-en (李承恩), alias Li Syong-kong (李祥光), was baptized in Hong Kong in 1859. Following in the footsteps of his father, he served as catechist in the Sai Ying Pun Hakka congregation from 1883 to 1888. He then emigrated to Sabah, North Borneo, where, under the auspices of the Basel Missionary Society, he organized a congregration of Hakkas. He married Lin Loi-kyau, a daughter of the Revd Lin Khi-len. She was a teacher at the girls' boarding-school at Sai Ying Pun from 1882 to 1894.

Li Tsin-kau had one daughter, Li En-kyau (李恩嬌), born in 1860 and baptized as an infant. She attended the Sai Ying Pun school and also taught there from 1877 to 1902; in addition, she carried out volunteer church work among the women.

The services rendered by the several generations of the Li family to the congregations and schools of the Basel Missionary Society well repaid the initial interest and attention which the young Li Tsin-kau had been given when he first turned up in Hong Kong in 1853 as one displaced because of his connection with the leader of the Taiping movement.

The details of the family of Li Tsin-kau were taken mainly from the archives of the Basel Missionary Society and from a mimeographed paper entitled 'Geschichte der Hongkonger Gemeinden' kindly lent to me by Dr James Hayes.

8. Letter from Legge dated 26 September 1853, *Archives of the London Missionary Society*, South China, Box 5, Folder 3, Jacket C, and *Yearly Report of the Hong Kong Mission* dated 25 January 1854, Jacket D. For a brief note on Keuh A-gong, see Carl T. Smith, 'A Register of Baptized Protestant Chinese 1813–42', *Chung Chi Bulletin*, No. 48, 1970, p. 24. For a note on Ng Mun-sow, see Carl T. Smith, 'Dr Legge's Theological School', *Chung Chi Bulletin*, No. 50, 1971, pp. 16–22.

9. Letter from Legge dated 28 January 1869, *Archives of the London Missionary Society*, South China, Box 6, Folder 2, Jacket C, and letter from Wong Fun dated 8 May 1857, Folder 1, Jacket A. Another missionary estimate of Hung Jen-kan is the testimonial the Revd John Chalmers sent to the Revd Rudolph Lechler, *Basel Missionary Society Archives*, Vol. IV, 1857–62, letter written from London Mission House, Hong Kong, dated 24 December 1857: 'I have great pleasure in giving my testimony to the Christian character of Hung Jin, the relative of Hung Sew Tsuen, who, since his return from Shanghai in the year 1854, has been in the employment of our mission; first as a Christian teacher, and afterwards as a preacher and assistant missionary. His general behaviour has been such as becomes the Gospel; the work which we have given him to do, he has always executed to our satisfaction and not only so, but his zeal for the promotion of the cause of Christ has been marked. He is a young man of superior abilities, and I hope he may yet be honoured to labour successfully in the preaching of the gospel to his countrymen for many years.'

10. Letter from Chalmers dated 5 June 1858, *Archives of the London Missionary Society*, South China, Box 6, Folder 1, Jacket B.

11. Letter from Legge and Chalmers dated 11 January 1859, *Archives of the London Missionary Society*, South China, Box 6, Folder 1, Jacket C, enclosing a translation of a letter from Hung Jan: 'Translation of Hung Jan's last letter, sent from Shanghai by Mr. Muirhead, who received it from a Chinaman who had been with Lord Elgin's expedition up the Yangtze. He wrote in [*sic*] 170 or 180 miles on that river below Hakow.' Letters from 'Shau Kwan, Nan Gan [both on the northern boundary of Kwangtung], one from the capital of Keangse, one from imperialist camp at Yaou Chow [north of Keangse]' are mentioned as having been written by Hung Jen-kan.

12. Letter from Legge dated 24 August 1860, *Archives of the London Missionary Society*, South China, Box 6, Folder 2, Jacket C, and letter from Legge dated 14 January 1861, Folder 3, Jacket B.

13. Letter from Legge and Chalmers, 14 January 1857, *Archives of the London Missionary Society*, South China, Box 6, Folder 1, Jacket A.

14. Legge family papers, letters dated 28 March 1861 and 24 March 1871, *Archives of the London Missionary Society*.

15. For identification of Hung K'uei-hsiu, see Jen (Chien) Yu-wan, '太平天國洪氏遺裔訪問記', (Record of Visit with Descendants of the Taiping Hung Family), 太平天國雜記 (Taiping Kingdom Miscellany), No. 4, 1935, and 羅香林 Lo Hsiang-lin, 客家史料滙篇 (Historical Sources for the Study of the Hakkas), (Hong Kong, Institute of Chinese Culture, 1965), p. 409.

16. Hong Kong school report, 14 February 1875, 'Teacher Schui Thin will shortly change places with Fung Khui-syu in Tschong Hang Kang, because the last as a son of a Tai Ping Rebellion King, cannot stay anymore in the mainland without danger to the life of himself and family', *Basel Missionary Society Archives*.

17. Hong Kong school report, 16 April 1873, *Basel Missionary Society Archives*, and letter from Lechler dated 2 October 1865, *Die Evangelischen Heidenboten*, January 1866.

18. Chinese Mission Yearly Report, 1885, *Basel Missionary Society Archives*.

The ship *Dartmouth* left Hong Kong on 25 December 1878 and arrived at Georgetown, British Guiana, on 17 March 1879. Among its five hundred and sixteen emigrants were seventy Christians.

19. Kuo Ting-i (郭廷以), *Daily Record of Historical Events of the Tai Ping Kingdom* (Chungking and Shanghai, Commercial Press, 1946), appendix, p. 24.

Notes to Chapter 5

1. 'Sun Yat-sen as Middle School Student in Hong Kong', *Ching Feng*, Vol. XX,
No. 3, 1977, pp. 154–6. In the register of the China Congregational Church (Kung
Lei Tong (公理堂)), the three young men are registered as follows: No. 2 孫日新 (Sun
Yat-sen), No. 4 陸忠桂 (Luk Chung-kwei), and No. 5 唐宏桂 (Tong Wang-kwai).

2. *Missionary Herald*, 12 April 1912.

3. The American Board mission opened three day-schools, which were listed as
grant-in-aid schools in 1884. These were Bridges Street, teacher, Sung Yuk-lam, with
an assistant, ninety-three boys; East Street, teacher, Chau Cheung-tai, twenty-
eight boys; and Station Street, teacher, Chau Tsing-tsun, forty-one boys. The
school on East Street had been taken over from its former patron, the Revd Ho
Kau, of the London Missionary Society congregation. It was closed in 1887, and its
teacher, Chau Cheung-tai, replaced Tsing-tsun at the Station Street school. The
same year, the American Board mission took over the management of two schools
from the Presbyterians. One was the school on Queen's Road West, where Hager
had opened a Sunday school on 1 September 1883, the other was a school in Hing
Lung Lane.

4. The biography of Jee Gam and the careers of his children illustrate the rise of
a poor immigrant boy to a position where he could provide university education for
his children. They, for their part, returned to China to contribute to the new China
of Sun Yat-sen.

Jee Gam accompanied an uncle to San Francisco. He first found a situation as a
house-boy. Dissatisfied with his wages, he went to work in a factory. One Sunday,
he found his way to a Chinese Sunday school. The superintendent of the school was
attracted by the boy's appearance and manners and introduced him to the family of
the pastor of the church, the Revd George Mooar. He was taken into the family as
a servant, but was soon considered part of the family circle. In 1870, with two other
Chinese, he joined the Oakland Congregational Church. He soon became a leader
in Christian work among the Chinese. In 1871, he returned to China to marry a
bride who had been chosen for him. A son was born, but died. To console the
bereaved mother another boy was adopted. Jee Gam returned to California, leaving his wife in China. Later, he sent for her to join him, but his father suggested
that it would be better for him to take a second wife in California. Jee Gam replied
that this was against his principles as a Christian. He persisted and his wife was
allowed to join him.

He returned to China in 1876 to take his wife back with him to California. She
was not a Christian, but when Jee Gam transferred his membership from the First
Congregational Church, Oakland, to the Bethany Congregational Church, in 1884,
she was baptized and received into membership with him.

In 1895, the Congregational Association of Chinese Christians requested that Jee
Gam should be ordained. He had been doing the work of a pastor for twenty-five
years. The date of the ordination, 19 September, was the anniversary of the date on
which he had begun his Christian work in California.

In addition to the son adopted in China, Jee Gam had nine children; all were
baptized. One of his sons, Jee Shin Fwe Pong Mooar, having received a medical

degree from the University of California, went to Tientsin, where he practised as an eye surgeon. Another son, Jee Shin Yien Luther MacLean, received an MA from Harvard University and later joined the Ministry of Finance of the Chinese Republic. All the other children who grew to maturity received a good education in one way or another and all except one returned to China.

Jee Gam was planning to spend his old age on Chinese soil but died on his way home within a day's journey to Honolulu. His body was returned to China for burial.

5. *The Pacific*, Vol. 32, No. 8, 21 February 1883.

6. *The Pacific*, Vol. 32, No. 9, 28 February 1883.

7. Lo Hsian-lim, 'The Spread of Christian Faith and Its Influence on the Course of Modern China, as seen in the Chinese Genealogical Records' (中國族譜所記基督敎之傳播與近代中國之關係), *Journal of Asian Studies*, Vol. VII, No. 1, 1969.

8. See the following articles by Carl T. Smith, 'A Study of the Missionary Educational Philosophy of Samuel R. Brown from the Perspective of Inter-faith Encounter', *Ching Feng*, Vol. XII, No. 2, 1969, pp. 2–19, 'The Chinese Church in a Colonial Setting: Hong Kong', *Ching Feng*, Vol. XVII, Nos. 2 and 3, 1974, pp. 75–89, and 'The Early Hong Kong Church and Traditional Chinese Family Patterns', *Ching Feng*, Vol. XX, No. 1, 1977, pp. 56–60.

9. *American Missionary*, Vol. XXII, No. 9, 1878, p. 281.

10. Fung Foo (1849–1934) was another of those Chinese boys in the United States who came under church influence and received an English-language education.

Fung Foo (馮扶), alias Chung-ling (鍾靈) or Pat Sun (拔臣), an orphan, was shipped out as a coolie to Cuba at the age of 15. Instead of working in the sugarfields as a labourer, he became a house-servant. After completing his service, he drifted up to New York City. There he came under the patronage of the superintendent of the Five Points mission and was sent with two other Chinese boys to study at Howard University at Washington, DC. The Hong Kong obituary of Fung Foo states that he was educated at Harvard, but this is an error. Howard was a school founded for the education of blacks and was associated with the American Missionary Association.

After completing his studies, Fung Foo went to San Francisco, where he became a helper in the Congregational Chinese Mission sponsored by the same society. His services were of considerable value and he helped to draft the constitution for the Chinese Young Men's Christian Association.

While at Howard, he had written to the Secretary of the American Missionary Association, which was financing his studies, stating, 'I am preparing myself to be a teacher, and will go back to my country to teach my people of this language'. His youthful resolve was realized, for after returning to Hong Kong in 1881, he became a teacher at the Government Vernacular School at Sai Ying Pun. Its successor is King's College, Bonham Road. Later, he was appointed as Headmaster. He served in the Hong Kong government school system until his retirement.

He married Kwan Uet-ming (關月明), the eldest daughter of Kwan Yuen-fat, an elder in the London Missionary Society congregation. Fung Foo was therefore related by marriage to Wan Ping-chung, whose wife was a cousin of Uet-ming. Fung Foo was a deacon in the To Tsai Church(formerly the London Missionary Society congregation and subsequently the Hop Yat Church) and was later ordained and became an elder. In the later years of his life, he assisted in the organization of Ying Wah College and established a free school at Castle Peak, New Territories, for poor boys.

11. Lee Sam was a convert of the California mission which had sent the Revd

C. Hager to Hong Kong. He accompanied Hager to Hong Kong and assisted him in establishing the mission there. He also sold and distributed literature on behalf of the American Bible Society.

12. This was the Central Government School, later Queen's College, in which Sun Yat-sen was enrolled in March 1884.

13. Either this is a misprint or Hager did not hear the name clearly. Miss Harriet Noyes founded True Light College in Canton in 1872. Its successors are the Hong Kong True Light School, Tai Hang Road, Hong Kong; the Kowloon Chan Kwong (True Light) Girls' School, Kowloon Tong; and the True Light English School, Waterloo Road, Kowloon.

14. Emily Hahn, *The Soong Sisters* (Garden City, New York, Doubleday, 1941), p. 5.

15. The account given by Miss Hahn of the young runaway stowing away on the cutter SS *Schuyler Colfax* and being befriended by Captain Charles Jones does not agree with the facts uncovered by Ensign A. Tourtellot and published in an article 'C.J. Soong and the US Coast Guard', *US Naval Institute Proceedings*, Vol. 75, 1949, pp. 201–3. This states that he was shipped aboard the American revenue cutter *Albert Gallatin* and was enrolled in the coastguard by its captain, Eric Gabrielson, in January 1879. See the article on Soong, Charles Jones, in the *Biographical Dictionary of Republic China*, editor Howard L. Boorman (New York, Columbia University Press, 1970), Vol. 3, p. 141.

16. Cambridge, Heffer and Sons, 1949, p. 277.

Notes to Chapter 6

1. It is difficult to know what date to give to the origin of the Tung Wah Hospital. In 1869, an organizing committee of concerned Chinese was formed. In 1870 (the usual date given for the foundation of the hospital), the Tung Wah Hospital Ordinance was passed and the foundation stone was laid by the Governor. The hospital was formally opened by the Governor on 14 February 1872.

2. Colonial Office Records, Series 129–23, 19 February 1848.

3. Colonial Office Records, Series 131–3, 4 November 1856.

4. See the studies by Chung-Li Chang, *The Income of the Chinese Gentry* (Seattle, University of Washington Press, 1962) and *The Chinese Gentry: Studies in their Role in Nineteenth Century Chinese Society* (Seattle, University of Washington Press, 1955), and by Ping-ti Ho, *The Ladder of Success in Imperial China* (New York, Columbia University Press, 1964).

5. See the column 'Old Hong Kong', in the *South China Morning Post* of 12 July 1933.

6. Colonial Office Records, Series 129–12, 24 June 1845.

7. *Friend of China*, 6 November 1861.

8. George Smith, *The Consular Cities of China* (London, Seeley, Burnside and Seeley, 1847), p. 82.

9. Yen-p'ing Hao, *The Compradore in Nineteenth Century China* (Cambridge, Harvard University Press, 1970), p. 195. I have not been able to check the sources he cites.

10. These were Loo King (盧景), owner of Inland Lots 99, 102, and 103; Lo Lye or Alloy (盧儧), owner of Marine Lots 16C and 19; Loo Foon (盧寬), owner of Marine Lot 16D; Loo Sing (盧成), owner of Marine Lot 17C; Loo Chuen, alias Loo Chew, alias Young Aqui, alias Loo Choo-tung (盧昭), owner of Marine Lots 16A, 28A, and 35A. The family lived in Aqui's Lane, or, as it is now known, Kwai Wa Lane (貴華里), running from Hillier Street to Cleverly Street and lying between

Queen's Road and Jervois Street. Here, in 1872, lived Loo Wan-kew, Loo Yum-shing, compradore of David Sassoon, Sons and Company, and Loo Achew.

11. See 'The Districts of Hong Kong and the Name Kwan-Tai-Lo', *China Review*, Vol. 1, 1872, p. 333. This source also confirms the deleterious effect of Aqui's activities in Hong Kong: 'In 1843, when there were but few merchants or shop keepers, one Sz-man-king, unto whom those who were in distress, in debt, or discontented, resorted, opened a place for gambling along Chung Wan to which all among the fishing-boat people, who loved gambling, came.'

12. Quoted by R.M. Martin in his report dated 24 July 1844, in G.B. Endacott, *An Eastern Entrepot* (London, Her Majesty's Stationery Office, 1964), p. 97.

13. E.J. Eitel, *Europe in China* (Hong Kong, Kelly and Walsh, 1895), pp. 168–9.

14. G.B. Endacott, *An Eastern Entrepot* (London, Her Majesty's Stationery Office, 1964), pp. 96–8.

15. G.B. Endacott (1964), p. 107.

16. G.B. Endacott (1964), p. 96.

17. A Singapore house was a pre-cut timber house ready for assembly, imported from Singapore. At the time of the gold-rush in California, a similar type of house was shipped from Hong Kong to San Francisco in large numbers. The trade brought considerable profit to a number of Hong Kong carpenters.

18. Colonial Office Records, Series 129–12, No. 97, 10 July 1845.

19. Colonial Office Records, Series 129–7, 23 July 1844.

20. Colonial Office Records, Series 129–3, Treasurer's Report, 1847.

21. *Friend of China*, 5 January 1856.

22. Colonial Office Records, Series 129–78, No. 113, 24 August 1860.

23. Tam Achoy was survived by five sons: Tam Kung-ping, alias Tam Ping-kai, who died at Canton in 1887, Tam Mo-seen, Tam Yun-yeen, Tam Kee-chun, and Tam Lin-tai. The latter had been adopted by Achoy's fourth wife in 1865.

24. Tang Aluk was survived by a daughter, the wife of Hu Yu-chan; a son, Tang Tung-shang, alias Tang Pak-shan, died in 1899; and a grandson, Tang Yeung-mau, the only son of Tang Shau-shan, alias Tang Kau-chun. Some of the court suits revolved around whether the deceased son, Tang Shau-shan, was a natural or an adopted son of Tang Aluk. The family has retained many of its real estate holdings up to the present.

25. Colonial Office Records, Series 131–2, 14 January 1851.

26. *China Review*, Vol. 1, 1872, p. 171.

27. K.G. Tregonning, *Under Chartered Company Rule (Borneo 1881–1946)* (Singapore, University of Malaya, 1958), Chap. 1.

28. *China Mail*, 23 July 1891.

29. Cambridge, Harvard University Press, 1970.

30. *China Mail*, 17 October 1861.

31. For details on the Chiu (Hsu) family, see Hsu Jun, Chronological Autobiography of Hsu Jun, (徐潤, 徐愚齋自叙年譜) (1910). Republished in the series *Chung-Kuo ching chi shih liao ts'ing pien* (Taipei, Ching Tai Pien (食貨史學叢書), 1977).

32. See Carl T. Smith, 'The Chinese Settlement of British Hong Kong', *Chung Chi Bulletin*, No. 48, 1970, pp. 30–1.

33. For a note on Cheung Achew, see *Chung Chi Bulletin*, No. 45, 1968, p. 11.

34. *China Mail*, 9 December 1858.

35. *China Mail*, 19 December 1871; 7 February 1872.

36. *Daily Press*, 4 November 1868.

37. Li Chin-wei (ed.), *Centenary History of Hong Kong* (香港百年史) (Hong Kong, Nan Chung Printing House, *circa* 1947), p. 271.

38. *Daily Press*, 23 April 1880.

39. *Daily Press*, 23 April 1880.

40. *Archives of the London Missionary Society*, South China, Box 8, 23 September 1876.

41. Report of Charles St. George Cleverly, Surveyor-General, for the year 1848, Colonial Office Records, Series 133–5.

42. The name of Ho Tsun-shin does appear on a list of contributors to the Berlin Missionary Society Chinese Vernacular School Fund in 1868 and 1869.

43. For reference to these various aspects of the career of Ho Shan-chee, see *Daily Press*, 24 July 1868, 20 September 1878; *China Mail*, 28 February 1882.

44. For details of the career of Ho Kwan-shan, see *Daily Press*, 4 October 1871.

45. *China Mail*, 28 August 1891.

46. A biographical sketch of Ho Kai can be found in G.H. Choa, *The Life and Times of Sir Kai Ho Kai* (Hong Kong, The Chinese University Press, 1981).

47. *Hong Kong Telegraph*, 3 September 1891.

48. The information on the family of Wu Ting-fang is taken from the Archives of the Presbyterian Missionary Society, New York. The exact relationship is deduced from evidence rather than having been directly stated in the sources. At the marriage of Ng Achoy and Ho Amooy on 14 January 1864, at St. John's Cathedral, Hong Kong, there were two Chinese witnesses, Ho Tsun-shin (father of Ho Mooey) and Ng Akwong (presumed brother of Ng Achoy and former student of the Presbyterian Mission School).

49. See the biographical notice written by Wu Ting-fang, *Daily Press*, 28 August 1905.

50. Lo Hsiang-lin, *Hong Kong and Western Cultures* (Tokyo, Sobunsha, 1963), pp. 49–50.

51. *Daily Press*, 2 February 1874. A biographical notice of Wang T'ao appears in A.W. Hummel, *Eminent Chinese of the Ch'ing Period* (Washington, DC, United States Government Printing Office, 1943), p. 836.

52. *Daily Press*, 20 February 1864.

53. *Wah Tsz Yat Po*, 7 August 1902. Details of the life of Wong Shing are from various references to his activities in reports of missionaries in the Archives of the London Missionary Society.

54. For a biographical account of Leung Tsun-tak, see Carl T. Smith, 'Commissioner Lin's Translators', *Chung Chi Bulletin*, No. 42, 1967, pp. 32–5.

55. For a more extended biographical account of Wei Akwong, see chapter 3 above and Carl T. Smith, 'An Early Hong Kong Success Story: Wei Akwong, the Beggar Boy', *Chung Chi Bulletin*, No. 45, 1968, pp. 9–14.

Notes to Chapter 7

1. Ho, Ping-ti, *The Ladder of Success in Imperial China* (New York, Columbia University Press, 1962).

2. Samuel W. Williams, *The Chinese Commercial Guide* (Hong Kong, A. Shortrede, 1863), p. 162.

3. Letter from S.W. Williams dated 18 May 1834, *Archives of the American Board of Commissioners for Foreign Missions*, 16.3.8, Vol. 1.

4. Williams (1863), p. 162.

5. George Endacott, *A History of Hong Kong* (London, Oxford University Press, 1964), p. 127.

6. *Daily Press*, 30 January 1883, 19 February 1883, 16 January 1890.

7. Carl T. Smith, 'An Early Hong Kong Success Story: Wei Akwong, the Beggar Boy', *Chung Chi Bulletin*, No. 45, 1968, pp. 9–14.

8. Carl T. Smith, 'The Formative Years of the Tong Brothers, Pioneers in the Modernization of China's Commerce and Industry', *Chung Chi Bulletin*, No. 10, 1971, pp. 81–95.

9. Carl T. Smith, 'The Emergence of a Chinese Élite in Hong Kong', *Journal of*

the Hong Kong Branch of the Royal Asiatic Society, Vol. 11, 1971, pp. 74–115; and *Hua-tze Jih-pao*, obituary notice (in Chinese), 7 August 1902.

10. Smith, 'Chinese Élite', 1971, p. 108.

11. Reference to service in the Chinese customs is based principally on lists of Chinese clerks of 1876 and 1880 appearing in circulars from the Inspector-General, China Imperial Customs. For a fuller account of Ng Mun-sow, see Carl T. Smith, 'Dr Legge's Theological School', *Chung Chi Bulletin*, No. 50, 1971, pp. 16–20.

12. Smith, 'Chinese Élite', 1971, p. 103 ff.

13. A copy of the report on the preparatory school and theological seminary in Hong Kong is held in the library of the Archives of the London Missionary Society in London.

14. Colonial Office Records, Series 129–82, No. 106, 30 October 1861.

15. *Daily Press*, 3 October 1866. See also Marriage Record Book, St. John's Cathedral, Hong Kong.

16. Smith, 'Chinese Elite', 1971, p. 107.

17. James W. Norton-Kyshe, *The History of the Laws and Courts of Hong Kong* (Hong Kong, Noronha and Company, 1898), Vol. 2, pp. 237–40; *China Mail*, 28 November 1874, 2 January 1875.

18. Knighthood was the ultimate badge of élite status. Knighthoods were not given to the Chinese until the early twentieth century.

19. *Hong Kong Telegraph*, 14 July 1881.

20. *Hong Kong Telegraph*, 23 June 1881.

21. *Hong Kong Telegraph*, 20 September 1881.

22. W.C. Hunter, *The* Fan-kwae *at Canton* (London, Kegan, Paul, Trench and Company, 1882), pp. 50–4.

23. *Chinese Repository*, Vol. 14, 1845, p. 297.

24. James W. Norton-Kyshe, *The History of the Laws and Courts of Hong Kong* (Hong Kong, Kegan, Paul, Trench and Company, 1882), Vol. 1, p. 288.

25. Norton-Kyshe (1882), pp. xiii–xviii.

26. Norton-Kyshe (1882), pp. xix–xxvi.

27. Smith, 'Chinese Élite', 1971, pp. 110 and 104 ff.

28. Norton-Kyshe (1882), p. 545.

29. Smith, 'Chinese Élite', 1971, pp. 101–2.

30. The biographical data for Wong Fun were gathered mainly from the Archives of the London Missionary Society.

31. A list of the graduates of the College of Medicine for Chinese, together with comments, appears in Hsiang-lin Lo, *Kuo fu chih ta hsüeh* (Sun Yat-sen's College Life) (Taipei, *Shang wu yin shu kuean*, 1959).

32. See Henry J. Lethbridge, 'The District Watch Committee, the Chinese Executive Council of Hong Kong', *Journal of the Hong Kong Branch of the Royal Asiatic Society*, Vol. 11, 1971, pp. 116–41.

33. See Henry J. Lethbridge, 'The Evolution of a Chinese Voluntary Association in Hong Kong: the Po Leung Kuk', *Journal of Oriental Studies*, Vol. 10, 1972, pp. 33–50.

34. Henry J. Lethbridge, 'A Chinese Association in Hong Kong: the Tung Wah', *Contributions to Asian Studies*, Vol. 1, 1972, pp. 144–58.

35. See Sing-Lim Woo, *The Prominent Chinese in Hong Kong* (香港華人史略) (Hong Kong, 版影印, 1937).

36. Carl T. Smith, 'Compradores of the Hong Kong Bank', in Frank H.J. King (ed.), *Eastern Banking: Essays in the History of the Hongkong and Shanghai Banking Corporation* (London, The Athlone Press, 1983), pp. 93–111.

37. Lethbridge, 'The Tung Wah,' 1972, pp. 144–58.

38. Carl T. Smith, 'Ng Akew, One of Hong Kong's Protected Women,' *Chung Chi Bulletin*, Vol. 46, 1969, pp. 13–27.

Notes to Chapter 8

1. The relationship between missionaries and indigenous people and culture is a well-travelled area and nothing new is presented on the subject here. It is, however, useful to look at the question as it worked itself out in a particular place.

2. The status of the Bishop was changed in 1875. The Cathedral was disestablished and disendowed in 1892. The Anglican Bishop is still fifth in precedence in the protocol list of the Government. He follows the Chief Secretary and precedes the Roman Catholic Bishop and the members of the Executive Council.

3. General report of missionaries dated Macau, 22 March 1841, *Archives of the London Missionary Society*, South China, Box 4, Folder 2, Jacket A.

4. Letter from the Revd S.W. Bonney dated 29 January 1847, *Archives of the American Board of Commissioners for Foreign Missions*, 16.3.8, Vol. 2, No. 188.

5. George Smith, *A Narrative of an Exploratory Visit to Each of the Consular Cities of China, and the Islands of Hong Kong and Chusan, in Behalf of the Church Missionary Society, in the Years 1844, 1845, 1846* (London, Seeley, Burnside and Seeley, 1847).

6. Letter dated Hong Kong, 10 August 1867, *Archives of the London Missionary Society*, South China, Box 6, Folder 5, Jacket A.

7. London Missionary Society, Yearly Reports, Box 1, 6 February 1868.

8. His picture is the frontispiece of W.H. Medhurst's *China: Its State and Prospects* (London, Snow, 1838). A brief notice of Choo Tih-lang appears in A. Wylie, *Memorials of Protestant Missionaries to the Chinese* (Shanghai, The American Presbyterian Mission Press, 1867), p. 40. Reprinted by Ch'eng Wen Publishing Co., Taipei, in 1967.

9. Letter from Mr Gillespie dated Hong Kong, 27 February 1847, *Archives of the London Missionary Society*, South China, Box 4, Folder 5, Jacket E.

10. Letter from Wong Fun dated Hong Kong, 8 May 1857, *Archives of the London Missionary Society*, South China, Box 5, Folder 4, Jacket C.

11. The merchants of Canton involved in the opium trade were generous contributors to the Morrison Education Society, the Medical Missionary Society, and the Society for the Diffusion of Useful Knowledge. All these were organs for the missionary effort.

12. *Chinese Repository*, Vol. V, 1837, p. 546.

13. Letter from E.C. Bridgman dated 11 February 1837, *Archives of the American Board of Commissioners for Foreign Missions*, 16.3.3, Vol. 1A, No. 33.

14. *Friend of China*, 25 August 1842.

15. *Friend of China*, 25 August 1842.

16. See Stuart Creighton Miller, 'Ends and Means: Missionary Justification of Force in Nineteenth Century China', in *The Missionary Enterprise in China and America*, edited by John K. Fairbank (Cambridge, Harvard University Press, 1974), pp. 249–82.

17. *Missionary Magazine*, Vol. 10, 1847, p. 164.

18. *Missionary Magazine*, Vol. 15, 1852, p.5.

19. Letter from the Revd S.W. Bonney dated Canton, 10 March 1847, *Archives of the American Board of Commissioners for Foreign Missions*, 16.3.8, Vol. 2, No. 191.

20. *Archives of the London Missionary Society*, Box 5, Folder 4 (special folder).

21. The Revd Robert Morrison arrived at Macau on 4 September 1807. On the day he was married, 20 February 1809, he accepted the position of translator to the East India Company. Officially, the Company did not import opium on their ships, but they did not prohibit its growth in India and derived income from its

sale to 'free merchants' who brought it to China. Thus, indirectly, Morrison was allied with the trade.
22. *Christian Advocate*, 13 July 1832.
23. Letter from the Revd S.W. Bonney dated Canton, 4 January 1847, *Archives of the American Board of Commissioners for Foreign Missions*, 16.3.8, Vol. 2, No. 187.
24. Letter from the Revd S.W. Bonney dated 7 February 1847, *Archives of the American Board of Commissioners for Foreign Missions*, 16.3.8, Vol. 2, No. 191.

Notes to Chapter 9

1. George Smith, *A Narrative of an Exploratory Visit to Each of the Consular Cities of China, and the Islands of Hong Kong and Chusan, in Behalf of the Church Missionary Society, in the years 1844, 1845, 1846* (London, Seeley, Burnside and Seeley, 1847), pp. 508–9.
2. Loren E. Noren, 'Urban Church Growth in Hong Kong 1958–1962, Third Hong Kong Study', Hong Kong, mimeographed, undated.
3. Church Missionary Society Archives, China, CH/O–44.
4. Yen-p'ing Hao, *The Compradore in Nineteenth-century China* (Cambridge, Harvard University Press, 1970).
5. Hong Kong Blue Book 1879, Report of the Director of Education.
6. *The Outpost*, Diocese of Victoria, January 1925, p. 12.
7. Smith (1847), pp. 505–6.
8. Smith (1847), pp. 512–3.

Notes to Chapter 10

1. Hui-chen Wang Liu, *The Traditional Chinese Clan Rules* (New York, J.J. Augustin, 1959), published for the Association for Asian Studies.
2. William H. Medhurst, *China: Its State and Prospects* (London, Snow, 1838), p. 338.
3. *China Mail*, 20 July 1871.
4. *China Mail*, 20 July 1871.
5. Report on women's work by Miss Rowe, *Archives of the London Missionary Society*, Decennial Reports, 1880–90, Hong Kong.

Index

ABEEL, DAVID, 23, 224
Aberdeen University, 158
A-bi, 215
Advisers to Government, 10, 11, 52, 63, 68, 133, 139, 160, 161–7, 168, 170, 183, 192, 193
A-fa, dentist, *see* Le A-sam
Afuh, 214
Ah Loo, 214
Ahone, Julian, 7, 188, 215
Ahop, 221
Ah-Yang, 225
A-kap, 79
Akow and Company, 112
Alan, Henry Martyn, 57
Aldersey, Miss, 70, 71, 216
Alice Memorial Hospital, 131, 160, 161
Aling, 24, 37, 221
All Saints' Anglican Church, 5
Allied Commission at Canton, 150
Alum, William, 52, 56, 57
Alun, 221
Aman, 52, 54
America, *see* United States of America
American Baptist Church, 212
American Baptist Mission, 3, 187, 213, 214, 215, 216, 217; church at Bangkok, 215, 216, 217
American Bible Society, 45, 90, 231
American Board Mission congregation at Bridges Street, Hong Kong, 88, 90, 91, 96; *see also* China Congregational Church
American Board Mission School, Bridges Street, 8, 90, 229; in Hong Kong, 229; Sai Ying Poon, 89; Singapore, 65, 70, 135, 142, 146, 214, 215
American Board of Commissioners for Foreign Missions, 6, 7, 52, 54, 56, 58, 64, 70, 71, 92, 94, 135, 143, 212, 213, 214, 215, 217, 229
American Commissioner to China, 28, 60, 157
American Consul at Singapore, 70
American Methodist Church, 102, 210
American Missionary Association, 92, 93, 230

American Presbyterian Mission, 35, 40, 70, 89, 215, 216, 217; school at Hong Kong, 89, 229
American Trading Company of Borneo, 118
Amoon, 226
Amoy, 215
Ancestors, 167, 185, 196, 197, 201, 202, 203
Andersen, N.P., 73; Anderson, Mrs N.P., daughter of Tsang Lai-sun, 73, 74
Andersen, Ruth K. (Mrs Donald R. McEven), 74
Anderson, Agnes, 154
Anderson, Catherine, wife of Ho Sai-wing, 154
Anderson, Charles (Carl) Graham, 154
Anderson, Charles Graham Overbeck, 153
Anderson, Edith, 154
Anderson, Ernest G., 154
Anderson, G.C., 153
Anderson, Henry Graham, *see* Hung Kam-ning
Anderson, Henry M. (Dr), 154
Anderson, Hugh G., 154
Anderson, Irene Teresa, 154
Anderson, James G., 154
Anderson, Joseph Overbeck, 153
Anderson, Mabel, 154
Anglican Church, 4, 8, 172, 197, 199
Anglo-Chinese College, *xvi*, 4, 38, 55, 130, 134, 142, 143, 147, 148, 149, 213, 214, 215
Anglo-Chinese School for Chinese Boys, 142
Annam, 118, 200
Anstey, Thomas Chisholm, 157
Anti-Christian agitation, 189, 190, 203, 204
Archbishop of Canterbury, 136
Arrow lorcha incident, 66, 81
Asam, *see* Yeong Lan-ko
Ashun, 214
Assing's *Daily General Price Current*, 134
A-tei, 215

Canton and Hong Kong Telegraph
 Company, 130
Canton Guild, Shanghai, 50
Canton mission hospital, 41
Chalmers, Revd John, 82, 83, 131, 207,
 228
Chan, convert of Roberts, 6, 7, 217
Chan Achoy, 150, 151
Chan Afook, 162, 165–6
Chan Akuen, 111
Chan, Alice Martha, 163
Chan Atow, see Tsun Atow
Chan Ayin, see Chan Oi-ting
Chan Ayow, see Mrs Daniel Richard
 Caldwell
Chan Chun-poo, 112
Chan Hok-lam, 220
Chan Iu-ting, see Chan Yau-lok
Chan Kam-ying, see Alice Martha Chan
Chan King-ue, 161
Chan Lai-sun, see Tsang Lai-sun
Chan Lai-tai, 130
Chan Man-ng, see Alice Martha Chan
Chan Man-shing, see Chan Quan-ee
Chan Oi-ting, 132, 133, 151, 198
Chan Pat, 163
Chan Quan-ee, 40, 162, 163
Chan Shut-cho, see Chan Quan-ee
Chan Su-kee, George, 137
Chan Sz-wa, see Chan Yau-lok
Chan Tai-kwong, 7, 136, 137
Chan U-fai, 162, 166
Chan Wei, 163
Chan Yau, 163
Chan Yau-lok, 152
Chang Ye, 215
Chaochow, Kwangtung, 62
Chartered Mercantile Bank of India,
 London and China, 126; see also
 Mercantile Bank
Chau Cheung-tai, 229
Chau Tsing-tsun, 229
Chau Wan, see Chow Wan
Cheang Luk-u, 51
Cheefoo Convention (1876), 71
Chek Chin, 217
Chek Ete, 214
Chek Han (How?, Ho?), 214
Chek Hwa, 215
Chek Kok, 215
Chek Team, 217
Chek Yet, 215
Cheltenham College, England, 159
Cheong Achew, see Cheung Achew

Cheong Assow, 127
Cheong Tscheng-sai, 69
Cheung Achew, 66, 122, 226; his
 widow, Cheung Chew Shi, 226
Cheung Chau, 3
Cheung Kam-cheong, 112
Cheung Mui, Mary, wife of Tam Tin-
 tak, 150
Cheung Mung, 226
Cheung Po-chai, 107
Cheung Tsun, 226
Chicago, Illinois, 94
China coast culture, 11, 34, 69, 74
China Congregational Church, xvi, 6;
 see also American Board Congrega-
 tion at Bridges Street
China Merchants' Steam Navigation
 Company, 23, 49, 50, 51, 122, 147
China Railway Company of Tientsin,
 164
Chinam, 110, 111, 112, 116, 117
Chinchew (Fukien) merchants, 112, 113
Chinese Ambassador to the United
 States, 130, 132, 133, 159, 198
Chinese American Commercial Com-
 pany, 131
Chinese Christian Churches Union,
 Hong Kong, 202
Chinese Christian Union, 5, 8, 76, 179,
 215, 216
Chinese Church at Singapore, 217
Chinese community leadership, 69,
 103, 105, 107, 109, 114, 121, 128,
 131, 135, 153, 168, 192, 225
Chinese Consul-General, Havana, 133,
 198
Chinese Consul-General, San Fran-
 cisco, 131, 159
Chinese contract labour, 47, 48
Chinese diplomatic service, 130, 131,
 132, 133, 144
Chinese Educational Mission, 23, 24,
 36, 71, 73, 97, 100, 101, 135, 147,
 183, 216
Chinese Engineering and Mining Com-
 pay, 133, 151
Chinese Evangelization Society, 190
Chinese family, 167, 168, 185, 186,
 195–203
Chinese Government abuses, 25, 26,
 40, 219
Chinese Government schools, 129, 143;
 of foreign language, Shanghai, 28,
 71, 134; Tientsin, 143

250 INDEX

Szechuan, 55

Sz-man-king, see Loo Aqui

TAI, ASSISTANT TO REVD HAMBERG, 217

Tai Hung-chi, Imperial Commissioner, 102

Tai Ping Shan, Hong Kong, 4, 107, 109, 114, 122, 123, 225

Tai Ping Shan Chapel (London Mission), 4

Tai Ping Shan government school, 149

Taiping rebellion, 5, 8, 73, 75–87, 103, 114, 117, 133, 133, 136, 227

Tam Achoy, 104, 109, 114, 115, 123, 124, 225, 232

Tam Kee-chun, 232

Tam Kung-ping, 232

Tam Lin-tai, 232

Tam Mo-seen, 232

Tam Ping-kai, see Tam Kung-ping

Tam Pui, Nam Hoi District, Kwangtung, 149

Tam Sam-tshoy, see Tam Achoy

Tam Shek-tsun, see Tam Achoy

Tam Tin-tak, 150, 151

Tam Yun-yeen, 232

Tan Le-chun, 217

Tang Aluk, 104, 115, 232

T'ang Ching-hsing, see Tong King-sing

Tang Kam-chi, see Tang Pak-yeung

Tang Kau-chun, see Tang Shau-shan

Tang Kwan, 215

T'ang Mao-chih, see Tong A-chick

Tang Pak-shan, see Tang Tung-shang

Tang Pak-yeung, 120

Tang Shau-shan, 232

T'ang T'ing-chih, see Tong A-chick

T'ang Ting-keng, see Tong Afu

T'ang Ting-shu, see Tong King-sing

Tang Tui, 217

Tang Tung-shang, 232

Tang Yeung-mau, 232

Tanka, see boat people

Tanyau, 221

Tarrant, William, 108

Taylor, Revd John, 213

Teum Chi, 216

Theological Seminary, London Missionary Society, Hong Kong, 4, 40, 148

Tientsin, 49, 73, 118, 143, 146, 147, 161, 164, 220, 223, 230

Tin Sau, see Hwang Tin-sau

Ting Jih-ch'ang, 11–14

To family of Wing On Company, 201

To Kwa Wan, Kowloon, 3

To Tsai Church, xvi, 4, 183, 199, 230; see also London Missionary Society Chinese Congregation

Tomlin, Revd Jacob, 213

Tong A-chick, 19, 23, 24, 34, 36, 37, 38, 39, 40, 41, 42, 43, 44, 45, 46, 47, 48, 49, 50, 146, 220, 221, 222, 223

Tong Afu, 34, 36, 40, 50

Tong Akü, see Tong King-sing, 34, 36, 40, 41, 43, 44, 220

Tong A-tow, 220

Tong Hop Shing, 44

Tong K. Achick and Company, 47, 220

Tong Ka, Heung Shan District, Kwangtung, 35, 220, 221

Tong Kam-sing, 122

Tong King-sing, 34, 36, 40, 41, 43, 44, 49, 50, 51, 147, 220, 221, 223

Tong Mow-chee, see Tong A-chick, 34, 36, 49, 50

Tong Phong, 88

Tong Sing-po, 44

Tong Ting-keng, see Tong Afu

Tong Ying-shing, see Tong Afu

Tourtellot, A. (Ensign), 231

Tracy, Mr, 71

Translators, 10, 11, 38, 52–63, 144, 145, 146, 147, 152, 170, 181, 199, 224, 235

Treaty of Nanking, 2, 38

Triads, 55, 56, 108

True Light Girls' School, Canton (Miss Noyes' school), xvii, 99, 186, 231

True Light schools in Hong Kong, 231

Tsae A-heen, 212

T'sae A-ko, 212

Tsang, Daisy, daughter of Spencer Tsang Lai-sun, 73

Tsang, Elijah, son of Tsang Lai-sun, 73

Tsang Lai-sun, 69–74, 216

Tsang, Ruth A-tik, wife of Tsang A-sun, 70, 71, 72, 73

Tsang, Spencer, son of Tsang Lai-sun, 73

Tsang, William, son of Tsang Lai-sun, 73

Tsen (Chan) A-lin, 84

Tsen (Chan) En-min, see Tsen A-lin

Tsen (Chan) Tchuy-khuyk (Ch'iu-chu), see Tsen A-lin

Tseng Kuo-fan, 161

Tseung Sz-kai, 162, 166